STUMBLING INTO INFINITY

STUMBLING INTO INFINITY

An Ordinary Man in the Sphere of Enlightenment

MICHAEL FISCHMAN

New York

STUMBLING INTO INFINITY
An Ordinary Man in the Sphere of Enlightenment

Copyright © 2011 Michael Fischman. All Rights Reserved.

ISBN 978-1-6003-7648-1 (trade paperback)

First Edition

Published by
MORGAN JAMES PUBLISHING
1225 Franklin Avenue, Suite 325
Garden City, New York 11530-1693
Toll Free 800-485-4943
www.MorganJamesPublishing.com

Excerpts of copyrighted material by Sri Sri Ravi Shankar used by permission of the Art of Living Foundation.

Cover design by Supriya Gupta. Back cover photo by Michael Lloyd. Interior design by Jeffrey Ainis, www.ragingpages.com. Set in Garamond Premier Pro.

Printed in the United States of America

Library of Congress Control No. 2009928756
Stumbling into infinity: an ordinary man in the sphere of enlightenment / Michael Fischman. — 1st ed.

Author royalties are donated directly to the Art of Living Foundation, a global non-profit educational and humanitarian organization.

A Reading Group Guide is available at www.stumblingintoinfinity.com.

If you do not change direction,
you may end up where you are heading.

— LAOZI (LAO-TZU)

CONTENTS

CONTENTS

STUMBLING
INTO INFINITY

Prologue

"You're a very lucky man, Mr. Fischman," said the short, stocky ticketing agent as he squinted at his computer screen. "You must know someone who can work miracles." He typed rapidly on his keyboard. "For no apparent reason," he declared, "you've been upgraded to first class!"

He looked up with a big grin. Removing his reading glasses, he extended his arm and gave me my ticket. I smiled back and nodded my head, acknowledging that I knew I was lucky. But there was no time to explain. I needed to get to the plane.

In a few days, I would find myself in a giant dusty field in Bangalore, India. But I wouldn't be alone. Looking out at more than 2.5 million people over three days, I would be sitting on a stage with kings, presidents, movie stars, religious leaders from several faiths, and more than a thousand musicians (who had barely rehearsed). They would all be there for the Art of Living Foundation's twenty-fifth anniversary and the fiftieth birthday of its founder, His Holiness Sri Sri Ravi Shankar. It was nothing I could have imagined when I first met Sri Sri on that wintery day in 1979, when only a handful of people had even heard of him.

Now, I had boarded the plane, and could finally close my eyes. I was exhausted. I drifted into a sort of half-sleep, thinking about the long and unlikely journey that had brought me to this moment.

But my reverie didn't last long.

An attractive, middle-aged woman suddenly plopped herself in the seat next to me, banging my knee with her purse. Her perfume was sweet, and a bit overpowering.

"Do you fly often?" she asked, as she adjusted her skirt and made herself comfortable.

I am usually eager to meet new people, but that night I simply needed to keep my eyes closed. A flight attendant joined the conspiracy and interrupted my brief silence by reminding me to buckle up, and offering some warm roasted cashews and something to drink. My seatmate saw my open eyes as an opportunity.

"I have a real fear of flying," she explained, removing a pill bottle from her purse. "Well, it's not the flying itself," she said, clarifying her phobia, "it's taking off that really terrifies me."

She placed some pills on her tongue and washed them down with red wine. "I usually take Valium to help me relax when I fly," she explained. Speaking nervously, she asked, "What do you do for a living?"

"I help people relax and get rid of stress," I said, aware of the irony. But my answer felt incomplete. In any case, she was no longer listening.

She squeezed her eyes closed and sighed heavily, as the plane started rolling down the runway. Grabbing my arm, she moved closer. "I'm sorry," she said meekly. "I can't help myself. I don't want to die."

"Don't worry, we're safe," I assured her. And in a few minutes she fell asleep, clutching my arm.

I have often wanted to explain the life I lead more fully. But, in some ways, it is a life I barely comprehend myself, and certainly one I would never have predicted or even imagined for myself.

In fact, if you had told me when I was growing up that someday I'd write a book about the grace of an enlightened teacher, I wouldn't have believed you. For one thing, school was such a struggle that writing a book would have seemed impossible. But mostly, the idea of an enlightened teacher or guru was completely foreign to my Western upbringing.

Like many New Yorkers who identified themselves as belonging to the tribe of people known as the Jewish Middle Class, I grew up knowing the kind of future that would make my parents proud. I would have a successful career as a lawyer or doctor, a home in the suburbs with a tree-dotted backyard, and maybe a swimming pool to relax in during the hot summer months. I'd have a beautiful wife who would shop at upscale malls, and two adorable children, each one the brightest and most popular in their class. Yet, over time, this destiny became increasingly less attractive.

Perhaps you could blame it on my generation. As a baby boomer growing up in the sixties and seventies, idealistic, revolutionary, and counter-cultural ideologies filled my head with hopes of a better world. After reading such popular books as *Autobiography of a Yogi,* by the Indian mystic, Paramahansa Yogananda, and *Be Here Now,* by psychologist and former Harvard professor Dr. Richard Alpert (better known as Ram Dass), I was more interested in attaining a state of nirvana and enlightenment than in studying for my chemistry finals and graduating from college.

I knew vaguely that in India and in many Eastern traditions the spiritual guru is a normal feature of family life. But, like many Westerners, I was generally independent-minded, and assumed that, in spiritual matters, most people found their own way. Certainly, there was nothing to suggest that I would someday become a friend to a great spiritual leader, much less the head of his U.S. organization.

I started writing this book as a way to answer the many questions I've been asked about the early days around His Holiness Sri Sri Ravi Shankar. As someone who had an intimate seat at the beginning of a great spiritual movement, I wanted to convey some of the magic and mystery of those early years — little-known stories, private moments with Sri Sri (*Shree Shree*), and the extraordinary combination of wisdom and innocence I saw in him.

But looking back on the events that led me to Sri Sri, I began to see my life in a new light. The challenges and experiences were like puzzle pieces that started to fit together, and a picture emerged that I hadn't seen before. I had been a seeker of knowledge throughout my childhood and early adult life, believing, or hoping, that some truth existed that would melt away life's confusions and traumas. But on meeting

Sri Sri, my life turned upside-down. Eventually, I would come to the realization that, for me, love — unconditional love — was more fulfilling and transforming than finding truth.

As Sri Sri once said, "The great souls make you drink the water you are already carrying with you." It was life-changing to discover, during meditation, that joy and transcendence was actually something that was available inside me. Finding that it could be experienced outside of meditation was a revolution.

In writing this story, different eras and their flavors came to life again — the world of Orthodox Jews I grew up in; twenty years of teaching meditation and breathing to people around the world; the traumas and triumphs of self-discovery in the Caribbean and Jerusalem; the spiritual traditions of India that became so meaningful to me; and the remarkable atmosphere around the enlightened master I fell in love with.

As I write this, I am president of Sri Sri's Art of Living Foundation in the U.S. However, this is my personal story.

I have done my best to stay true to the events as I remember them. It is possible that some details have been distorted by memory. A couple of names and event details were changed to protect the privacy of certain individuals, and the time between some events has been compressed.

As you will see, for me, the spiritual journey has not always been easy. Being on this path has brought out both my finest and my worst qualities. However, throughout this journey there has been an underlying sense of grace and many mysteries I can't explain.

I offer this book in gratitude, with the hope that it will inspire others to explore a life of greater fulfillment and unconditional love.

Michael Fischman
Boca Raton, Florida, 2010

Part One

CHAPTER ONE

The Disappearance of Faith

ONE NIGHT, WHEN I WAS about three years old, while my parents and sister were asleep in our cramped, one-bedroom apartment in the South Bronx, I awoke before dawn and saw Grandpa. Transparent as a mist of smoke, he stood still in our bedroom doorway. With his white hair, crystal-blue eyes, pencil-thin mustache, and his double-breasted pinstripe suit, he looked as though he wanted to say something to me, but he couldn't speak.

I didn't know why he was there, and his appearance frightened me. I was so scared that I screamed. I remember my sister, Sharyn, sitting up in bed, and pointing at the doorway, howling. The sound of her screaming terrified me even more.

All this noise woke my parents, but they didn't seem to see Grandpa, and they didn't understand what was wrong. Incapable of explaining, we continued to cry and scream. It took some time to calm us down, but finally, after some warm milk and cookies, we were able to go back to sleep.

Maybe it was because our parents wanted to protect our innocence that they kept Grandpa's death a secret. It was a long time before I understood why he was no longer around. And it was many years before I realized that Grandpa's death had coincided with the time of his mysterious visit.

I was born on September 11, 1954, in the middle of a hurricane. New Yorkers had been glued to their radios and newspapers for several days, with the New York Weather Bureau predicting the worst storm in the region's recorded history. Thousands of people along the Eastern Seaboard were evacuated, and the Navy abandoned hundreds of aircraft and warships.

My mother would often remind me that I was born in a double-eyed hurricane, as if this added uncertainty explained my nature.

As far back as I can remember, I was preoccupied with death; aware that I wasn't going to live forever. I would lie in bed buried beneath my covers, hold my breath, and imagine what it would be like to be dead. Would I live under the earth in a coffin for the rest of eternity? Was there really a heaven? More frightening than the loss of my body was the prospect of losing my mind. Who would I be if I didn't have my thoughts, memories, or feelings?

Whenever these terrifying thoughts arose, I panicked. I prayed to God, hoping that if I never fought with my sister again and listened to my mother when she told me to turn off the TV, maybe then I wouldn't have to die.

My mental storms calmed on our yearly vacations at the Shady Nook bungalow colony in upstate New York, even my thoughts about death. But once we were back among the tall buildings, crowded streets, and the rumbling of the elevated subway cars, my fear of death would return. After only a few days, our vacation seemed like a far-away dream. And I knew that, just like our summer vacation, my life would someday be over. I was desperate to understand why we had to go through life at all if someday it had to end.

I couldn't speak to my parents about my fear of death. When I tried, they didn't know how to respond. My mother, a heavyset woman with blue eyes and a protruding chin, did not want to talk about such things. She would hold me close, pull my head to rest against her cushy breasts, and stroke my forehead. *"Shush!"* she would say, looking into my eyes. "You are just a child. Why do you worry about such things?"

My mother thought it was unnatural for a young boy to be obsessed with such gloomy thoughts. To change the subject, she would turn on the TV and encourage me to watch a show with her.

My father, Sol Fischman, liked to lounge around in pajamas while he listened to the radio or read the Yiddish daily newspaper, *The Forward*. A Holocaust survivor who had emigrated to the United States in his late thirties, he simply kept quiet when I mentioned my fear of death. He spoke often about his past and told stories about the war, but there was a dark cloud around him when the topic of death came up.

Over time, I became increasingly determined to understand the meaning of life and death. I longed to find truth, to find God.

When I was six, my father sent Sharyn and me to an Orthodox Jewish school called Yeshiva Torah Ve-Emunah to learn about our heritage, laws, and traditions.

Riding to school on a dilapidated yellow school bus that smelled of leaking gasoline and our driver's cigarette smoke, I usually entered the *yeshiva* (school) feeling nauseous and wanting to go home. My queasiness continued throughout the day. The gloomy décor didn't help. The classroom walls were a pale lime-yellow, and the rooms were dimly lit by low-hanging, exposed, incandescent light bulbs. Accumulated layers of paint sealed most of the windows, so fresh air was a rare commodity. The only thing modern about our school was the frosted windows that prevented outsiders from looking in — and kept us from looking out.

We began our day with prayers and lessons on the *Chumash* — the five books of Moses (the Bible). My favorite story was about Abraham, the father of monotheism, partly because, unlike me, he was able to stand up to his father. According to Jewish tradition, Abraham was born in Babylonia, the son of Terach, an idol merchant. From his early childhood, he questioned the faith of his father and sought the truth. He came to believe that the entire universe was the work of a single God and began to teach this belief to others. Abraham tried to convince his father of the folly of idol worship.

One day, when Abraham was left alone to mind the store, he took a hammer and smashed all of the idols except the largest one.

He then placed the hammer in the hand of the largest idol. When his father returned and asked what happened, Abraham said, "The idols got into a fight, and the big one smashed all the other ones." His father said, "Don't be ridiculous. These idols have no life or power. They can't do anything." Abraham replied, "Then why do you worship them?"

I remember the rabbi telling our class that all of the Jewish souls from all times were actually present on Mount Sinai and heard the voice of God when the law was given to Moses. The rabbi told our class that, in biblical times, God chose the most worthy of all people, the Jews, to receive his law, the Ten Commandments. He explained that somehow our ancient souls, which contain this memory, bind our people together as a nation, keeping us close to God.

As an adult, I became aware that questioning is an honored part of the Jewish tradition. But as a small boy, I was met with stern looks from the rabbis when I questioned the stories of my religion. "Rabbi, was Moses really a prophet of God, or did he mess up somehow?" I asked. "If Moses was such an extraordinary person who could receive direct communication from Almighty God in the form of a burning bush and the Ten Commandments, how was it that he could lead his people into the Promised Land but not enter the Promised Land himself?" My teachers would usually greet such questions with a forced smile, followed by a frown.

The rabbis at my yeshiva were strict and harsh. If we were slow learners or misbehaved, they thought it was amusing to pull our ears or pinch our cheeks until we screamed. For more serious crimes, they struck us with rulers, sometimes using a special double-thick ruler. Since I couldn't learn at the same pace as the other students (due to what I later learned was dyslexia), I was punished often.

Nevertheless, I still loved learning about my heritage.

Unlike most boys, who thrived on sports trivia about Mickey Mantle and Roger Maris, I was attracted to stories about the rabbis who were considered *tzaddiks,* men of God. They were leaders, learned in Jewish law, loving toward family and community, at peace with themselves, and one with the Divine. More than anything, I wanted to be like them, inspiring people and living fearlessly in communion with the Divine, beyond mundane existence. This goal of Jewish life was, for me, the only thing worth striving for.

I began to love God, feeling His presence with me always. I was certain I'd become a rabbi, a man of God, and follow in the footsteps of such tzaddiks as King Solomon, Rabbi Akiva, or the Bal Shem Tov, the father of the *Chassidic* sect of Judaism.

This love affair with God lasted until I was eight, ending with the death of my maternal grandmother.

By her standards, Grandma was successful. She had brought five children into the world, and I was one of more than a dozen grandchildren.

Grandma had come to live with us when I was seven, four years after Grandpa died. As a young woman, she and my grandfather were among the lucky ones who had been able to travel to America and escape the Russian pogroms — the massacres and riots against Jews that were instigated by Russia's czarist government. The pogroms brought destruction to personal property and murder to the lives of many Jews. Grandma would weep as she told me horrible stories about the soldiers and policemen who had terrorized her family.

She was my closest friend and companion; the one who'd perfected the art of matzo ball soup and stuffed cabbage, and who sometimes protected me from my dad. Sometimes when we sat together watching the evening news, she would praise me during the commercials. "You know you're a very sweet boy, *Michaela*," she'd say in her thick accent, stroking my face with her coarse, wrinkled fingers. "You're different than the other grandchildren. When you grow up you're going to do something important. You'll be able to help people and make them happy." I'd nod my head, not fully sure what she meant or what she was seeing in me.

But as time passed, Grandma played with me less and less. She became frail and bedridden, and eventually needed constant nursing care and attention. I would sit beside her and hold her hand, but her blank expression was nothing like the loving Grandma I knew.

One day, after Grandma's nurse left her room, I sat in the chair by her bed, held her limp hand, and searched her impassive face for signs that she remembered me. Even though it was summer in New York, she wore a pink flannel nightgown and had a hot water bottle near her feet. A white porcelain bedpan and a roll of toilet paper sat close to her bed, and the smell of rubbing alcohol permeated her room.

Then, without warning, her breath stopped. I ran to tell the nurse and my mother what had happened, hoping they could do something to revive her. But I knew that Grandma was gone. I stood shaking, as though I'd been dipped in ice water. I'd seen death.

The burning, gnawing pain in the center of my gut was unbearable. I cried so much that I couldn't breathe. It no longer felt safe to love anyone, not even God.

I sought hope by asking the head rabbi at our school if there was anyone — a pious or learned man, a tzaddik, or even a rich king — who had learned the secret of living forever. The rabbi scowled as if I was sacrilegious, telling me to go back to class and stop being so foolish.

During third grade, my family moved to Mosholu Parkway, a more affluent Jewish neighborhood in the Bronx. It was too far to travel to the yeshiva, so we were enrolled in the public school and continued our Jewish education by attending Hebrew school in the late afternoons.

After the loss of my grandmother, life held less and less meaning, and school became harder. I had problems adjusting to the ethnic diversity of the new school and felt like an outsider. Like others, I was afraid of the gang members. Being short, Jewish, and, at the time, overweight, I was often picked on and beaten up after school, and once, even threatened with death. A poor reader and an atrocious speller, I also found it difficult to keep up with the class. Yet I excelled in verbal skills and was always chosen as the lead in class plays.

Partly as a reaction to living with a family of immigrant refugees, I developed the skill of speaking clearly. I had an innate ability to engage people and make them laugh when I told stories. As a teenager, I had thoughts of becoming a radio announcer or TV host, but had no real idea of where my abilities would lead.

Although I disliked school, there was one teacher who inspired me. It was 1964, and my whole fourth-grade class was enamored with Mr. Schwartz, our young social studies teacher. He had a goatee and dressed in a soft corduroy jacket, knitted tie, and Hush Puppies. His light-brown hair hung below his ears and made him appear a bit shabby. Everyone thought he must be a beatnik, but I thought he was cool.

One day during a lesson on Asian history, he spoke to the class about karma and reincarnation.

"This is the wheel of birth and death," he said, drawing a circle on the blackboard. "Hindus and Buddhists believe in the law of *karma,* the law of action and its results. Whatever you do binds you to this wheel of life and death again and again. The only way to get off this wheel is to have a centered mind and live an earthly life of good deeds, devotion, and prayer to God. Otherwise you have to keep coming back, lifetime after lifetime."

This was the missing link, the knowledge I had been looking for. I wanted to shout and shake everyone in the class and tell them, "Can't you see? This is it! We don't really die. We just leave the body for a little while. Then we come back to learn more lessons, one day — hopefully — finally getting it." I felt so relieved and wanted to learn more.

I didn't realize then how significant this realization would turn out to be, planting a seed that would blossom in years to come.

My thoughts about death, and now karma and reincarnation, were nearly impossible to share with my family, especially with my father, who was very Old World and conservative.

I was also frightened of my dad and shied away from telling him anything that he could react against or might upset him. He was easily angered, and I never knew how he might take something I said or did. I was terrified when my father became enraged, since it would only be a matter of time before his stinging hand would meet my face.

My father would hit me for little things, like snipping off my bangs, getting dirty while playing, or frightening my sister. Sharyn and I were trained to be on our best behavior when he was home.

One time, when my father saw the poor grades on my report card, his face turned red with rage. He went mad, unbuckled his belt, and growled at me to lie down on my bed. He had done this before. I buried my face in a pillow. I could hear his heavy breathing and the sound of the belt slipping out of his pants. I wished someone would save me, but no one could stop my dad when he got like this. Not even my mother. Then came his command to pull down my pants. I guess his intention was to whip my bared behind, but he was indiscriminate as he beat me, and I screamed into the pillow.

Sometimes I bled. Most of the time my skin would burn like fire from the blisters and bruises. My mother would comfort me and tend to my wounds. She prevented me from going to school until the bruises healed, embarrassed and afraid to let the teachers and other children see. I was ashamed too. I swore that if I had kids I would never do this to them.

When he wasn't losing his temper or reprimanding me, he would cuddle up on the couch and tickle me with his unshaved whiskers, and I knew he loved me. But when he turned his rage on me, I would search his eyes for that love and wonder why it wasn't there.

When I was eleven, I did something wrong in school, and in the evening my dad found out. He grabbed me by the ear and dragged me into my room. He pulled out his belt and terror came over me. But instead of beating me, he simply said, "You're too big for this now."

And with that, it was over.

Maybe someone had intervened, the school principal, or perhaps a teacher.

A psychologist might look back on his abusive behavior as a symptom of post-traumatic stress disorder from the war. But for me, the trauma was long lasting, making me afraid to take risks, and affecting my self-esteem and relationships for many years.

I rarely spoke about these events with my father, even as an adult. Once, when I was about twenty years old, while out to dinner, he brought up how he had treated me, and expressed how awful he felt. He looked down at the table and fidgeted with the saltshaker. There was sadness in his eyes and heaviness in his breath. I soon moved the conversation to another subject. I didn't have the heart to make him feel worse. It was clear that he had also been a victim.

Born in 1914, in Czestochowa, Poland, to a middle-class Jewish family, my dad stood only five-foot four inches, with a bald head, barrel chest, and a well-defined *Ashkenazi* (Central/East European Jewish) nose. He and his younger brother, my Uncle Terry, survived the Second World War together and were very close. The last time they saw their parents and sister alive was the night after *Yom Kippur* (the Day of Atonement), the most solemn of the Jewish holidays. His parents hid in their apartment as my father and his brother got in the selection line for the Nazi work camps.

The Nazis would not allow any Jew with a deformity or handicap to work, so my father cleverly hid his younger brother's clubfoot from the Nazis by forging his brother's work documents and surrounding him with a cluster of friends who looked hardy and robust. This worked, and probably saved my uncle's life.

During the first few years of the war, my father and his brother lived in a Jewish ghetto, but they were later transferred to a concentration camp that manufactured ammunition. Dad and Uncle Terry escaped from the camp one night while walking to an adjacent factory for work detail. In the dark, they hid themselves by lying in an abandoned field, waiting nervously for the armed guards and their work team to disappear into the factory. When it seemed safe, they walked into the city and made their way to the train station, only to find that it was more dangerous to be Jews on the streets of Poland than to be in the camps. They managed to sneak back into the camp, where they remained until liberated at the end of the war.

Often, when I was alone with my dad, he would tell me the story of his final hours in the camp, and his eyes would project a sense of pride. "We could all see that the war was coming to an end. Most of the Nazi officers and guards had left the factory where we worked. Many of the Jewish boys ran for their guns, but I was more practical. I went for the commandant's clothes. I put layer upon layer of suits and coats on my body. It was so heavy, I could barely walk. I almost got myself shot when the Jewish boys saw me walking around wearing the commandant's fine Italian Borsalino hat and coat. They thought I was him!"

He told the same stories over and over. But each time I would listen intently, in fascination, knowing that these stories were important to him. It was our way of being close, of bonding.

There was sadness when he spoke about his parents. He always impressed upon me how much he loved and honored them, and I felt, by comparison, that my love for him and my mom was mediocre and never enough.

My father had focused much of his life on survival. He faced economic challenges with his business and frustrations and disappointments with his family.

When he spoke about the atrocities of the war, most of the stories emphasized his cleverness and practicality in the face of adversity, rather than the degradations he and other Jews had endured. He tried his best to teach me what he learned about survival, and, like many Jews of his generation, he hid his emotional scars. To my father, know-how, *chutzpah,* and money — not faith — were crucial to survival in any situation, especially during war. When I was a child, it seemed odd that he attributed his survival to his wit and resources rather than to God. As I grew older, I felt burdened by his emphasis on the importance of money, and I knew that the focus of my life would be different.

Unlike my father, my mother never told me much about her life and rarely shared personal thoughts. But she was much more modern and easygoing than my dad.

My parents had different views on child rearing, which was often the source of their disagreements. But whenever there was an argument, my mother was the first to drop it. "Don't hold on to a grudge," she told me. "If you do, you will be the loser."

While walking with her on the streets of New York, she would lock her arm in mine as though I were escorting her. She encouraged me to walk on the curb side, telling me that was the right thing to do when I was with a woman. "Always respect women," she'd say. "Then people will respect you."

When I was a boy, she would take me to movie matinees, where we almost always shared a large box of chocolate bonbons. Although Mom kept a strictly kosher home, she would be flexible with rabbinical law on our days out, treating my sister and me to Chinese food almost every Sunday.

Mom was born in Chicago, in 1911. To help her avoid anti-Semitic prejudices and assimilate more easily into American culture, her parents legally changed her Yiddish name, Chana, to Claire.

My father met my mother not long after he and his brother arrived from Europe in 1950. Soon after, the Fischman brothers became the successful owner-operators of a kosher delicatessen and restaurant in the Bronx, and later in Queens.

Eventually, the whole family slaved away in the deli — my father, uncle, mother, aunt, cousins, sister, and me. From the time I was twelve until I went to college, I spent most of my weekends working in "the store," wearing a white apron and selling frankfurters with mustard and sauerkraut. No matter how hard I tried to get rid of the lingering odor, my friends would constantly tease me, saying that I needed to find a new deodorant and that I smelled like pastrami. Many times on my way home from work, stray dogs would run after me, as though they'd found a juicy bone or a fresh piece of meat.

My family responsibilities in the store meant that I missed many opportunities to be with my friends. But I did not have to work during the summer, when my parents would send me to a "sleep-away" camp that was nestled in the Catskill Mountains near Monticello, New York. Camp was eight weeks of fun and fresh air. Although I was not very good at sports, I was the ringleader of mischief and practical jokes.

In high school, I received several art awards, won prestigious contests, and was encouraged by my teachers to study art as a career. And, in 1972, I received a partial scholarship to study art at the State University of New York's Purchase College.

Dorm life at college turned out to be a lot like going to camp, and being an art major provided a lot of time to socialize and investigate the world of recreational drugs. Being a counter-culture hippie, I considered psychedelics and marijuana ways to expand consciousness, and I quickly made them part of my life.

But I felt lost. I questioned my purpose in life and the reason I was going to school. The academic classes I took were hard for me and I was too embarrassed to seek help for my learning problems. I cut classes and hiked alone in the woods that surrounded the campus. Nature brought me peace. The stillness of the trees and the colors of autumn leaves consoled me. I prayed to God to make me a better person and to give me a clear direction.

Then, in the middle of my freshman year, on a cold and dreary December day, I found out that my mother, at age sixty-four, had suffered a heart attack. By the time I arrived at the hospital, the doctor had already pronounced her dead. I was met by my grieving aunts and uncles, who told me the news. "Mommy's dead. She died ten minutes ago."

I wanted to cry but I couldn't. I felt cold and hot at the same time and thought I would faint. Breath would not exit or enter my lungs.

I never expected my mom to die so early in life, and I couldn't comprehend that I would never see her again. I felt as though I had a massive stone inside me. The entire universe was collapsing into my stomach. Life was again showing me that it wasn't safe to be loved or to love someone. If I did, God would only take that person away.

I missed my mother immediately, weeping for hours at a time. I thought of her ironing the family's clothes late at night while speaking on the phone to her sister, who lived only three blocks away. They spoke about everything — all the time. I never understood why they needed to speak for such long periods when they had just visited a few hours earlier. But Aunt Ruthy was more than a sister, she was my mom's best friend and confidante. After Mom passed away, Aunt Ruthy was there for me too, my emotional support.

I was devastated that I never got the chance to see my mom or say good-bye before she died. Confused and depressed, I dropped out of college to stay home with my grieving father. At school, staying out late and partying with friends had been a way to have fun and rebel. Now I did those things to suppress the pain of my mother's death.

I had no tools or guidance to help me through it. Sharyn and Dad were tight as clams, totally mute on their feelings about Mom's death. I didn't know where to turn. It would be many years before I had an opportunity to release my grief.

Dad wanted me to participate in the traditional Jewish bereavement period. I was expected to recite the Mourner's *Kaddish,* the prayer for the dead, at the temple for a year. Sitting next to my father in the early morning hours, hung over from the night before, I questioned the purpose of this mourner's ritual. My eyes would wander around the dimly lit *schul* (synagogue), watching the congregation of mostly older men *daven* (pray), their lips moving rapidly, whispering, almost silently, the Hebrew words they knew by heart. There was no need to open the prayer books they cradled close to their chests.

The traditional mourner's prayer simply praised the sanctity and glory of God, and seemed to have nothing to do with my mother's death. Maybe the ritual was intended to help feel communion with God or the community at a time when a person's faith might be low, but the words and repetition did not console me or help me understand what had happened, and hardly anyone seemed to empathize with my pain. I felt resentful and separate from the congregation.

I asked our rabbi about the deeper meaning of this prayer, but his explanation was vague and confusing. Or maybe nothing would have gotten through to me at that time. Still, I hoped that if I repeated the prayer long enough, my grief would be relieved or I would feel the presence of God, but nothing happened.

Thinking about others in my family who had passed away, I was aware of the inevitable: eventually, I would die too. More than ever, I had a longing to know God and understand the meaning of life. And maybe that was the one of the purposes of the Kaddish.

As I sat on the hard wooden pews, I felt queasy from the smell of stale morning breath that permeated the room. Dad would sit in the synagogue with his eyes closed, holding his prayer book tightly. I assumed that he was remembering the good old days, when he would go to the temple where his father was a *hazzan* (the cantor, who leads the sung prayers). I knew that if he could read my mind, he'd be disappointed. I really only went to the temple with him to make him happy.

Despite my feelings, I stayed with my father, attending synagogue with him in the morning and partying with my friends at night. Instead of being a support and consolation for each other, Dad and I battled. I couldn't adjust to his stubborn, conservative nature, and he couldn't handle living with a rebellious hippie like me.

One day, he laid down the rules: "No more just hanging around and coming home all hours of the night. From now on, you have to be home at eleven on weeknights and twelve on weekends. And cut your hair! You look like a woman with your hair growing below your shoulders!"

Finally, he threatened to throw me out of the house. "You have to either get a job or go back to school!" he declared.

A few weeks later, I moved out and started a new job in New York City's garment center.

My cousin Leon was a highly accomplished designer in the fashion industry, and since I'd been an art student, he believed he could mold my talent and help me get a job as a textile designer. I apprenticed with my cousin for a little while, eventually landing a job at a small studio on Seventh Avenue, in the heart of the garment center. I enjoyed being creative, making designs that would eventually get printed on fabrics that appeared in the stores.

I shared my new apartment in Flushing, Queens, with two guys — a bartender and a professional musician who played bass in a jazz band.

I liked my new friends and my new freedom. Eventually, I bought a used car, went back to school at night, and started dating a beautiful girl. Everything appeared to be going well. Yet inside I was miserable. Life was becoming monotonous. I felt detached and uncomfortable with myself. I often found myself tuning out an unfulfilling world by sitting in front of the TV and watching reruns. Something was missing.

In a short time, everything fell apart. I was like a Hank Williams Country & Western song. My girlfriend broke my heart by having an affair with my best friend. Then the car I'd just purchased was stolen. I was a success as a textile designer, with promotions and pay increases. But what began as a promising and creative career, now just felt repetitive.

I was part of a generation that was more active than most in pursuing a meaningful life and a better world. That spirit, and an ever-increasing backlog of painful experiences, made me think that there might be a better way to live my life.

Hoping for some guidance, I entered psychotherapy. I chose a traditional Freudian analyst, but was quickly turned off by the oversimplified connections he was making between my childhood and my life as a young adult. I felt that there must be a better way to heal and grow and overcome my limitations, but I didn't know how to find it.

Strangely, it was curiosity about an old friend that finally propelled me into a life-changing sequence of events.

CHAPTER TWO

The White Album

PERHAPS IT WAS MY GUARDIAN ANGEL, good karma, coincidence, or old-fashioned good luck that caused an ex-girlfriend to call with the news that she had run into my old buddy, Kevin. She gave me his phone number and insisted I call him. She explained that Kevin had recently returned from several months on a meditation retreat in Livingston Manor, New York, and had gone through a huge transformation.

Only a few days earlier, I'd been lying on my bed, staring at a poster on my bedroom wall, with a stream of thoughts about becoming a recluse, discovering peace of mind, and meditating in a cave. These thoughts were unusual for me, but, for some reason, they brought some comfort.

The poster had come with the Beatles' *White Album* and included some thumbnail pictures of the Beatles' time in India with spiritual master Maharishi Mahesh Yogi. I'd been a Beatles fan since they first appeared on the *Ed Sullivan Show* in 1964, and I and had all their records. The Beatles had dabbled in Eastern mysticism. Maybe meditation was the answer I was searching for.

Still, I hesitated to call Kevin.

Kevin and I bonded instantly when we first met in our high-school gym class. We were fourteen years old. He was tall and scrawny, and I was short and plump. Ill-suited as athletes, we were two outcasts, constantly ridiculed for our appearance and our lack of physical coordination. We hung around together after school, rode our bicycles in Flushing Meadows Park, drank cherry Cokes, and told lies about girlfriends we never had.

But by the time we graduated, Kevin had become a handsome, charismatic young man and was popular with girls. The last time we met, he was an outlaw guitar-playing hippie type, with his hair pulled back in a ponytail like Willy Nelson. He had a thick beard that erased his neck, wore motorcycle boots, and his keys jingled like a tiny carillon as they dangled from a silver chain on his belt loop.

I never expected Kevin to become attracted to a spiritual path. I tried to imagine him wearing a white robe, with his legs twisted in a lotus position. After so many years of not speaking to each other, and with so little going on in my life, I felt uncomfortable calling him. But I was also intrigued.

After several days, I decided to give him a call. I wanted to find out what he had gained from meditation. Had he experienced nirvana? He sounded happy to hear from me and wanted to get together as soon as possible. I was still apprehensive, but invited him to my apartment for dinner.

Kevin looked different. He was poised, had a warm smile, and his eyes were clear and radiant. He was clean-shaven, well groomed, wore freshly pressed chinos and a long-sleeve blue dress shirt, and brown wing-tip shoes. He looked very conservative. I twitched nervously, scratched my head, and smoked one cigarette after another as I listened to him talk about meditation.

He had spent the last two years at a Transcendental Meditation (TM) retreat center. And having completed the first phase of training to become a TM teacher, he was eager to tell me how meditation worked and what he'd learned about TM's founder, Maharishi Mahesh Yogi — the same Maharishi I had been looking at on the Beatles poster.

"Meditation allows the mind to experience its true nature, which is bliss consciousness," he explained. "Through meditation, you get to experience your inner Self or Being."

I had read very little about meditation, and the language and the concepts he was using were mostly foreign to me. Kevin was definitely serene, and he seemed to know what he was talking about, but it was all a bit abstract to me, and I thought he was throwing pearls to swine. But after giving some rehearsed-sounding analogies from physics, he explained that our pure consciousness was like a movie screen, with our thoughts and experiences projected on it. If the screen is dirty, full of stresses and strains, the images are not as clear and enjoyable. Meditating, he said, helps you clean the screen and also experience that pure consciousness by itself, which he said was very blissful. That explanation, at least, was something I could relate to.

Meditation, he assured me, would soothe my nervous system, and I would be able to experience a deeper state of rest than sleep. "Then, as the nervous system is freed of stress," he said, "you begin to experience real joy. You're more relaxed, and self-awareness happens more frequently. You begin to experience higher states of consciousness in day-to-day life. And this happens naturally and effortlessly, without drugs or alcohol."

The change in Kevin was speaking louder than his words. I couldn't help comparing his relaxation to my nervousness. His peace and centeredness is really what won me over. This was what I had been waiting for, what was missing in my life. I could eliminate the stress and fatigue, elevate my energy, and expand awareness. With a clear mind, I could know truth, which I believed would lead me to God.

In November 1976, the Saturday after Thanksgiving, I arrived early at the Forest Hills TM Center on Queens Boulevard to be initiated into meditation. A young woman greeted me with a smile. She introduced herself as Susan and informed me she would be my meditation instructor. (Kevin couldn't initiate me because he wasn't a full-fledged teacher yet.)

Susan guided me into a room that was permeated with the sweet fragrance of incense. We walked over to a table that had been prepared for a traditional ceremony she would do before my instruction. The flame from a small candle dimly lit the room. She motioned for me to stand near her and told me that she was going to perform a ceremony of gratitude to the masters of Maharishi's tradition who had kept this wisdom of *mantra* and meditation alive through the ages.

After the ceremony, Susan softly gave me my mantra, a Sanskrit sound that, when used correctly, vibrates subtly, allowing the mind to go into meditation effortlessly. She indicated that we should sit with our eyes closed, and, with only a few words, I was meditating on my own.

At first, my mind wandered with broken images from my past. I was not experiencing bliss. In fact, I was quite uncomfortable and restless. I saw my grandmother's face, and I had memories of being a child in my mother's arms. I feared that I would never calm down. I repeated my mantra, fully doubting I was doing the practice correctly. Then, surprisingly, my mind began to settle, and I felt a warmth come over my body. I began to feel relaxed and was reminded of the time I'd been given ether as a child, just before my tonsils were removed. I continued to meditate, and within a short time, all my thoughts vanished, I was in a void. I had lost all track of time. I thought only three minutes had passed, but when Susan brought me out of meditation she told me that I had been there for more than twenty minutes. The world looked completely new, vibrant, and crystal clear. I never imagined that an experience like this was possible.

Meditation seemed natural to me once I started, and I soon experienced the benefits of regular practice. Without much effort, I became completely drug-free, started an aerobic exercise program, and stopped smoking cigarettes — all within three months. I also started wanting healthier foods, and after six months or so, I lost my desire for meat and became a vegetarian.

With less negativity in my mind, my energy and enthusiasm were on the rise and my creativity was blossoming. After starting a job at another large textile company, I was quickly promoted to head designer of a large menswear division.

The benefits of my new routine were obvious, and I wanted to explore meditation further. I took several weekend retreats, where we meditated more, could ask about our practice, and watched videotapes of Maharishi Mahesh Yogi explaining the mechanics of meditation, its value in daily life, and growth into higher states of consciousness. I looked forward to hearing stories about Maharishi and his teacher, Swami Brahmananda Saraswati, in the same way I had relished the stories of the *tzaddiks,* the great rabbis of Judaism, in my childhood.

Maharishi came from a lineage known as the *Shankaracharya* tradition. His master had been honored as the Shankaracharya of the North, in Jyotir Math, one of the four seats of learning set up long ago by Adi Shankara, the highly revered eighth-century saint who had traveled throughout India, reviving the *Vedic* knowledge of one underlying and permeating reality of life.

These four spiritual centers were set up by Shankara as a unique and ingenious way to preserve this wisdom for all time. I have been told that the seat of the North is considered the most prestigious of the four seats. It was the first seat that Shankara created, and was originally held by his most devoted disciple, Trotaka. It was eventually occupied by Maharishi's master, Swami Brahmananda Saraswati, who Maharishi always referred to as Gurudev. *Gurudev* means great or divine guru, and is a common way for people in India to refer to a cherished master. Offering the Shankaracharya's seat to Gurudev was recognition that he was a *Brahma gyani* — a fully realized knower of truth.

Before Gurudev, the seat had been vacant for more than a hundred and fifty years, since no one had been deemed worthy to fill it. However, Gurudev had himself repeatedly refused the seat for two decades. Finally, and without explanation, he accepted, and, in April 1941, at the age of seventy, he was inaugurated as Shankaracharya of Jyotir Math.

Gurudev was born in the northern province of Uttar Pradesh to an affluent and respected family. Rajaram (Gurudev's childhood name) was a mature and precocious child. Different from most children, he was not interested in toys, new clothes, or even playing cricket with the other kids. His best friend was his grandfather, who died unexpectedly when Rajaram was only seven. His grandfather's death had a profound effect on him.

Realizing that life was only temporary, at age nine, he left home and dedicated himself to knowing the eternal Self. The legend is that he traveled to the Himalayas on a quest to find the perfect master. During his journey he met many *sannyasins* (renunciates) and masters, but no one that measured up to the standards he had set. After five years of wandering in the mountains, he found his guru, Swami Krishanand Saraswati, who lived in a region called Uttar Kashi, often called the Valley of the Saints.

At age thirty-six, after being initiated into *sannyas,* the vows of a Hindu monk, Gurudev left his master for a cave near Amarkantak, in central India, where he retired into blissful solitude. Stories about him say that the peace and serenity he exuded was so great that wild tigers walked peacefully for miles around his cave. Although he was rarely seen for the next forty years, word of this enlightened saint began to spread throughout India.

Kevin gave me a photo of Gurudev, which I placed in a gold frame and kept on the night table near my bed. I liked burning a candle and incense near his picture when I meditated. Sometimes after meditation, I would hold the picture in my hand and gaze at it. There was so much serenity in this holy man's eyes. I felt closer to him than I did to Maharishi.

My TM teacher, Susan, happily shared the stories she knew about Gurudev, Maharishi, and the tradition of masters. She told me that Maharishi was a physics student at Allahabad University when he first saw Gurudev. One night, while Gurudev was making a rare appearance in a nearby village, Maharishi, along with his uncle and a few friends, went to see this highly revered saint to receive his *darshan* (blessing). Maharishi sat on the veranda of a rural house in pitch dark, not knowing that he was actually sitting near the saint he had come to see. But, soon, the distant headlights of a passing car swept across the porch, and the young student momentarily saw the face of the sage who was to become his master. In that fraction of a moment, Maharishi said his heart surrendered and he committed his life to serving Gurudev.

While having dinner at an Indian restaurant in Greenwich Village, Kevin told me more, explaining that before accepting Maharishi as a student Gurudev insisted that Maharishi finish his physics degree. As soon as he completed his university studies, Maharishi joined Gurudev and was initiated into the monastic order. It was about six months after Maharishi became a monk that Gurudev accepted the position of Shankaracharya of Jyotir Math.

But Maharishi soon discovered that being the youngest and newest monk had its disadvantages — he hardly ever got to see his master. He wanted to spend more time with Gurudev, but the large number of learned people around him made it difficult. Instead, Maharishi arranged to start cleaning Gurudev's floors. He prepared his meals, did his laundry, and, eventually, was answering his mail. He became so in tune with his master that before Gurudev could ask for a drink of water, Maharishi would drop the broom and say, "I will get it for you," and run off. He even slept on the floor outside Gurudev's door, in case his master might need something during the night.

On a video I saw, Maharishi explained that Gurudev hardly ever asked him to do anything. So to learn his master's mind, he would test Gurudev's reactions. Maharishi would perform an action to see how Gurudev responded. Then he would take another action and watch Gurudev again. Within two-and-a-half years, Maharishi had completely attuned his heart and mind to his master. He is said to have sat as the master sat, spoken as the master spoke, and thought as the master thought.

After what Maharishi called "twelve years that flashed by," Gurudev left his body. Following his *Mahasamadhi* (final transcendence at death), the body was placed in a stone casket and lowered into the Ganges River. Maharishi dove down alongside the casket to make sure it was aligned properly. Maharishi stayed under water for a very long time, and many on the shore began to worry that they might have lost him, too. After some time, he surfaced, took a deep breath, and again dove into the water. Finally, Maharishi resurfaced and climbed into the boat that was waiting for him. Many years later, when Maharishi recalled this event, he explained that as he followed the casket, he too dropped the body and went with Gurudev. But Gurudev brought him back to life. He told Maharishi that his work in this world was not yet through and gave him the responsibility of spiritually regenerating the world.

After Gurudev's passing, Maharishi retired to a cave in Uttar Kashi, high in the Himalayas. After two years of silence in that Valley of the Saints, a thought kept coming up that he should go to a particular town in South India. The other saints in the area tried to dissuade him, but the thought persisted. So Maharishi left the Himalayas and went to the holy city of Rameshwaram, and then to Trivandrum, where he was asked to give a series of lectures. During these lectures, he began to teach what he called Transcendental Deep Meditation. And this was the start of his Spiritual Regeneration Movement.

My relationship with Maharishi was very different than the relationship he had with his Gurudev. My link to Maharishi was through a television screen. Though I had not yet met him in person, my heart filled with devotion as I watched him through the new medium of that time — videotape.

I was inspired by his mission to bring meditation and enlightenment to the average man. But sometimes I wished I could actually spend time around Maharishi. I had heard that spending time around an enlightened master would speed up one's growth, like one flame lighting another, and help a person with his or her spiritual blind spots. But I assumed that not everyone needed to have that experience, at least not in person. Most meditators seemed to be growing spiritually without that direct interaction.

After I had been meditating for a year or so, I was reading the *New York Post,* and saw an article about Maharishi's TM-Sidhis Program. The article explained that *siddhi* is a Sanskrit word for perfection, and that one who attains such perfection or yogic abilities is called a *sid-dha*. Through a series of powerful advanced techniques, individuals could accelerate their growth toward enlightenment — bliss consciousness — and at the same time create a vibration that would contribute to world peace. This was what I had been waiting for my whole life. Maybe this was my calling. I would get enlightened and, in the process, I would help the world.

I took a leave of absence from my job and was able to complete the entire training in five months. During the course, we were told that practicing the program in large groups would amplify the effects and be even more powerful. I felt such bliss and energy that, several months later, in late 1979, I took my next step by joining fifteen hundred TM *siddhas* from all over the United States at Maharishi International University (MIU) in Fairfield, Iowa.

I was excited by the idea of meditating in such a large group. There was already some research that indicated that even a small number of people practicing these techniques had been correlated with a reduction in crime in several cities.

As I drove toward the campus, I could see a Golden Dome under construction. It was a geodesic dome, a structure developed by Buckminster Fuller in the late 1940s that provides an enclosed space, free of structural supports. Maharishi had thought such a structure would be perfect for the large programs he envisioned.

Most of the participants were attending the conference for a week during their winter vacation. However, I planned to stay for at least a year, dedicating myself to exploring deeper states of consciousness while creating world peace.

On the second day of the conference, I heard a rumor that Maharishi would be coming to MIU. I'd heard this sort of rumor on large courses before, so I didn't pay much attention. But when I walked into the meditation hall for the evening program, the stage now supported a special sofa and the distinct pencil-thin microphone I had seen on film. The fragrance of the many colorful flowers erased any lingering doubt. I had seen Maharishi many times from the waist up on videotape. Now, I would have a chance to meet the man who had affected my life so profoundly.

A few moments later, Maharishi glided through a hushed but excited crowd to the stage. He sat silently, looking at the hundreds of people who had gathered to see him. A feeling of bliss pervaded the hall, and I felt goose bumps all over my body. Maharishi looked older and smaller than he had seemed in his photos and tapes. His hair and beard, now creamy white, made him look even more like a holy man. With the white curtains, his white robes, and white hair and beard, I felt as if I was in heaven among the clouds. A strong vibration rose up my spine and a pulsation between my eyebrows spread like an electrical current throughout my body.

Maharishi greeted the crowd in his distinctive warm voice with, *"Jai Gurudev."* (He used this salutation to attribute glory and reverence to his own guru and the tradition of Vedic masters.) He asked people to come to the microphone to share their experience of practicing the new program in a large group. I was too shy to share. I simply sat listening, my eyes fixed on the man I admired so much.

The following day, there was a gala inauguration ceremony for the Golden Dome that was under construction. The ceremony took place outdoors under the still roofless dome, on an especially cold Iowa winter day. We gathered in our heavy coats to watch three Vedic pundits chant hymns from the Rig Veda.

The word *Veda* is Sanskrit for "knowledge," but implies the knowledge of the whole range of creation and how to experience it in consciousness. Maharishi explained that the *Vedas* are ancient knowledge that predates modern history. They were cognized by a number of ancient seers and passed down orally for thousands of years. The significance of these Sanskrit scriptures is not only in their content, but also in the vibrational quality they produce when chanted.

It was so cold that day that two of the three pundits were wrapped in layers of warm shawls and blankets over their flimsy robes, and they sat near a small electric heater to keep from shivering. The third pundit, seemingly unaffected by the freezing cold, wore only his thin silk

Indian robes and a serene, tender smile. He had soft, almond-shaped eyes that sparkled with compassion as he watched the crowd huddle together to stay warm. He took his time and looked at everyone. For a few fleeting moments I thought he was looking at me. I felt excited and happy about that. There was something special about him. Toward the end of the event, someone finally persuaded him to take a shawl, and I was glad someone was taking care of him.

Later that afternoon, I walked to the meditation hall, bundled in my winter coat, carrying my cushion and blanket under my arm. As I walked, I could see the pundits being driven around the campus in a huge white Cadillac.

A feeling of calm came over me as I stopped to watch them. Through the back window of the car, I could see the blissful face of the young pundit who had refused blankets during the ceremony. As he smiled and waved to the small crowd that had gathered, his twinkling eyes caught mine. I felt a warm breeze brush against my skin. His innocent gaze penetrated my heart and tears welled up. They weren't tears of sadness, though. In a few moments I began to weep.

I was stunned at my reaction. Who was this man and why was he having such a strong affect on me?

A senior TM teacher told me that the young pundit was named Ravi Shankar, and that he was quite dear to Maharishi. For many years, that moment stayed in my heart, filling me with warmth and love.

I stayed at MIU for the next six months, meditating every day, in the Dome when it was completed. During the first four months, I lived in town, working at various businesses run by meditators. To make life easier, I decided to join the university staff and live on the campus.

My job was at the university farm, growing tomatoes and zucchini, and looking after the dairy cows. For a young Jewish man who had spent his whole life in New York City, living in the Midwest as a meditating farmer, without subway trains and skyscrapers, seemed incredibly surreal. I felt like a character in my own movie. There was something fulfilling about this life.

However, after a while, my old mental patterns returned I started to question why I was in Iowa. There was no doubt that my meditations were deep, but I still had the same feelings of inadequacy and separation from others that I'd felt before dropping out of college. I couldn't relate to the isolated community in Fairfield, and I didn't want to become another overzealous meditator.

To me, the community seemed narrow in its focus. I appreciated their sincerity, but I still had desires I wanted to fulfill. I wanted to feel more integrated, have fun, maybe get married and start a family. I needed a break from chasing enlightenment. And with all the meditating I had done, I was still no better at dealing with feelings.

But I didn't leave. Instead, I started becoming unruly and hanging out with a few other like-minded New Yorkers. We acted rowdy and immature, coming late to our jobs, having food fights in the dining hall, and singing *Amazing Grace* at the top of our lungs at all times and places for days on end.

Eventually, our small rebellious group was called into an MIU administrator's office. We were told that we were "unstressing too heavily," and that our gross behavior was detrimental to Maharishi's work. With no previous warning, and absolutely no discussion, we were given twenty-four hours to leave campus.

I had grown uncomfortable at MIU, and my behavior was clearly off, but I had given up my job and my apartment in New York to participate in Maharishi's desire to have large groups meditating together. The coldness of the university's response was a shock.

I felt a deep sadness as I prepared to leave. I couldn't believe how thoroughly I'd sabotaged my desire to serve and grow. I was orphaned from the meaning and purpose I'd found, with no idea what I would do next.

The last thing left to pack was my photo of Gurudev. Placing it in my suitcase, I had a surprising feeling of gratitude and relief. But I had prayed for an opportunity to feel a sense of purpose, help the world, and grow in higher consciousness. I wondered if I would ever get another opportunity like this.

CHAPTER THREE

A Taste of India

DRIVING THROUGH THE ROLLING HILLS of Iowa, on my way back to New York, I began to get a perspective. I was still angered and disappointed by the way I'd been treated, but I wasn't blaming Maharishi or questioning the value of his techniques.

Overall, I was pleased with the direction I had taken in my life. I was now twenty-six, and I had learned to meditate, met Maharishi, and had experienced refined states of consciousness. Intuitively, I sensed that this was just the beginning and that eventually I would need to explore other aspects of personal growth. But for now, continuing with my meditation program was still my highest priority.

Back in the material world, it didn't take long for me to reorient. I had to focus on earning money, and I soon had a job as a freelance designer. I enjoyed being back in the big city. I got involved in a new relationship, Kevin and I grew closer as friends, and I started reading books about metaphysics and spiritual teachers. I was ready for my next step. A desire to spend time with yogis and mystics started to percolate.

And then, within six months of my return to New York, Maharishi announced a six-week Vedic Science conference, to be held in New Delhi, India. He expected to have several thousand people meditating and practicing their advanced techniques together during the course. I was hesitant to resume my relationship with the TM movement so soon after my MIU experience, but I was sure Maharishi would be there for this program, and I looked forward to another chance to be in his presence.

It was November 1980, and India was a much different place than it is today. I was excited about my first trip outside of North America, but I was unprepared for the conditions that awaited me. After a forty-two hour chartered plane ride from New York with two hundred and fifty other meditators, the chaos and confusion of the New Delhi airport overwhelmed me. With the lack of air conditioning, the heat and humidity was especially uncomfortable, and the resulting combination of body odors and mold nauseated me.

Making our way through the pandemonium, we finally found our luggage, heaped in a huge pile in the center of the waiting room. Fatigued and miserable, I longed for a bed. But we had to wait two more hours while TM representatives sorted our luggage and organized transportation to our rooms.

On the rickety airport bus we were segregated by gender for housing. Women were housed in comfortable hotels, while most of the men were sent to stay in the countryside, at Maharishi Nagar — Maharishi's rustic ashram outside of Delhi, in the town of Noida. I was among a lucky group of three Americans and seven Italians who were arbitrarily assigned to a small guesthouse situated on a quiet road on the outskirts of Delhi.

Maharishi arranged the inauguration of the Vedic Science conference to coincide with *Diwali,* the annual fall festival of light that honors and celebrates, among other things, Lakshmi (the goddess of wealth and other forms of abundance), and the victory of light over darkness within each person. An elaborate Vedic ceremony was planned for that evening.

It was pitch dark by the time the seven of us arrived at what we were told was the site of the ceremony. With just a few lanterns to light our way, it appeared that the ashram was totally barren —a huge empty parking lot in the middle of nowhere. After walking aimlessly for a while in the dark, we were greeted by some Indians, dressed in traditional white robes, who led us to an enormous tent covered with colorful Indian tarps.

I could hear Maharishi's familiar voice speaking to the crowd in a language I assumed was Hindi. It took me a while to spot him among the many dignitaries on the stage. The current Shankaracharya of the North was there, along with his full entourage. Near Maharishi were several pundits, and sitting directly to his right was a man whose face I recognized. It was the young pundit in the white car — Ravi Shankar. The one who had refused blankets to stay warm at MIU while he chanted Vedic hymns.

Nearly six thousand people crammed into the enormous tent erected for the ceremony. Among them were approximately twenty-five hundred Vedic pundits. Many looked worn and ragged, which did not match my image of refined Vedic priests. After the *Lakshmi puja* (a traditional ceremony performed on Diwali), shawls and Indian sweets were offered as gifts to the pundits, dignitaries, and the three thousand meditators. Suddenly, I noticed a commotion among the pundits, and many started pushing their way to the stage, grabbing as many gifts and sweets as they could carry. Maharishi turned his head away, rolled his eyes and laughed, as a huge Indian man jumped down from the stage to protect him and the other dignitaries, pushing the crowd back with a long wooden pole. It wasn't at all the way we expected pundits to behave. The Americans and Europeans were especially perplexed, and a little frightened.

The next day we set off to meet with Maharishi for the beginning of our conference. The owners of *The Indian Express,* Delhi's most popular newspaper, had donated their new vacant office building, still under construction, for the conference.

Inside, I found myself sitting so close to Maharishi that I could see the whites of his eyes. This was what I had come for. After a few moments, an aide brought him some juice, and I watched as Maharishi brought the silver cup to his mouth. Watching Maharishi perform this simple act felt intimate, like he was sharing a part of his personal life.

Because I'd never had any one-to-one interaction with Maharishi,

I never thought of him as my personal master. For many like me, who started TM after it had grown into a large organization, he seemed more like a world teacher than a personal guru. TM was promoted as a do-it-yourself technique. Even though I longed for a more intimate relationship with a master, I knew that at my level in the TM hierarchy it would be nearly impossible to get outwardly close to him. And yet his communication with us felt personal.

Maharishi had been a guru to his original group of followers in the beginning days. But by the time I came along there were so many people, and that kind of relationship seemed impractical. However, Maharishi had laid out such a well-defined program, I concluded it wasn't necessary to have a personal guru in order to evolve. In fact, I laughed at people who had a guru, thinking they were weak and incapable of making decisions for themselves.

Two weeks after we arrived, on a day that my group moved from our guesthouse to the ashram at Noida, word spread that a riot had broken out. We heard that a group of angry pundits had overturned one of our buses and set an administrator's car on fire. The pundits were refusing to cooperate with Maharishi or the movement organizers.

The chaos and unruliness of the situation frightened some of the course participants. A few women I knew were calling their airline to see if they could go home early. I realized that my earlier impression of these pundits had been well founded.

Though most of us didn't know it at the time, it turned out, to the horror of the organizers, that most of these pundits were not really pundits at all. Maharishi's grand plan had required that as many pundits as possible be recruited for the conference in order to perform the *yagyas,* the ancient Vedic ceremonies that enliven the laws of nature and bring blessings to the participants and the world. Behind the scenes, some overzealous and less scrupulous organizers had essentially bribed these people to move to Maharishi Nagar. Many had sold their homes and livestock, and traveled from distant villages for the promised reward of high wages, good food, and some minor Western-style comforts for themselves and their families. The false pundits heard that the conference organizers were about to discover what took place and would ask them to leave. Terrified of losing what they were promised, they panicked. They fought among themselves and then turned into an agitated mob that would not listen to reason or take direction from the movement authorities.

Ravi Shankar, the young pundit I had seen at MIU, took it upon himself to remedy the explosive situation. Confident that he could resolve the conflict peacefully, he wanted to speak to the angry mob directly. Many of the TM-movement organizers pleaded with him not to do that, warning that it wasn't safe and that he would literally be risking his life.

The enraged group gathered with sticks and torches. Rumors had spread that Ravi Shankar was against them, and they started shouting at him and threatening to set him on fire. He approached their leader and convinced him to let him address the crowd for thirty minutes. After that, he said, they could do what they wanted to him.

Despite the peril, he stood silently and looked at the people with love. No one made a move. A thousand faces were waiting to see what he would do next. "Jai Gurudev," he said. And then, without any use of force or authority, he simply explained that the yagyas were highly specific. If done well they were extremely helpful and powerful, but if done incorrectly they could actually be harmful, both to the world and to those who performed them.

He assured the group that no one would be made to leave, explaining that the ashram needed all types of skills, not just pundits. It did not matter if they were cobblers, stonemasons, or farmers, they would all be given whatever they had been promised in return for work. And to make sure only qualified pundits were chanting, any pundit who wanted to perform the yagyas would be tested.

This seemed to satisfy the group, and he was easily able to separate those who were trained as pundits from those who were not. Within a short time, he had defused what could have been a crisis for Maharishi's movement.

Compared to the challenges that faced Maharishi and the young

Ravi Shankar, the problems and discomforts I was experiencing during that time were small and inconsequential. Yet, along with the joy of being in Maharishi's extraordinary presence came the daily struggle with the physical conditions on the course. My lungs burned from the harsh smoke of burning dung patties that blew into the conference rooms from the campfires of the squatters below. And my body ached from sitting for hours on the hard concrete floor. The Indian squat toilets were an unbearable inconvenience for me. And the minute I left the building, I was surrounded by grabbing beggars.

Maharishi was giving us an in-depth understanding of the essence of Vedic knowledge, but for many of the Westerners, the course became an exercise in survival. Meditation was the simplest practice of our day, a stark contrast to the constant adjustments demanded by the physical environment.

An infirmary was set up on the sixth floor of the *Indian Express* building, looking more like a battle scene from *Gone With the Wind* than a Vedic conference. Sanitation and hygiene became a real problem, and hundreds of Westerners soon lay in beds in the makeshift infirmary, mostly suffering from dysentery, with many wishing they were home. I became fastidious about everything I ate. I ate only rice and *chapatti* (flat bread). I became so neurotic that when I ran out of purified water I brushed my teeth with Limca, a brand of Indian soda pop.

As wonderful as it was to be with Maharishi, to see him in person, to meditate, and hear his knowledge, I was thoroughly relieved when it was time to go home. I missed New York. I had lost fifteen pounds. I was tired of worrying about where my drinking water came from and about parasites. I wanted to relax in the comforts and conveniences of a developed country again.

My friend, Kevin, greeted me on my arrival back home and was shocked at how thin, stressed, and exhausted I looked. "This, after being with Maharishi for a month?" he asked. I couldn't explain. I was so glad to be home.

India was great — once. But I promised myself I'd never go back.

CHAPTER FOUR

The Dharma Hunter

Ahhh…. IT WAS A RELIEF to be back under the familiar canopy of the
New York skyline. There was a shift in my awareness. Now that I was
back from India, I lived with a heightened sense of gratitude for simple
things, like drinking water directly from the tap or breathing air that
was (comparatively) free of toxic smoke and pollutants.

However, after a few weeks, my perceptions and feelings of gratitude
dulled. I was once again caught up in daily routines.

Then, on December 8, 1980, a report came through my car radio
that John Lennon had been shot dead outside his Manhattan apartment building. I couldn't believe what I heard. I felt it personally. Tears
streamed down my cheeks as I listened to the details of the tragedy.
I was so overwhelmed with sadness that I had to pull my car off the
road and stop.

For me, John Lennon was more than a rock star. He was a force that
had inspired the culture to embrace a social revolution.

While attending John Lennon's vigil in Central Park, I thought about
my life and realized that I was overly concerned with myself, consumed
with my own affairs. I wanted to move ahead and grow, to be more than
just another New Age meditator. I wanted to make a difference and
contribute to the world in some way. I knew it was time for me to find
a new direction and take greater responsibility in my life.

Dharma is the Sanskrit word for the work or activity most in tune with a person's nature or purpose in life. I needed to find my dharma. But I didn't know how.

Bored again with the fashion industry and my freelance work, I wanted a change. One of my housemates helped me compose a resume, and within a few months I got a job marketing graphic-arts cameras to the advertising and printing industry.

After a year, and some smooth talking, I landed another job, as an account executive for Ogilvy & Mather, one of the world's most prestigious advertising agencies. Along with an office on Madison Avenue came the financial rewards that allowed me to move into my own apartment, purchase a brand-new car, and dress in fine fashion.

There were many perks that came with being an account executive for an advertising agency. My boss encouraged me to entertain my clients, giving me an annual expense account that exceeded what most schoolteachers earned in a year. However, the excitement of a virtually unlimited expense account, dining at the finest restaurants in New York, and having front-row seats to the latest Broadway shows soon wore off. Five years earlier, this kind of life would have been very attractive. Now, as a meditating vegetarian who abstained from alcohol, I was a fish out of water. When entertaining my clients, I was appalled to watch them drink double martinis at lunch and then go back to work.

I stuck it out for a few years, but I was getting frustrated. I became increasingly fed up with the bureaucracy of the corporate world, and with the superficial, impersonal relationships I had with my clients. My heart still longed for something greater. Wherever I turned, I was reminded that I needed to find my purpose in life.

The desire to find my dharma began to burn like a blazing fire. I thought that a new career might fill that void. So I started reading books about how to find the perfect job, and spent a lot of money on employment counselors who administered aptitude tests that came to no conclusion. Thinking that I needed more creativity in my life, I enrolled in pottery, photography, and vegetarian cooking classes. I now had a new recipe for artichoke salad, some colorful ashtrays, and even got lost in the darkroom — but still I had no direction in life.

Each time a spiritual teacher came to New York, I would sit through the lecture, and then, at intermission, I would privately ask for guidance in finding my dharma. I would receive a polite smile and some cryptic, mystical message. "You can't but live your dharma." Or, "Your dharma will find you." Perhaps this was profound knowledge, but it didn't make any sense to me at the time, and it left me feeling more bewildered.

Confused, I longed to find an answer. Thinking that California was the hub of the New Age movement, I felt that there must be something waiting for me there. Maybe I would get involved in a seminar. Or perhaps by spending time with my dear friend and mentor, Charlie Lutes, I would find some answers.

Charlie was one of Maharishi's first devotees in the United States. He was a highly evolved person who seemed to know things that most people didn't. Although I met Charlie in New York, he lived in Southern California's San Fernando Valley with his wife, Helen. Every Friday evening he gave public lectures on spirituality in West Los Angeles. Charlie was more than my spiritual mentor — he was my surrogate guru.

A former sales engineer for a major concrete manufacturing plant and construction company, Charlie Lutes was one of the founding members of TM's Spiritual Regeneration Movement. In 1959, he and Helen had become the first two people in the continental United States that Maharishi initiated into TM. In the early days, Charlie traveled several times around the world with Maharishi. And when the Beatles in Rishikesh, John Lennon affectionately referred to Charlie as "Captain Kundalini." Charlie proudly displayed a pin that identified him as a member of the U.S. President's Task Force.

Always a charismatic speaker, with a powerful spiritual presence, Charlie spoke to TM meditators about subjects that Maharishi did not generally address. Although he had been the TM movement's first president, many in the movement came to view Charlie as a renegade. But he played a significant role in inspiring people to stay on the spiritual path. People flocked to him, as he regularly traveled around North America, sharing knowledge about esoteric phenomena and spirituality that seemed to come from a deep level of knowing.

When I first met Charlie in New York, in 1978, he was already an older man. Impeccably dressed in conservative blue or gray suits and striped silk ties, Charlie had an air of certainty, and, despite his age, he retained a movie-star appearance that was a cross between Burt Lancaster, Cary Grant, and Nick Nolte. He spoke about the angelic kingdom, karma, astral travel, reincarnation, spaceships, faith, the coming Earth changes, and, always, about Maharishi and the importance of meditating. Whenever he spoke about God or a higher power, I noticed an unusual phenomenon. A small muscle would protrude between his eyebrows, and as it began to pulsate, a powerful energy would fill the room.

Because he was such a great inspiration for me, I spent as much time around him as I could, especially when he came to New York. Entertained and intrigued by his engaging personal stories, and his direct and often humorous delivery, a small group of us would often gather around him after his lectures and join him for dinner. In addition to his fascinating insights about Maharishi, Charlie's stories ranged from his experiences as a high-ranking amateur boxer in his youth to his involvement in the secret military intelligence when he was in the service. He even alluded to his past lives — supposedly he was Alexander the Great, and, in another life, the Roman legionnaire who speared Jesus to relieve him of his pain on the cross. Knowing Charlie, all these stories seemed totally believable.

When he was in his mid-thirties, he experienced symptoms similar to a stroke. He was rushed to his doctor's office, only to be pronounced clinically dead on the examining table. As Charlie left his body, he heard a voice on the other side tell him that he could leave now, but if he chose to remain in the world he could perform a great service to humanity. Charlie chose to return to the world, and miraculously came back to life. Within a few years of this near-death experience, Charlie was secretly invited to become part of the School of Mysteries, which, as he would humorously comment, "was a very mysterious school." For years, he met weekly with a teacher in an empty apartment that contained only two chairs and a card table. According to Charlie, his teacher was an adept, able to take him into the astral realms and show him many subtle levels of creation. Heaven and hell, the birth and destruction of the universe — Charlie had the opportunity to experience these great mysteries for himself.

His main purpose in giving public talks was to inspire TM meditators to continue meditating. "Stay on the path," he would exclaim. "The trouble with our meditators is that they take the initiation of every guru that comes into town — every Tom, Dick, and Harry. Stay on one path. You're already on the path of liberation! You're on the highest path. So don't get caught digging a new well when you're so close to reaching water."

Charlie was strongly against mixing different paths and traditions, saying, "When you mix different paths and lineages, your aura gets snarled with different vibrations." Practicing different forms of meditation, he told us, would only cancel out the benefits received from each path. "It is like learning many languages at the same time and yet not being the master of any."

Since I couldn't interact in person with Maharishi, Charlie played the role of surrogate guru. Many spiritual teachers came through L.A. in those days, and I would occasionally see them speak. But, as Charlie encouraged, I didn't take their initiations. If it were not for Charlie Lutes, I might not have continued meditating.

In the spring of 1985, I quit my job, loaded up my car with a tent and sleeping bag, and drove across the United States to California.

Driving down California's magnificent Pacific Coast Highway, I could feel I was getting closer to my destiny. Somehow, I knew tremendous growth and changes lay only miles ahead, in Los Angeles. The lush scenery along the coast felt like home to me.

I wound up living in the San Fernando Valley for six months, until

I finally found a rent-controlled apartment in Santa Monica through my new friend, Chris Reed.

Chris had arrived in Los Angeles about a week before I did. We met at one of Charlie's Friday-night talks. A chemical engineer from Colorado and a fellow meditator, Chris was a little nerdy, with his wire-rimmed glasses, black denim jeans, and shirts that were at least a size too large. His love of music had brought him to L.A. to study at the Guitar Institute of Technology in Hollywood. I played the harmonica, so every now and then we got together to jam and play the blues. He was an average player who had trouble keeping the beat. It was his compassion and sincerity that won me over, and we quickly became close friends.

Within a few months, Chris and his new girlfriend, Judy, encouraged me to enroll in a personal-development workshop that they told me was designed to help people get in touch with their emotions. Chris believed that to develop more fully, it was essential to take steps toward emotional healing. We both knew meditation was extremely beneficial, but we didn't feel that it was healing our emotional scars as quickly as we wanted.

The workshop was designed and led by Barbara De Angelis, an attractive self-help author I knew from the TM movement. She had many intuitive insights into the dynamics of personal relationships. I was able to process suppressed emotions, and people at the workshop seemed to like me. They told me I was warm-hearted, intelligent, and funny, which instantly boosted my self-esteem. As a result of my learning difficulties and my dismal performance in school, my father had hammered it into me that I was a stupid person who would undoubtedly become a failure in life. I had heard this so many times that I fully believed it. With the help of the workshop, I was able to reverse years of conditioning. For the first time in my life, people were seeing me as an intelligent, strong person. I now had new friends who shared my interests in life and who wanted to live with an open heart.

Many parts of my life improved, but I was still dissatisfied with my career and at a loss to know my purpose in the world. I had recurring thoughts of serving people and teaching meditation. I also toyed with the idea of going back to school to become a therapist. I believed that I had a talent for working with people and for helping them. Confused, I was unable to make a decision.

I decided to visit a well-known channel/psychic and see if the information resonated. Speaking for my "guides," the psychic told me that my confusion about my purpose was due to my lifetimes as a monk in France and Prussia. He said, "At those times, you were controlled through fear, eliminating any passion that might lead you astray from God. In this lifetime, your challenge is to become more human and be in touch with your desires and with what makes you happy. You allowed yourself to have all your desires burned out of you by your spiritual preceptors. You were left with a misunderstanding of the vows of celibacy and dispassion."

An intense feeling of anguish gnawed in the pit of my stomach and I began to weep. Memories of past relationships flashed before me, and I realized that there was something in me that might have contributed to these failed relationships.

On the lighter side, he told me that my guides said I came into this world with two gifts: teaching and humor. They said I had a natural ability to convey knowledge through storytelling. "Or, if you choose, you can create great fame and fortune for yourself by standing in front of groups of humans, making jokes and creating laughter."

Most of my adult life, I hadn't given much thought to my ability to make people laugh. As a child, people told me how much I made them laugh. My aunts and uncles thought I was the next Jerry Lewis. But as I grew up, that natural humor was harder to find. Were the guides right? Could I actually become a professional comedian?

I enrolled myself in a school in Beverly Hills and took improvisation classes. It's amusing to think that I took a class to be funny. Real humor comes when you are in the moment and natural. But after a while, I did hone my timing and began to feel more comfortable with the idea of being a comedian. I liked making people laugh. As time passed, my ego became more involved in the process, and I felt the need to constantly be funny. My wit became more biting and sarcastic, and I began to hide behind comedy.

I had moved to California to get in touch with myself, grow spiritually, and find my purpose. But I was lost in my need to impress others and receive recognition.

I had become more free, emotionally, and now I wanted to contribute and get closer to people. I wanted to make people happy, but being a professional comedian wasn't the way. Perhaps there was some truth to what the guides had said about my ability to convey knowledge.

I was making small steps, but I sensed that something bigger was in store.

Part Two

CHAPTER FIVE

When the Student Is Ready...

BRIGHT SUNSHINE AND A VIVID BLUE SKY replaced the early morning fog, giving way to a typical Southern California day. Finding bare cupboards and an empty refrigerator, my stomach directed me to the local health food store for groceries and breakfast. Taking the scenic route, I gazed at the ocean from the open window of my car, the cool sea breeze brushing against my face. My mind was particularly calm. Despite some false steps, it seemed as though there was a force watching over me, propelling me in the right direction.

Browsing among the aisles of the Santa Monica Food Co-op, searching for the perfect wheat-free, sugar-free cookies (that were, hopefully, not taste-free), I ran into a beautiful blond-haired woman I'd met at Charlie Lutes's Friday-night lectures. Claire Atkins looked radiant.

We made small talk for a few minutes, and then she told me about a seminar she had just taken in Montreal. She spoke with the enthusiasm of a child in a candy store. She said that her new teacher, Pundit Ravi Shankar, whom she called Punditji, would be arriving in California in three months and staying for several weeks. He would be conducting a program called the Art of Living Course in Santa Barbara, Santa Monica, and, finally, in San Francisco, before flying back to Montreal for an advanced residential retreat. "Just come and meet Punditji," she said. She told me he'd spent time with Maharishi and had been one of his favorites. "You'll love him, he's great!"

I found out later that *Punditji* was a title of respect and endearment usually given to a Vedic priest. Claire said it was what Maharishi called him.

She handed me a sort of brochure as if to explain. As a former advertising executive, my immediate reaction was to critique the graphics and content. I was not impressed. It was nearly illegible and poorly designed. The name, Pundit Ravi Shankar, sounded familiar, and I wasn't sure why. I knew he wasn't the musician, but I had a hard time seeing his face in the photograph. It looked like a third-generation photocopy. I thought that if I were involved with this organization, I would have designed a better, more sophisticated brochure with more appeal.

From what I could see, with his long hair and beard, he looked a lot like a young Maharishi. The brochure said that he was the "fully blossomed flower of existence, whose spiritual teachings were known for their unusual depth, simplicity, love, and skill." It explained that his parents discovered that, at age four, he was able to recite the jewel of Vedic texts, the *Bhagavad Gita,* and that he had studied with many renowned spiritual masters. By age eighteen (having skipped some grades), he'd graduated with a degree in physics from Bangalore's St. Joseph's College, and had completed traditional Vedic studies. He also started some charitable organizations and schools that served the needy in rural villages in India.

While the brochure was poorly designed and lacked any substantial information about the workshop, something intrigued me. I wondered if this was the reason I had moved to California. In any case, I had an odd certainty that I wanted to meet Punditji and take his course.

I began to mark the days on my calendar. And a few days before his arrival in Santa Barbara, I decided to get more information. I called the number that appeared on the back of the brochure, and a soft-spoken person with a kind voice answered the phone. His name was Jeff.

"Can you tell me about this Art of Living Course?" I asked.

"Well," he said with gentle enthusiasm, "it allows you to experience the nature of your own Being. We do a number of techniques and processes during the workshop that help people eliminate toxins and bring the mind into the present moment."

"I can appreciate being in the present moment, but how does it work?" I asked.

"It's through the various processes and techniques," he replied. "They help people unfold and experience more joy and more emotional freedom."

"Jeff, can you be more specific, more concrete?" I insisted. "What do you actually do in the course?"

He tried his best to explain, but his answers were vague. I simply couldn't understand what the course was about.

"Jeff, listen, I appreciate your time, but it all sounds very wishy-washy to me. I was involved in an emotional seminar for the last two years. I want to have more of an understanding of what is actually done in this workshop. If you can't tell me, is there anyone who can?"

"No," he said, and I could tell he was becoming irritated. "Maybe this is not for you. I'm not sure you're ready for something like this. It could be too subtle for you."

I was stunned by his response. He was obviously not a salesman.

Frustrated by our conversation, I decided to be prudent and wait until Punditji came to Santa Monica. I wasn't about to drive all the way to Santa Barbara to take a course I knew nothing about. However, for some reason, I still continued to mark the days.

Finally, on July 1, 1988, Punditji arrived in Santa Monica, where a small massage school would be the site of a public talk. I entered the hall and laughed to myself, realizing how small and unorganized this Art of Living really was. Only fifteen people had shown up to hear him. There was no stage, just a small lounge chair covered with a white sheet. To the left of the chair, on a low cloth-draped table, was a small bouquet of flowers and a portable cassette machine to record his talk.

Piles of used towels and massage mats were crammed in the back of the hall, and the odor of massage oil filled the air. I began to feel nauseous as I waited for him to arrive, and I soon decided I should probably leave before he got there.

But suddenly, my body was covered with goose bumps. My mind went numb, as if I'd entered a silent void. I could barely breathe and I thought I was going to pass out. I looked up and noticed that Punditji had entered the hall. He looked familiar.

As he walked to his seat, the room became calm, and for no apparent reason I began to feel lighter and more joyful.

Punditji sat silently in his seat, looking into the eyes of each person in the room. As he looked into my eyes, I felt a shock of recognition. This was the same pundit who had stood up to the angry mob in India and who had come to MIU with Maharishi so many years before, had looked at me through the window of the white Cadillac, and made me well up with tears. His gaze had stayed in my heart all these years. I was so thrilled to see him, and suddenly, I was eager to hear everything he had to say.

He cleared his throat and made a funny little high-pitched sound. "Hmmm?" he began. "There are three types of communication. When two people talk head-to-head, little is gained. When communication is heart-to-heart, words don't matter much. When we communicate soul-to-soul, from the level of silence, much more is gained. We convey more through our presence than through our words."

Again he sat silently, and took his time looking at us. This time, the silence was deafening and lasted longer than before. I began to fidget. But after a while, I got lost in his appearance. He reminded me of Jesus, with long, black hair that fell below his shoulders, a full beard, and dark-brown loving eyes that twinkled as he sat in silence.

He was impeccably dressed in all-white Indian clothes. He wore a long, white *kurta* shirt with a small Nehru collar, and a white South Indian-styled *dhoti,* the traditional skirt-like cloth, with a gold-colored border, which was gracefully pleated like a sari and fanned out on his chair. Although it was warm in the room, he was wrapped in a thin cotton shawl with a small gold border that matched his dhoti. Around his neck he was wearing a traditional gold-strung 108-bead *rudraksha mala* (prayer beads).

Again, I drifted.

"Now," he said, "what is happening in your mind? Are you all here? One-hundred percent mentally here? Are you aware of the dialogue that is going on in your mind as I am speaking? Mind may be saying 'yes, yes' or 'no, no.' Are you aware?" He was silent for a few seconds. "Most people's minds are either in the past or in the future, regretting the past or feeling anxious about the future. This constant vacillation of the mind is what causes stress in the nervous system. Are you aware of the chatter in your mind? Just see what is happening in your mind right now."

Again, he sat in deep silence. I looked around the room at everyone else to see what they were doing during this silence. I thought of when I first met him at MIU, and I began to wonder about the seminar that was coming up. As I focused on my mental activity, the chatter began to slow down. I became relaxed and my mind became very still. I wasn't thinking about anything. It was like I was meditating with my eyes open.

"What's happening now?" he asked, which only amplified the silence. "Just observe your breath, how it flows. The first thing we did coming into this world was to take a deep breath in. Then you started crying. The last thing we will do is breathe out and make others cry. The first act of life is inhalation, the last act is exhalation. Throughout life, we breathe in and out, but we have not observed our breath. The breath has a great secret to offer."

Punditji told us that eighty-five percent of the impurities in the body are released through the breath and that most people use only thirty-five percent of their lung capacity. Coming from him, these statistics sounded authentic and indisputable. Then he said that every emotion in the mind had a corresponding rhythm of breath.

I thought about my breath and how it changed when I got angry. I noticed how soft and slow I was breathing as I sat, fully relaxed by this time, listening.

"Can you control your mind from the level of the mind?" he asked. "No. Fear comes automatically. Many times, you tell your mind there is nothing to be anxious about, and still there is anxiousness. When you experience unpleasant emotions, you don't know what to do. You go here and there or do this and that, but the negative feelings don't leave you. Sometimes it may take several days or months to get over anger, jealousy, hatred, or fear. If you attend to your breath, you can very quickly get over the negative emotions," he said, "because breath is the connecting link between the body and the mind, between the inner world of silence and the outer world of activity. Mind is abstract and breath is more tangible. Doing some breathing techniques will help."

He put things so simply. He was wise and silent yet light and flowing, with a very sweet presence. I wasn't sure I understood everything he said, but I knew I liked him. Not once during his talk did he try to sell the course. In fact, by the end of his talk, I still had no idea what the Art of Living Course was about.

After the talk, I went up to him, and I could feel his peacefulness. I told him that my meditations had become a little dull and that I wasn't going as deep as before. He smiled and looked into my eyes reassuringly. "You are planning to come to the course, aren't you?" he said. "Then come. You will learn some knowledge about yourself. It will help you."

And with that, he left the hall.

As I was getting ready to leave, I noticed two women who were dressed quite conservatively, struggling to get Punditji's lounge chair into the trunk of an old, blue, and slightly bruised Mercedes-Benz. I stopped to help them and surprised myself by asking them where Punditji was staying while he was in Santa Monica.

They were friendly and introduced themselves. One of the women, Janael McQueen, invited me to come to the house where Punditji was so I could spend some time with him. Then the other woman, Michèle Krolik, suggested that I follow their car so I wouldn't get lost. I was taken by their friendliness and accepted their offer.

When I arrived at the house, I sat patiently, hoping I would be able to speak to Punditji. But I only saw him for a few seconds as he walked down the corridor to his room.

Michèle kept me busy for most of the evening, telling me about Punditji and the course. She was only slightly more informative about the workshop, but she encouraged me to register and said that I would love spending time around Punditji. I left the house feeling a bit spacey and excited, and not sure what to expect.

I was surprised by the small turnout for the workshop. Including my friend Chris Reed and me, there were only 14 people taking the course. Five of these participants were traveling around California with Punditji and were repeating the course in each city they visited.

The workshop was held at Shanti Mandir, a small meditation center behind a supermarket, just off Ocean Park Boulevard in Santa Monica. There was no air-conditioning, and the room was hot and poorly ventilated. It seemed like a noisy place to hold a course. I could hear dogs barking in the background and the sound of city buses.

I don't remember much about that first evening, except the joy I felt sitting in Punditji's presence. He had the personal, non-guarded openness you might see in a child. He clearly came from a deep place, but in such a kind and natural way that it was easy for me to feel close to him. I left the course that evening wanting more.

The second session took place on *Guru Purnima,* the auspicious full-moon day of devotion and gratitude to one's guru or spiritual lineage. I felt fortunate to be taking a workshop with Punditji on that day, though I hadn't thought of him as one of the masters of the tradition.

During the Guru Purnima celebration, he chanted traditional Vedic hymns and spoke briefly about the significance of a master in one's life. Listening and watching him, my vision started to blur. He began to look transparent and ethereal. Then his face changed and became Hanuman (the monkey-featured deity, who is considered the embodiment of devotion and service). I rubbed my eyes in disbelief. How could this be happening? Maybe it was the dim lighting?

Then, in a few moments, his face transformed again, this time into an ancient holy man who resembled a picture I had drawn when I was a child. I had a feeling I was seeing Punditji as he may have looked in a previous life. I became more absorbed in the vision, and slipped into a deep state of meditation.

That night, I had vivid dreams of Punditji taking care of me and nurturing me, like a mother would nurture a child. When I awoke, I couldn't wait to return to the course.

It was now the third session, and Punditji was going to teach us a technique he called *Sudarshan Kriya*. In 1982, he had come out of ten days of silence and seclusion with the knowledge of this technique. He told us that *su* means proper, *darshan* means vision, and *kriya* is a purifying action. Through specific actions of the breath during Sudarshan Kriya, we would be able to get a proper vision of who we are. The technique would give us an experience of our own nature — our Being.

"There is a rhythm in nature," he explained. "Seasons come and go in time. First there is winter, then spring, then summer, then autumn comes. There is also a rhythm to our bodies. We get hungry at certain times and sleepy at certain times. There is also a rhythm to our breath, a rhythm to our thoughts, a rhythm to our emotions. In Sudarshan Kriya, all of these get harmonized with the rhythm of our Being. It's like the difference between noise and music. In music, we create a harmony with the different sounds."

He told us that with Sudarshan Kriya, the *prana* (life-force energy) goes to every cell of the body, eliminating negative emotions and toxins that have been accumulated over the years. "After the practice, you will see how much lighter, freer, and more joyous you feel."

I had been practicing the TM-Sidhis Program for many years, and I doubted that there could be anything more powerful than that. But my first experience of Sudarshan Kriya was mind blowing. I had a myriad of physical sensations that felt like being on a roller coaster. I became hot, and I started perspiring. Then, within a few moments, I was freezing cold and shivering. My whole body was tingling with energy, as though I was plugged into an electrical socket. Tears rolled down my cheeks, though I wasn't sad. Later, I was laughing hysterically but for no apparent reason. With all this activity, I was surprised to find my mind in a state similar to meditation — very calm and serene.

After the process, I was smiling from ear to ear. I felt light, as though my body was floating in space. I was completely relaxed, and my mind felt free. I'd had some good experiences when I was meditating, but I'd never had an experience like this. There were no unnecessary thoughts clouding my mind. I wasn't troubled by the past or the future. I understood what it meant to be present, to be living "now."

Punditji told us to come back the next day to go through the Sudarshan Kriya again. "It takes two times doing Kriya for the rhythm of the Being to be set," he said. It was an exhilarating experience and I was glad we were going to do it again.

During the course, Punditji spoke to us informally and gave us plenty of opportunities to ask questions. I felt relaxed with him and enjoyed the intimacy of the small group. In a later session, he told us, "In India, when this all began, people would ask me to speak, to lecture. I said I only talk one-to-one. So the organizer of one of the programs said, 'All right, you talk one-to-one and we'll all sit in the room.' I said, 'All right, sit.' Since then, I have never changed my style. I'm still speaking one-to-one."

He was so charming and irresistible, I had to sit as close as possible to him. There was plenty of time for each course participant to speak and interact personally with him.

When it was my turn, I asked the question that had been burning inside me for so long: "How can I find my dharma?"

"Hmmm?" Again, he made that wondering sound. This time his sound was soothing to me, as though charged with compassion. Instead of answering further, he invited me to join him and a few other people at Indira and Yogen Thakar's house for dinner.

The Thakars were an Indian family living in Torrance, just south of Los Angeles, who had not yet taken the Art of Living Course but enjoyed having holy men visit their home. Indira came from South India and spoke Kannada, the same language as Punditji. She was excited to have a holy man in her home who could speak in her native tongue.

As we entered the Thakar's home, Indira performed the traditional *aarti* ceremony, which is usually done when a swami or holy man enters a home. She anointed Punditji with some sandalwood paste between his eyebrows and then circled incense and a camphor flame in front of him, followed by a sprinkling of flowers.

They gave us a tour of their home. Hindu deities and scenes from the Indian epic, the *Mahabharata,* were on the walls of each room, and there was an aroma of Indian spices. They proudly showed us their *puja* room, the place where they did prayer and meditation. On their temple shrine was a framed picture of Punditji, surrounded by flowers. It was apparent that they held him in high regard and considered him a saint. It was obvious to me that he was an exceptional person, but was he a realized master? This was something that I had not contemplated until that moment.

It was a magnificent summer evening — sitting in the backyard with Punditji, eating South Indian food, and hearing "spiritual gossip," as he put it; an informal potpourri of wisdom. We felt part of his family.

When we drove away from the Thakars' house that evening, I sat with Punditji in the back seat of the car. As he looked out the window, I decided that this was the perfect opportunity to ask him my personal question. This time I decided to phrase it differently.

"Punditji, I have always been confused about my career. I'm not happy with my job, and I feel as though I am supposed to be doing something else. I have put a lot of energy and time into finding my dharma, but I still feel stuck and frustrated and don't know what I should be doing with my life."

"Oh, you don't need to worry about that," he said smiling. "You will be traveling around the world and teaching Sudarshan Kriya."

Was he crazy? His words were shocking and brought up many fears. My mind began to race, imagining what it would be like. There was no way that I was going to become a teacher and live an austere life out of a suitcase. I wasn't at all interested in becoming a monk like him.

I was so infuriated by his reply that I could feel the heat rising from my head. I sat back in my seat, folded my arms across my chest, and pouted. I thought about the TM teachers I knew, and remembered how frugally most of them had to live. The local teachers I knew slept on the floor of the meditation center on thin foam mattresses and sleeping bags, and they rarely had enough money to purchase even the bare essentials. Instead, they were always planning for their enlightenment and going on extended residence courses. However much good they were doing, I considered them losers on some level. I was clearly not going to live that life.

I sat silent and angry for the rest of the ride. The peace I'd felt an hour earlier was gone. Convinced that he was mistaken and didn't have an understanding of my dharma, I reminded myself that he was only someone who was teaching a simple breathing technique.

The next morning, I contemplated whether or not I should finish the course. I was convinced that Punditji didn't have a clue about my purpose in life, and there seemed to be no point in continuing. Then the doorbell rang. It was Chris. He wouldn't take no for an answer and insisted that I finish the course. He waited for me to take a shower and we drove to the course together.

As soon as I walked in the room, I felt at home. I realized that there was something unique about Punditji that I couldn't resist. He was kind and charming, intelligent and wise, patient and compassionate. But I also felt how much he liked me. He enjoyed having me around. With most people, I felt that I needed to do something in order for them to like me. I'd use my sense of humor to make people laugh, thinking they would like me more. But with Punditji it was different. He didn't seem interested in my qualities, he was interested in me. I felt free to be myself.

When I shared this with Chris, he said that it didn't take a genius to see that Punditji was a "giver not a taker," as he put it. Chris was right. Punditji clearly didn't want anything from me, or anyone else. Although I didn't comprehend it at the time, he wasn't really treating me differently than anyone else. In his presence, everyone felt a sense of intimacy — understood, special, and loved.

My experience of Sudarshan Kriya was even more fantastic the second day. I was amazed at how quickly my irritable feelings disappeared. I was centered again, and I could already laugh at how I'd reacted to what Punditji had said.

After the workshop, Punditji's organizers needed to leave so they could set up his program in San Francisco. As they said good-bye to him, they voiced a concern about logistics. Michèle wanted to know who would lock up the hall, return the key, and drive Punditji to the airport the next day. I listened with half an ear as she voiced her concerns. I knew that someone would volunteer to help.

Suddenly, Punditji looked at me with a smile and said, "Michael can take care of all that. Just give him the key to lock up and I will go with him in his car."

Oh, no, I thought. Please don't volunteer me. I didn't want to get involved and caught up with any group — or even worse, be seduced into being a teacher. But Punditji was so genuinely charming and I felt so blissful around him. He had just given me this precious gift of Sudarshan Kriya. He looked right at me with his big brown eyes and flashed a smile. How could I say no? It was only locking the door and driving him, right?

"OK, sure. I would love to help," I said. "I'll return the key tomorrow after I take Punditji to the airport."

Instantly, the key to the hall was handed to me. I felt I was going through an initiation. I was being empowered, a mantle was being passed. I maintained a fairly nonchalant attitude, but I was both excited and scared. What was I getting myself into?

After I locked the hall, Punditji, Chris Reed, and Claire Atkins got into my car and we toured Santa Monica and Beverly Hills for a while. I drove to the beach, and we walked with him and watched him dip his feet in the ocean. He looked regal and ancient as his long hair blew in the wind, and was also playful as he enjoyed the ocean air.

Later that evening, we drove to the house where Punditji was staying. While Claire prepared something for Punditji to drink, Chris started asking about his relationship with his girlfriend, Judy. I was surprised by the responses. Punditji spoke to Chris as if he'd been counseling him and Judy for years. He seemed to know all the patterns and details of their relationship. Chris went on and on about the problems he was having with Judy. Finally, he asked: "Punditji, do you think I am with the wrong partner? Maybe Judy isn't the one for me and I should just find someone else."

Punditji was sitting cross-legged on the couch, lightly holding part of the *mala* that hung from his neck. He swung his beads playfully around in a circle, looking at Chris with a gentle gleam in his eye.

"If you know how to row a boat, you can row any boat," he said. "But if you don't know how to row, changing boats won't help. Changing the relationship does not solve the issue. Sooner or later, you will be in the same situation in any relationship.

"Most people look everywhere for a perfect relationship," he added, "but few look deep within themselves, to the place from where we relate. What is your relationship to yourself? Who are you to yourself?"

"Yes," said Chris, "but Punditji, I'm getting bored with the relationship."

Punditji smiled and acknowledged Chris's question. "People think, 'Oh, I am single, I am so bored being by myself. I need a companion, I need a relationship.' If you are so bored by your own company, think about how much more boring you must be for someone else. And two people bored with themselves getting together, they completely bore each other!"

We all laughed. It seemed like you could talk to Punditji about anything.

Punditji got up and we followed him onto the veranda. It was a cool summer night and we all sat down together. The moon was reflecting in the gentle ripples of the nearby pool.

But Chris still had a questioning look on his face. Punditji smiled and twirled his mala a couple times.

"See," said Punditji, "if your relationship is based on personal need, it may not last long. Once the need is fulfilled, on a physical level or on an emotional level, the mind will look for something else and go somewhere else. If your relationship is from the level of sharing, then it can last longer."

I thought about my last relationship. Neither of us had come from a space of serving, we had both been demanding and selfish. Even though

I had done a lot of emotional work on myself, I still seemed to lack whatever it took to be successful in a relationship.

"People often find relationships that fulfill certain needs," said Claire. "What's wrong with that?"

Punditji seemed to enjoy her directness. "When you're looking for security, love, and comfort from your partner, you become weak," he explained. "You are on the receiving end. When you are weak, all the negative emotions come up and you become demanding. Demand destroys love. If we just know this one thing, we could save our love from getting rotten. It's the limited awareness of ourselves, the limited experience of love, that encapsulates you in a tiny compartment where you start suffocating. We can't even handle the love we are asking for because we have never probed into the depth of our own mind, our own consciousness."

It was getting late, and Punditji told us to rest, though I didn't feel tired or have any desire to leave. We said good night, and I told him I would be back at 10 a.m. to drive him to the airport.

I woke up early the next morning so I could try out my new breathing techniques. They only took a little while, but the effects were wonderful. The Sudarshan Kriya breathing was more like an advanced meditation technique. Afterward, my mind was as quiet as a whisper and my regular meditation happened in such an effortless way, such a contrast to what I'd been experiencing. Usually it took quite some time to settle down during meditation, but with the Kriya it was completely different. And as I continued to do the practice over the next few weeks and months, this experience grew, and I found my meditations became more pleasant and profound.

While I was eating breakfast, Chris called. He was obviously enjoying Punditji as much as I was, since he'd decided not to go to work that day and wanted to come along for the ride.

After picking up Punditji, we drove to a large health-food store near Venice Beach. It was fascinating to watch Punditji browse the aisles, amazed at the variety of items. He was so innocent and everything seemed like a surprise to him. We purchased a few things for him to bring back to India, and then we were off to the beach for a short walk before going to the airport.

Although he spoke cryptically, Punditji explained that we had been with him before, in a past life, at an ashram in India, exploring the nature of consciousness and growing closer to God. He implied that he had been our teacher. Somehow it seemed right. I imagined myself in saffron robes, living in the forest, meditating in bliss. It felt familiar.

But he quickly returned to the present and started asking us questions about the AIDS virus. Chris and I were of no help, as we knew very little about it at the time. "We need to help these people," said Punditji. "We need to bring the Kriya to them. This knowledge can help them a lot. Maybe we could organize a course for them. Look into that while I'm gone, Michael."

We said good-bye at the airport, and tears began welling up in my eyes. I held them back so Chris wouldn't see. I didn't know how I could feel this way after such a short time.

On the ride home, Chris and I were silent. As we drove down Lincoln Boulevard, I felt expanded and there was a pleasant stillness inside. Everything looked alive and vibrant. I was happy and content, and also sad that Punditji was gone. Yet I could still feel him with me. I couldn't help wondering where I was headed.

CHAPTER SIX

Journey Into Stillness

THE NEXT DAY, I woke up feeling very clear. Some of the inner stillness I'd felt after Sudarshan Kriya and during my ride home from the airport continued to linger through the day. I was noticeably more productive at work and found time to do things that I had been postponing for a long time. And I didn't feel my usual afternoon sluggishness.

But my main thoughts were about Punditji, how sweet he had been, the knowledge he'd shared, how he had included me and made me feel part of him. Enthusiasm bubbled up when I thought of him. I was excited about life. I had similar feelings when I was in love, but now I was centered, at ease, and self-confident. It was perplexing yet soothing at the same time.

I realized it was no use. I decided to drive up to San Francisco to be with him and take the course again. I called my office and spoke to my boss, telling her I had a family emergency. Growing up with my father I had developed a talent for excuses.

Judy, Chris's girlfriend, also wanted to take the course, and agreed to share the gas and driving. I called ahead and asked one of the organizers if they could find a place for us to stay while we were in the Bay Area. Arrangements were made for us to stay with Marr and Joan Goodrum, two gracious and hospitable people who lived just across the bay, in Oakland.

Judy and I arrived late to the hall on Thursday evening. Again, the course was being held in an unsuitable place. The room was dimly lit, dilapidated, and too small. However, this time I didn't care much about the environment. My focus was on Punditji. The course had already begun and Punditji was speaking. My heart felt light and full. I was so excited to see him. As we entered the hall he gave me a big smile, reassuring me that I had made the right decision to drive up.

We took our seats, and within a few minutes, Chris walked in! He told me later that he couldn't stay away either, and decided to fly up at the last minute.

As I looked around at the people listening to Punditji share his knowledge, I noticed a quiet smile on nearly every face. His voice was calm and almost feminine, with its softness and fairly high register. His pleasant accent and inflections added to the appeal of his message, and he spoke in an intimate way that was easy to understand.

I'd never witnessed anything as fascinating as the way Punditji conducted his program. His style of teaching was very informal. Although the knowledge he shared was often profound, he spoke casually and conversationally. In fact, it was only after I had taken a few of his courses that I realized he was actually covering specific points.

Again, there was plenty of time for people to interact with him, share their experience, or clarify something they didn't understand. Each time someone spoke, Punditji would give his full attention, almost like a loving blessing. He phrased his answers in a way that clearly had special meaning to the individuals he was speaking to, but were also useful to the rest of us.

At one point, a woman told him that she was having a difficult time accepting certain individuals in her life. "Help me, Punditji," she said. "How can I overcome this?"

He replied as though he were speaking to an old friend. "I don't want you to do anything difficult. Just tell me, which is easier, accepting people or not accepting? When you don't accept, what happens?" He paused as she considered this. "You get upset. Isn't it? Who get's upset? You do."

Relieved, the woman began to laugh. "Oh, Punditji, you make it sound so easy."

"So at all costs, save your mind," he continued. "Whose mind? Your mind."

A heavyset man with a mustache, who seemed a bit reserved, asked a question from the back of the room. "Punditji, what is ego?"

"If you are unhappy, behind your unhappiness is your ego. You can't be unhappy without the ego behind it," he said. "We keep a line of separation. Ego is what causes the separateness, the barrier in us. A small child doesn't have an ego. Once, the criminals in a jail assembled and they all talked about who did the greatest crime. So one said, 'Oh, I blew up a bank.' Another said, 'I stole some secret papers from the White House.' The third criminal said, 'What!? You're talking childish. I stole ten dollars from my own pocket when I was sleeping.'" Punditji threw his head back, laughing. "There is even pride in stealing!" Punditji explained, enjoying the humor in his own joke. "You can steal from others, but how can you steal from your own pocket?"

"So how do you get rid of the ego?" asked the man from the back of the room.

"Ego cannot be erased," Punditji answered, smiling at the man, aware that his words were surprising. "It should just be seen, noticed, observed. Then you become natural. Just be aware of it. Your awareness will bring down any unnaturalness. If you are natural, you feel that belongingness; there is no other."

The next day, the course was moved to a beautiful Zen Buddhist center in San Francisco. Punditji hadn't been pleased with the venue either and had asked Michèle to find a new location. He taught the rest of the course sitting in front of a ten-foot white marble statue of Buddha on a huge lotus.

Taking the workshop a second time was even more powerful than the first. While doing Sudarshan Kriya, Gurudev (Maharishi's master) appeared before me in a vision. He beamed with radiance and blessed the work I was doing with Punditji. He made it known that spending time with Punditji would be a great boon to my spiritual development. After the Kriya, I had doubts about my experience, and thought that perhaps it had been a delusion. But when I shared it with Punditji, he nodded and told me not to doubt. "It is valid and a gift," he said reassuringly. "Come tonight to the *satsang* and we will talk more."

After dinner, Judy, Chris, and I drove to the satsang. Satsang is a Sanskrit word that literally means gathering in the company of truth or Being. It refers to people coming together with a master or with others on the path for a spiritual purpose, such as sharing knowledge, spiritual practices, and/or singing.

The satsang was held just outside the city, at Michèle's mother's home. I noticed that essentially the same people who'd been at the Thakars' house in Torrance had come together again here. I felt honored that Punditji had invited me, and I was looking forward to hearing more spiritual stories.

After sitting for a short meditation, Punditji sat in silence, gazing at each person, one by one. It was as though he was a shepherd, methodically inspecting his flock. We sat quietly for quite some time, until Punditji gave us the signal that it was OK to ask some questions — "Hmmm?"

Someone broke the silence and asked: "Punditji, I have been meditating for so many years now, doing service, eating right, doing yoga, and still I am not enlightened. It seems like it takes forever."

As Punditji began to speak, I pulled out a notebook and pen.

"There is a story," he said, smiling at all of us. "Once there was a great saint who had two disciples. One of them was an old man. He was a very ardent disciple who meditated a lot, and one day he asked the master, 'How long will it take for me to get enlightened?' The master said, 'You need another three lives.' Now this man got so annoyed. 'What? I have been practicing for twenty years. Do you think I am a beginner? Having practiced so long, another three lifetimes? No! No! It can't be.' He got so frustrated that he threw off his mala and shawl and went away in anger.

"The master approached his other disciple, who was a young boy, and said to him, 'You will take as many more lifetimes as there are leaves on this tree.' Listening to this, that boy started dancing, 'There are so many trees in this universe. There are only this many leaves on this tree. This is countable. Then one day it is going to happen.' It is said that on that very day the boy got enlightened."

I laughed to myself. Whenever I'd heard this type of story, it always had a similar ending — "then he got enlightened." But how does that happen, what is the trick? No one ever tells you that.

Punditji continued as if he was reading my mind.

"For enlightenment, the basic thing is patience, infinite patience. And readiness to wait, wait in love. This is very difficult. Usually we wait in frustration, getting frustrated more and more. Another type of waiting is waiting in love. That waiting does not bring frustration. In fact, every moment is joyful and full of enthusiasm. That type of waiting is a celebration. You see? You don't enjoy what you already have. You always look for the joy that you don't have. Your mind flows in that direction. So waiting itself is a very good *sadhana* (spiritual practice) that enhances the capacity for love, for acceptance. It increases the depth of our being. It's very beautiful."

Was that my problem? Did I lack patience? Maybe if I could let go, I wouldn't be so obsessed with finding my dharma and I'd feel more fulfilled with my life.

"This path is very complete," he explained. "It's not just some practice that you do a few hours a day, then regret that you aren't having the experience in your day-to-day life. Many people complained to me that their meditation practice was all right, but it did not bring change in their lives. That is why this knowledge is being brought out now. It's the right time. It integrates the knowledge and the experience of the Self into daily life. While walking, talking, sitting — all the time — that reminder, 'I am the Self,' gets established. On this path there is love, there is knowledge, and there is service, all integrated into one with the experience of pure awareness."

A few new people arrived from Santa Barbara and greeted him with flowers. He acknowledged their arrival and spoke to one of the new arrivals as though he knew him well — a tall, distinguished man with curly hair named Lloyd Pflueger.

"So what do you want to know, Lloyd?"

Lloyd grinned at being included so instantly. He was a tall, broad-shouldered man, with long curly hair and dark-framed glasses. He was working on his doctorate in religious studies at the time and felt comfortable around spiritual teachers. He wasn't shy about asking questions.

"Punditji," he said earnestly, clearing his throat, "could you please comment on the Second Coming of Christ? Is it the opening of the Christ light within each of us? Or will Christ physically return?" Boldly adding, "Do you have a direct role to play in the next millennium?"

"Some people keep waiting for the prophets to come," Punditji answered. "And this type of person has been there through the ages. Before Moses, people were waiting for the prophet to come. And when Moses came, not everybody thought he was the prophet. Some fully believed him, some half-heartedly believed, and some not at all. The same thing happened in Jesus's time. People still waited for the Messiah to come. Jesus came and left, yet still people waited. The same thing happened in Buddha's time. People had the premonition that an avatar was going to come. And then Buddha came. He lived for a long time and then left. Still, they were waiting.

"It needs an eye to recognize a prophet," he said. "It needs a subtle mind and a developed heart to feel the presence. Not everyone can do it. Those who cannot see and would like to wait can wait for a millennium to come! That is good also. As I said before, waiting itself is a nice practice."

What was I hearing? Was he a prophet? An avatar? A new Messiah? Is that what Lloyd was asking? I looked over at Chris and Judy, thinking they would have some response. But they were in their own world and just smiled at me.

Judy looked a little nervous and was whispering something in Chris's ear. After listening to what she was telling him, Chris seemed to push her to ask her question.

"Punditji," she asked apprehensively, with a bashful smile, "how can I free myself from my deepest worries and fears? I know that some of them are irrational, but they come up over and over again."

"Sit quietly," he said. "Do Sudarshan Kriya and meditation. Don't think that fear is somewhere deep inside you. Psychology has caused such an erroneous notion. People think that deep down inside there is some block, like fear or guilt. On the contrary, deep down in your center there isn't guilt, fear, or anger. There is only bliss and joy. Deep down you are wonderful. Never think that deep down you have all these anxieties. If you accept that concept as truth, it becomes harder to get over those emotions. They become more permanent. Those emotions are all on the surface level. Go deeper. At the center of your being you are a fountain of joy."

Looking at Judy, Chris nodded his head and raised his eyebrows, indicating, "I told you so." I smiled watching them, and then I finally decided to ask a question, too. Although I was afraid it might sound like a cliché, it was a question I'd often wanted to ask someone of this stature. "Punditji, what is the meaning of life? Can you tell us?"

"Ah," he said. "This you better find out for yourself. Don't ask me to chew your candy for you. It is not possible. Be with this question. I can tell you one thing, you are very fortunate that this question arises in your mind. One in a million people will sincerely get this question. It means that you have started your journey toward the light. Be with this question, and don't be in a hurry to get a ready-made answer from somebody. Go deep into your Self and you will find out."

His comments were helpful, but something deeper was happening to all of us. I felt as though we were being bonded together in love through a sort of magical grace.

Punditji was more than a dear friend and teacher. He was clearly a mystical being who exuded wisdom and compassion from every cell of his body.

The following week, Punditji was conducting an advanced residential course near Montreal, Canada, and I had to go. I booked my flight the day I got home from San Francisco, and then called my boss, around midnight, knowing I would reach her voice mail. I left a message saying that I needed more time off — the same family emergency. Two days later, Chris, Judy, and I were off for our next rendezvous with our spiritual friend.

At the airport, I met Jeff Houk from Santa Barbara. This was the same Jeff who got irritated with me on the phone and told me that I probably wasn't ready to take the workshop. He had a kind face and a warm smile, and his voice had a tranquilizing effect on my nerves.

Sitting on the plane together, Jeff and I had a much different experience than the one we'd had on the phone. Comparing our lives, we found that we had many things in common. We both had dominant fathers that we were constantly trying to please, we had both done TM, and we were both searching for greater meaning and purpose in our lives. We chatted most of the night, starting a friendship that has lasted many years.

Although my connection with Jeff was great, in other ways the trip to Montreal was a disaster. Chris had the idea that we could save some money, so we booked a red-eye flight that left Los Angles at midnight and arrived in Vermont at 6 a.m.

The plan was to rent a car and drive to Montreal that same morning, giving us plenty of time to rest before the course started. However, once we boarded the plane, the captain announced that they were having technical difficulties and our flight would be delayed. We were held hostage on the runway for several hours, in standard airline fashion, without ventilation, food, or water.

After landing, Chris and I had a fight in the rental-car office, and everyone stopped speaking to each other. By the time we arrived at the course site, we were exhausted and irritable. It turned out that the Canadian organization was just as disorganized as its American counterpart, and it was several more hours before we were finally assigned our rooms.

There were five of us from California joining thirty Canadians for this ten-day advanced retreat. The advanced course (now called the Art of Silence Course), was very different from the Art of Living Course. For one thing, for most of the course, we were in silence. Morning meditation began at five a.m., followed by yoga and a light breakfast. The rest of the day was spent with Punditji, who led us in guided "Hollow and Empty" meditations, based in observation and silent awareness.

I hated this meditation. It seemed completely pointless. My mind was filled with thoughts and I was in excruciating pain from sitting for hours on end. My back, knees, and hips were so stiff that I felt like I was a hundred years old. Whenever I opened my eyes during a session to peek, everyone else seemed to be blissful and deep. I was sure I was the only one who wasn't getting it.

It was also difficult for me to be in silence. My mind kept chattering and I was filled with doubts — about everything — the validity of the meditation technique, my ability to do it, and doubts about Punditji, too. Did he really know what he was doing? Or maybe he knew for most people but didn't know what would work for me. My mind rambled on and on.

In between meditations, my mind continued: The fat lady laughs too loud … That woman's sexy, I like her … Can't that tall guy sit still? I stuck a label on everyone, including myself. Self-judgment and blame came up. I felt separate and wanted to hide. I knew that most of these experiences were caused by release of stress. But the fuel for me to continue was Punditji's peaceful presence. Graceful, compassionate, caring, and kind, he spoke very few words but occasionally flashed me a glance and a smile.

However, within a couple of days, I began to settle down, becoming more and more silent. During the Hollow and Empty meditations, I started to experience a duality inside — both thoughts and awareness. I realized that I was not my thoughts and emotions. They had a life of their own, perpetuated by my own subtle cravings and aversions. The longer I sat in meditation, the more I found my thoughts disappearing.

There was an acute alertness of the space between thoughts and between each cell in my body.

I wasn't worrying, planning, judging, or craving. In fact, I lost my small identity almost entirely. The experience was gratifying and blissful. Toward the end of the course, it was almost like a constant meditation. There was little distinction between sitting with eyes closed, eating lunch, walking, or sleeping. I was just being.

Each evening after supper, we assembled in the meditation hall to sing and listen to Punditji share some knowledge. The thirty-five of us would sit cross-legged on the floor, huddled close to his chair, wanting to hear every word. The hall would be lit with candles, and the sweet fragrance of sandalwood incense filled the air.

Out of habit, I journaled in my notebook as he spoke. Most memorable was the night he explained the value of the Hollow and Empty meditation and his approach to handling emotions, which was different from anything I had heard before.

"Every emotion in the mind has a corresponding sensation in the body," he explained. "Usually, we link our emotions with an event. This reinforces the emotions. But when you de-link the event from the sensation, when you observe the sensation as a pure sensation, then emotions get transformed."

I thought of all the times I had processed my feelings at various seminars. It was extraordinary to think that someone could be free from the binding influence of emotions and events without reliving or directly processing the original incident.

"When we observe our body," he continued, "we find that certain emotions are linked with certain nerve centers (*chakras*/energy centers). The first center is at the base of the spine. When the energy is here, and it is moving upward, there is interest and enthusiasm in life. When the same energy moves downward, there is dullness, inertia.

"When the life-force energy moves up to the second center, in the genital area, it is expressed either as creative energy or as sex energy. The same energy manifests as creativity or procreativity. A person who indulges in sex all the time cannot be creative. The mind becomes feverish and then dull. Have you noticed that when you are creative, you don't think much about sex? Creativity and sex are connected; it's the same energy."

For a while, I'd enjoyed being a creative designer in the garment center, and wasn't preoccupied with sex or even concerned about having a girlfriend. Maybe the energy in my second chakra was simply moving upward at that time.

"When the energy moves upward to the navel center," he continued, "it manifests in four ways: joy, jealousy, generosity, or greed. Have you observed when you felt a sense of loss? Suppose you lost your boyfriend or girlfriend, or your investment in the market goes down — where do you feel it? When you lose something, there's a strong sensation in the pit of the stomach. It is the same with jealousy, something happens in the stomach region, there is a sensation there. Same with joy or generosity. That is why the statues of the laughing Buddha and Santa Claus both have big bellies. A big belly is a sign of generosity and joy."

I wasn't sure where I experienced joy or generosity, but I knew where I felt the sensations when my mother died or when one of my girlfriends broke up with me — in the pit of my stomach. Those sensations were so unbearable I couldn't tolerate them. I would engage myself in almost anything to avoid those feelings.

"When the same energy moves upward to the heart region," Punditji explained, "it manifests as love, hate, or fear. Fear is love standing upside down. Have you noticed that you will only have one of these emotions at a time? When a person is fearless, either he is in love or he is in hatred. When the energy moves upward, it manifests as love.

"And then when the energy moves to the throat region, it becomes gratefulness or grief. Something happens in the throat when you are grateful or sorrowful. You feel a choking sensation. When the same life force moves to the forehead region, it manifests as anger or alertness. Only a person who is very alert gets angry. One who wants perfection, who expects perfection in everything, loses his temper fast. A dull person never gets angry. When the same energy moves further up, to the top of the head, it only manifests in one way — as bliss.

77

"The downward movement of that energy leads to anger, which leads to grief. Grief leads to fear, fear leads to jealousy, a sense of loss, and continues. When the same energy moves upward, it leads the emotions upward. This upward and downward movement of the life force is happening on its own all the time, but we are unconscious of it. When you observe the sensations, unpleasant ones dissolve and transform into pleasant ones. Negative emotions drop off and become positive emotions, they are transformed into bliss."

It was some time before I realized that observing sensations was a subtle spiritual science. Over time, through repeated courses, and with the practice of Hollow and Empty meditation, I developed the skill of watching my breath and observing the sensations in my body, both pleasant and unpleasant. At first, I did this with the desire of discarding my negative feelings, but later moved on to just observing, without having any judgment about the sensations. Eventually, the observation of sensations and emotions became a regular part of daily life.

Each night of the course, Punditji encouraged us to sing together. Divya Prabha, a full-bodied woman with a round, creamy white face that made her look like a porcelain china doll, would lead us in Sanskrit *bhajans* — melodic call-and-response chants.

Divya had studied with other gurus before she met Punditji. She was a master yoga teacher and an incredible singer. Her voice had a deep, melodic resonance that was delightful and soothing to hear. When she sang bhajans, her guitar and voice evoked tremendous bliss and a strong feeling of connection, as though I was one with everyone in the room.

Divya had a spellbinding voice, and it brought me to a very pleasant state. But not understanding Sanskrit, the singing still felt foreign to me. I still retained a core of silliness, and the first couple times we chanted, I rolled my eyes at Jeff and the two of us giggled like little kids.

One night, Punditji explained the significance of chanting and why it was part of the program. He said that when we sang the same thing at the same time, it unified our "collective consciousness" and kept the chattering mind from going off on a tangent. Many of the songs were in the ancient language of Sanskrit and, being so old, the words resonated deep in our consciousness, which is also ancient. The words had various meanings, but he indicated that the very sound of the words has a purifying and transforming effect.

His explanation eased my hesitation and I felt more comfortable participating in the chanting. Each of the chants seemed to stimulate a different quality of consciousness. My favorite was *Om Namah Shivaya,* which seemed to bring me into balance. As I let go and sang from my heart, my mind got lost in its own expansion. I felt waves of love flowing throughout my body.

It was difficult coming out of the ten days of silence. I now relished it and wanted the experience to last longer. At first, speaking gave me a headache and I could only do it for a few minutes at a time. I was also at a loss for words when others spoke to me. It seemed unnecessary to talk.

On the last night of the course, after the evening meeting, I felt pulled to go up to Punditji's room. There was a small group that had gathered there, discussing how they could bring more people to this knowledge. Everyone was laughing and obviously enjoying being with him.

Punditji acknowledged me when I entered the room, giving me a big smile and a nod of his head. "Come, sit," he said. He was so warm and welcoming. I felt included.

I enjoyed the comfortable feeling in the room, as various people shared their ideas. Then someone started referring to a meditation technique. I was surprised to learn that Punditji taught a personal meditation technique, besides the guided meditations he led on the silent retreat. So far, I had put Punditji in the category of someone who helped me emotionally and physically and amplified the benefits of my meditation. These were things that Maharishi didn't teach. But now there was something with the name meditation. I was churning inside.

I was told that it was an effortless type of meditation, like TM, but was done in a more delicate way. But Charlie Lutes had told us that

TM was the highest form of meditation. How could there be two highests? This ran against everything I had grown to believe over the last twelve years.

It was the first time since I had met Punditji that I felt distant from him. I'm sure that he could see the change in my face but he didn't seem to respond. Although I had little idea of what the technique really was, I finally became so disturbed that I left his room and went to bed.

Conflicted about his teachings, and with a fear that I was straying from the path, I lay restless for much of the night. I was angry with myself for being so naïve. Punditji had become so dear to me, he felt like my best friend. I knew he wouldn't do anything to mislead me. But if he was wrong about this, what else was he wrong about? I had found his techniques and knowledge amazing. But what did I know?

It was not at all the way I thought the course would end. Unable to deal with these concepts, and filled with an inner struggle, when I said good-bye to Punditji the next day, I thought it could be the last time I'd see him.

CHAPTER SEVEN

The Alchemy of Doubt

ON OUR WAY HOME, the California group decided to stay at a house in Montreal that served as the first Art of Living Center in North America. It was an old, neglected house, the paint on the door was weathered, the lawn needed mowing, and the trash cans hadn't been emptied.

Pierre LaFlamme, a Canadian Art of Living teacher, lived there and greeted us at the door. A familiar fragrance filled the entryway; a sandalwood incense I liked called Nag Champa. It calmed and comforted my mind. Pierre smiled at me. He was a mostly bald-headed man with a white beard, and was unpretentious and kind. As he gave us a tour of the house, I kept thinking of Punditji. I was confused about my feelings. On the one hand, he was the most loving person I had ever met. On the other hand, he was teaching something different than Maharishi. But the love I felt was stronger than any ideology. I wasn't sure what to do.

We entered the large meditation room and my confusion amplified. Above the fireplace were photographs of various revered enlightened beings, including Maharishi and Gurudev. And, surprisingly, there was also a photo of Punditji. They were giving Punditji the same status as Maharishi and Gurudev. There was a sense of grace in Punditji's presence, but how could it be? Despite the benefits I felt from Punditji's courses, at the time I believed that Maharishi had a monopoly on enlightenment — or at least that no one was in his league.

I was at a loss. Had I completely drifted off the path? Was I harming my evolution by spending time with another master? I really needed to talk to Punditji and get this cleared up as soon as possible.

On the ride to the airport, I told Chris my concerns. I thought he would have the same doubts. But, to my surprise, he didn't.

"Look, you're feeling good, the Kriya definitely works. It makes meditation so much deeper, and I can't imagine anything more powerful than that advanced course. What's the problem? Punditji's great and he's helping everyone so much. There are so many things you can do to deepen your meditation."

Chris stopped for a moment and smiled. It was a warm, humid day in Montreal, and the car had no air conditioning. Chris wiped the perspiration from his forehead with the red plaid handkerchief he kept in his pocket. "Dude," he said, "if meditation couldn't be improved for someone, then why did you learn so many advanced TM techniques? There are some things we can't understand. Just enjoy what you've received."

Chris's manner made me relax a bit. I had definitely benefited from what I was learning from Punditji. My meditation was profoundly deeper and I had experienced a state of happiness that I had always been looking for. Why should I need more assurance?

But I did.

As soon as I got home, I tried reaching Punditji in New York. He was staying at Mani Poola's house for a few days before leaving for India and he had given me Mani's phone number. The Poolas were Punditji's first sponsors in the United States, and Mani had taken him on a tour of Detroit in early 1986. But very few people took the course at that time. It wasn't until that summer, when Lloyd Pflueger met Punditji at the home of Raman Poola, Mani's brother, in the high-desert town of Apple Valley, California, that word began to spread through the spiritual community in the U.S. Being a Ph.D. student in religious studies, as well as a dedicated meditator, Lloyd's network of friends and colleagues quickly learned about Punditji. I wondered what Lloyd thought about all this. Why wasn't he worried? I spoke to Mani, leaving a message for Punditji to call me back.

The next morning, I tried calling again, and this time Punditji answered.

"Yes, Michael, I was out for a walk and I could see you picking up the phone to talk to me so I came back in. I tried calling you yesterday and heard your answering machine. It was very nice," he said with a laugh. "I felt like I was in the heavens."

I was mortified. The recording on my answering machine was a joke I had recorded several years earlier, and made me sound like a sort of New Age guru. Soft sitar music from a Beatles record played in the background as I spoke with an Indian accent and paraphrased a passage from the *Ninth Mandala,* part of the ancient *Rig Veda:* "I am in the seventh heaven, in the seventh sphere, where the sun wanders at will, where wishes and desires can be found; that is where you can find me. So please leave a message and I will call you back as soon as I return."

I told Punditji my doubts about following him. I felt stupid telling him, but I needed clarification. "Punditji," I said, "I feel like I'm deserting the path that I've been on. And my meditator friends say that you're just a renegade teaching something that's not sanctioned."

He laughed, and then said, "Art of Living is separate. That does not mean that there is a conflict. I'm not saying that it's better or more special, or that it's higher or lower. No, no. Remove all these stickers and see the truth as it is. No enlightened master will be annoyed or angry with you if you improve your meditation, if you improve your life, and are able to expand your heart and live life more fully."

"But Maharishi said that if we meditated long enough we'd eventually get enlightened. Why would there be a need for anything else?"

"See," he explained, "thirty or forty years ago, masters gave the technique of giving you hope for the future — in five, ten, or perhaps in twenty years you will be enlightened. I'm not saying that was wrong. It was necessary at the time. The whole thing was based on motivation, 'What about me? What will I get?' Over time, it caused a lot of frustration in people. Many had been meditating for twenty years, and for all that time they were concerned with, 'What about me?' The element of surrender, the element of letting go, the element of love, was missing.

I thought that it was time for a change. It was necessary to touch people at the level of the heart. A push from there opens you up. That doesn't mean that it's in conflict. All conflicts are in our mind. We create conflict where there is no conflict. Do you see?"

I didn't. I couldn't absorb it. "So you're starting another movement, something different? It really is very confusing to me."

"I'll tell you a story, Michael," he said. "There were two enlightened masters living down the street from each other. Each had their own little hermitage. One was on the top of a hill and the other was down the road, at the bottom of the hill. People would naturally go to the ashram at the bottom of the hill first. When they asked the saint at the bottom of the hill what he thought about the ashram at the top of the hill he would say, "No, no, no, it's no good. Don't go there. It's hopeless. If you go there, you will be doomed! Never go there!"

As I listened to him speak on my cordless telephone, I got up from the sofa and walked over to the open window on the far side of the room. It was getting close to sunset and there was a cool breeze in the air. Birds were chirping as they congregated in the branches of a tree. I enjoyed Punditji's melodious voice and his entertaining way of telling stories. I was happy that he was taking the time to explain things to me with such patience and care. I was feeling close to him again.

"One person who was very brave," he continued, "went up to the ashram at the top of the hill and stayed with that saint for a while. He found that the saint on top of the hill was very wonderful. So one day, he asked that saint, 'Why is the saint on the bottom of the hill telling people not to come here, and saying that you are no good and will harm them?' The saint replied, 'Why don't you go and be with the saint on the bottom of the hill and find out for yourself?'

"So the brave man went down the hill and stayed with the other saint for a year or two. And he found that he was also a wonderful saint. So finally, one day, he asked that saint, 'Why is it that you tell people not to see the saint on the top of the hill, and you say such terrible things about him?' The saint at the bottom of the hill replied, 'You know, the saint on the top of the hill is my teacher, my master. We are actually very good friends. He told me to do this so that people who don't have courage won't go there. This way they will get filtered out.' The ways of masters are mysterious and mischievous," said Punditji.

They certainly were, I thought.

"Punditji," I asked, "is it really necessary to have a spiritual master to get enlightened?"

"Three things are very difficult to get," he said. "The first is a human birth. After acquiring a human birth, the second thing is having an interest in spiritual pursuits and practices. It's only a few people in a society who get this interest. Having this interest is a real blessing. The third thing is the company of the wise, the enlightened. It can be very difficult to find an enlightened master. For this, one has to wait. Infinite patience is necessary."

I was happy I possessed this desire for knowledge. I felt lucky to have had so many teachers help me along the path. But Punditji was something more than just another teacher in my life. He was opening me up in a way that no one else was able to before.

"There is only one Being, one Self, one life in this planet — not two," he continued. "This realization comes to you through the master. A living master enables the transformation to happen in you at such an enormous speed. He is only there to relieve you of your fear, your tensions, and narrow identities. When you see that there is somebody who can be so quiet and so undisturbed, so solid and so confident — somebody living in that state — you know that it's possible for you also."

A choking sensation developed in my throat. I had only known him a short time, but I often got this feeling around him, an overwhelming feeling of gratefulness that was so strong it prevented me from speaking.

"You don't need a master on the spiritual path if you don't need to interact with people," he said. "If you don't need friends, a spouse, family, or anybody to talk with, then you don't need a master. For a robot to get enlightened it is very easy, it doesn't require a master. However, a person needs to interact with someone to learn how to speak, study mathematics, or chemistry, or even how to drive a car. If you need help learning something that is so concrete, then you definitely need a guide on a journey into the transcendent, which is so abstract. You don't have to first make somebody your master and then walk the path. Once your life has been transformed, then you say, 'Oh, you led me. You are my teacher.' You shed tears of gratitude and you call that person Guru. It is a spontaneous happening. It's the love that carries the whole thing on — more smoothly than you can even comprehend."

I must have had a really stupid look on my face. The kind you get when you know that everyone around you thinks that you have been acting foolishly. I didn't have any more questions. I was speechless and could barely say good-bye.

I had already seen and experienced so many incredible things around him. But I'd been stuck in a paradigm that only allowed one person on Earth to be a realized master. A sort of dullness lifted. My mind was catching up with my experience. Maybe he was indeed an enlightened being who was bringing a new dimension of knowledge to the world.

After reading books and hearing stories about gurus, I had the impression that a realized master would be more mystical and spell-binding. I never thought that a master would be so loving, simple, and natural. Punditji was the most natural person I had ever met. I felt no fears around him, just unconditional love. There was so much freedom and lightness in his way of teaching.

It was dawning on me that Punditji was not just a wonderful teacher and friend, but actually my guru. I never imagined I would have a personal relationship with an enlightened master. I felt unprepared and unsure of what I was supposed to do. I was in uncharted territory. All I knew for sure was that I couldn't wait to see him again.

CHAPTER EIGHT

Sitting Close

AFTER OUR PHONE CONVERSATION, I left my apartment and walked
to the beach. The sun had set and I could see only silhouetted images.
Things appeared impersonal, yet filled with beauty. I took my shoes off
and dipped my feet in the ocean. The waves rushed onto the shore and
splashed me. My clothes got wet but I wasn't disturbed. I felt childlike
and carefree. My body was light and my mind serene.

I wasn't sure how things would work out with a guru in my life. But
I knew that I was embarking on a great adventure and my life would
never be the same. All the yearning to know the meaning of my existence was coming to fruition. I was no longer afraid of the future; there
was safety in knowing my life would be dedicated to spirituality. For
the first time since childhood, I felt that God was with me.

As the days passed, the excitement began to diminish and I started
thinking about more practical things. My first priority was to change
that message on my answering machine, just in case I received more
phone calls from enlightened masters.

The realization that I was under the care of a guru — that he was my
guru — grew stronger and felt more certain. It started feeling more natural to think of him as "Guruji," the traditional title for a spiritual guru.

I also realized that I had to decide if I would be going to India.
Guruji had invited me there for a teacher-training course he was giving

in the spring, and although I'd agreed to go, I needed to be realistic. Just before taking the last three weeks off, my boss had given me a promotion and a raise. I knew that if I took even more time off I would probably lose my job. I had also developed an intestinal disorder and my doctor was discouraging me from traveling to countries where hygienic conditions were poor. I decided it would be safer and more valuable for me to stay home. I began putting my attention on Guruji's return to California, scheduled for the coming summer.

When I was first introduced to the Art of Living, I was turned off by the lack of care and attention that went into organizing Guruji's visit. I knew that with more focus on details, we could have much better results. When I approached the local group about organizing Guruji's tour, I was surprised to find that most of the people felt comfortable taking a back seat and were happy to let me be in charge. Although we had only a shoestring budget, I put together an adequate marketing program, designed posters, placed ads in newspapers, wrote articles, sent letters to different organizations, and spoke to as many people as possible about his upcoming visit.

Within a short time, people started to phone in with inquiries about Guruji's talks. Slowly, everything fell into place. I felt confident that my promotional scheme was working and that the tour would be a huge success.

However, I had been so consumed with Guruji's visit that I hadn't been giving much attention to my job. Two weeks before Guruji's arrival, my boss called me in and fired me. I was actually relieved. Now I was free to spend six weeks with my guru as he traveled around North America.

Besides setting up his talks and finding a place to have the Art of Living Course, I remembered Guruji's request to organize a program for the AIDS community. Although I knew little about AIDS, I knew about an AIDS support group that was run by author and spiritual teacher Marianne Williamson. I had often gone to Marianne's *Course in Miracles* lectures and been inspired by her words. It had also been a place I went hoping to meet spiritually minded women. After one of her Sunday-night lectures, I approached Marianne and told her about my teacher, Sri Sri Ravi Shankar, and his desire to work with the AIDS community. Her response was very positive. She was more than happy to have him speak to her group in West Hollywood.

Finally, in June of 1989, Guruji returned to Los Angeles. I wasn't able to sleep more than two or three hours the night before he arrived. Yet in the morning I wasn't tired at all. I was filled with anticipation, like an excited and enthusiastic child.

Many of the same people I'd seen during his last visit, plus a few new faces, were waiting at the gate when I arrived. I walked directly over to Claire Atkins, who had encouraged me to take that first step to meet Guruji. She looked pretty, with a tanned face and rosy cheeks. She wore a new dress and held a bouquet of yellow roses. She greeted me with a hug and told me how glad she was to see me again. I felt the same way. I was grateful that she had prodded me into this new adventure.

Chris and Judy arrived a few minutes after me. Running through the airport as though they were lost, they seemed relieved when they found us congregated at the arrival gate. "We thought we missed him," Judy said, catching her breath. Chris, also out of breath, gave a nervous laugh and looked sheepish about being late.

The group was getting noisier, with people chatting and sharing stories about Guruji. I didn't want to socialize or get distracted, though, and my eyes stayed fixed on the gate. As more of our group started watching eagerly for a glimpse, the commotion settled down. Person after person came through the gate. But still no Guruji. Finally, after everyone else had disembarked, Guruji emerged.

"Jai Gurudev," said Guruji, as he gracefully entered the airport lounge. With his lively serenity and buoyant smile, it only took an instant to remember why he was so dear to me. Unrushed, he received flowers and greeted each person, as he easily made his way toward the exit. Although he had been sitting on a plane for twelve hours, he looked as radiant and bright as I remembered.

As I greeted him, he looked at me with an inquisitive grin. He said he had been expecting to see me in India and wondered why I hadn't come. I briefly told him about my situation at work and my recent health problems. He nodded, indicating he understood and said that we would talk more at another time.

I had meticulously mapped out the transportation details in advance so there would be no confusion at the airport. I planned to drive Guruji in my car to an interview I'd set up at a TV station in Orange County. But with all the excitement, my transportation plan was discarded and pandemonium ensued. As several people argued over who would drive Guruji in their car, John Osborne, one of Guruji's devotees from Santa Barbara, drove up to the airport exit and whisked the guru away in his new luxury sedan. Jealous, and frustrated that my plan (and guru) had been hijacked, I joined the entourage of cars on a high-speed car chase along the L.A. freeway, until we finally arrived at the station.

Guruji did not seem happy with the quality of the interview and cut his meeting with the reporter short. Although he wanted to expand his organization and share his knowledge, he seemed to have specific ideas about how it would be done. He was not interested in superficial interviews that misconstrued the purpose of his mission or presented him using cheap sensationalism or hype. Guruji was confident that even if we didn't advertise or do publicity, many sincere seekers would find their way to the path.

After the interview, I asked him if he would like to come back to my apartment to meditate and rest before we all drove to Santa Barbara for some weekend programs. I didn't think he would stay long, but I hoped he would at least stop in for a few moments and bless my home. He accepted my invitation and a small group of us went to my place.

Guruji was like a curious child as he walked around my apartment, scrutinizing all my gadgets and spiritual paraphernalia. Luckily, I had cleaned my apartment. He went into my bedroom and poked around in my closets and desk drawers. As he stood looking at the photos I had of him and the various masters in the tradition, he inquired, "Michael, you mentioned that your father was just here visiting you. Did you have all these pictures in your room then? It must have scared him."

I was a little embarrassed, but felt even more uncomfortable not telling him the truth. I sensed that Guruji understood all the conflicts

I had with my dad and could feel my emotional scars. "No, Guruji," I explained. "When my dad was here, I took them all down and put them in the closet."

"Good, good, good. And what is this poster on the wall?" He was looking at a poster of rock 'n' roll legend Little Richard. *"Awap bop aloomop awap bamboom!"* he read. "Is this some kind of new American mantra?" he laughed mischievously.

We walked into the living room and he took a seat on the couch. I was delighted to have him in my apartment, yet I was worried that he might be evaluating me. As he relaxed on the sofa, his eyes scanned the room as though he was searching for something to play with. He saw a photograph of Maharishi and the Beatles on my coffee table and asked me, "Who are those people with Maharishi?"

"This is a photo of the Beatles with Maharishi that was taken in India," I said.

"No, this photo was not taken in India," he said matter-of-factly. "In India we don't have the types of flowers that are in this picture."

I was surprised. That photo was one of my prized possessions. I had purchased it from a Beatles collector who assured me it was taken in Rishikesh.

"Have you ever listened to the Beatles, Guruji?" I asked.

"Beatles? No. I know they were with Maharishi, but I have never heard their songs. You want to play their music for me?" he asked.

I was flabbergasted that my guru actually wanted to listen to the Beatles with me. He got off the couch and sat down beside me on the floor as I brought my records from the cabinet. He looked at the album covers as though he were reading sacred scriptures. I played their song, *Across the Universe,* for him.

"Do you hear what they are singing?" he said excitedly. "'Jai Gurudeva.' Isn't it?" And then he listened intently to the rest of the song.

I pulled out the Beatles' classic *Sgt. Pepper's Lonely Hearts Club Band* album and showed him the picture on the jacket. I asked him if he recognized anyone among the array of people on the cover. I was amazed at his response. Without a moment of hesitation, he pointed his finger to the Indian saints in the picture, and said, "Here is Babaji, Sri Yukteswar, and Yogananda." (These are masters in the lineage of Paramahansa Yogananda.) I considered myself to be somewhat of an expert on Beatles trivia and couldn't have imagined that Guruji would be able to teach me about this subject too, but he went on to explain the symbolism of the cover design, and the references to Shiva and Mother Divine.

He wanted to hear more of their music, so I played disc jockey. As he listened to the songs *Within You Without You, Dear Prudence, Sexy Sadie,* and *The Fool on the Hill,* I explained that these songs were either written when the Beatles were with Maharishi, or were inspired by him in some way. He enjoyed the songs, but again trumped me, saying that *Within You Without You* must have been something the Beatles recorded before they met Maharishi, and that it was based on a traditional Indian raga.

I don't know how he came up with some of the information that day. After being with him for many years, I have observed that he could know almost anything about a subject if he put his attention on it, as though he were pulling it out of the consciousness.

As I sat with him beside me, all my apprehensions about being with a guru began melting away. I had never imagined that a relationship with a spiritual master could be so natural. There was such care and tenderness in his actions. I had always felt a pressure to make an impression on others so they would like me. But with Guruji it was different. I rarely felt a need to impress him or put on airs. I could just be myself.

I smiled so much that day that my jaw and cheeks began to ache. My mind became very quiet, with none of my usual need to control. I wasn't used to this type of feeling but I liked it. Guruji's love was so nurturing, I simply wanted to be a part of him.

⁓

After we meditated and had something to eat, we were off to Santa Barbara. Guruji was going to stay at Jeff Houk's new condominium in Montecito for a few days while he gave some public talks. Jeff invited

Michèle Krolik and me to help him while Guruji was staying there.

Guruji's room had been prepared for his comfort. His bed was a thin futon mattress that had been placed on the floor, as he preferred, and covered with white sheets and a soft cotton comforter. Near his bed we put photos of Maharishi and Gurudev, a cordless phone, notepaper and a pen, some bottled water, a small clock, and three cans of Pringles potato chips (his favorite brand at the time).

Since the public talks would not start until the next night, a group of devotees gathered in Jeff's living room for an intimate evening. Candles near Guruji's couch lit the room, and sandalwood incense filled the air. I didn't notice any particular type of person there. It was a collection of all sorts.

Although Guruji was the center of my attention, I liked to watch how others interacted with him. It was clear that everyone felt close and had their own special relationship with him. Guruji had a knack for making people happy and uplifting them. Sometimes it would just take a gesture or a few simple words. But there were moments when someone in the room was brash with him. It irritated me, but Guruji didn't seem to be affected. On the contrary, he laughed, and encouraged them. There was a feeling of freedom to be yourself that everyone enjoyed and relished.

One of the regulars, Old George (as some of us referred to him), was a man in his nineties who walked slowly with a cane. Guruji always made sure that George sat in a comfortable chair that was close so he could hear. "Oh, Punditji!" George protested with a smile and a voice that was shaky with age. He made a little show of being embarrassed by the attention but was clearly grateful for the care.

Katie, a college student, was there with her boyfriend, Jerry. I liked Katie. She was spunky and smart, and younger than most of us, but that had no bearing on her dedication and love for Guruji.

That night, her eyes were sad. She sat on the floor directly in front of Guruji, and leaning forward, she whispered something personal that only he could hear. She began to cry, as Guruji listened attentively, his face compassionate and poised. With a playful glimmer in his eyes, he reached for a piece of candy from a nearby bowl. Flicking his wrist like a magician performing a trick, the candy instantly landed in Katie's lap. Her face grew brighter and a smile emerged. She wiped her eyes with a corner of her sleeve, leaned forward, and placed her head on Guruji's lap. "Good, good, good," he said with tender assurance. "Everything will be all right," It was enchanting to watch Guruji comfort her with only a few words, a gesture, and a smile. Her spirits lifted, Katie went to the back of the room, sat next to her boyfriend, and closed her eyes.

Some small talk and laughter passed between Guruji and the group, like a family sitting together in their living room. After we sang a few bhajans, the room felt settled and Guruji took some questions. The last question that night was from Katie.

"Punditji," she said softly, "what holds us back from really being free, from being realized?"

"Hmm?" he said after a moment. His pause created a silent feeling of expansion in the room. "You crave pleasure," he said gently, "which in Sanskrit is called *sukha,* and you're afraid of sorrow, *duhkha.* You think everything should be logical and you're obsessed with desires. Sukha, duhkha, logic, and desire — these four things pull you backwards."

Guruji paused for a moment and reached for a flower, a rose bud.

"Isn't it amazing? Although pleasures have been momentary and have left you empty, yet one still hopes for more pleasure. This sukha — the craving for some unknown, unseen great pleasure — holds you back."

I watched him play with the rose in his hand.

"Another thing that holds you back is fear. What are you afraid of?" he said, as he looked into each of our eyes. "You're afraid of experiencing more sorrow. As a child, you cried so many times when a toy broke. But what happened to you? Nothing. You passed through that. You have passed through many stumbling blocks in life, which you thought were impossible. Yet you remained untouched by any of them. You were shaken at that moment, but later on you found that you are as complete as you were before."

The door opened, and it was Chris and Judy. Guruji acknowledged them briefly with his eyes, and they quickly sat down.

"And then there is a desire for more," he continued. "Wanting more and more and more. We burn with desire and this burning with desire does not allow you to relax into the peace of your being. Desire means that the present is not okay. When I get this or have that I'll be happy. Hanging your mind in the future is one way to be miserable. Unless you let go of the desires, you can never find peace, you can never rest in divine love."

Guruji smiled at me, and then he twirled the rose a bit. I was stunned. The rose, which was just a bud when he took it from the vase, was now a fully blossomed flower.

"When you are able to let go, then you blossom. Every bud takes its own time to bloom. Don't force a bud to become a flower," he said, pointing the rose toward me and smiling innocently.

I giggled and looked around the room. No one reacted. Was I the only one in the room who had witnessed this small miracle? Or was my mind playing tricks on me?

"You live in a very logical world," said Guruji. "Every step in your life is measured. You justify everything that you do and all your experiences. You try to capture your experiences through logic, through reasoning."

He definitely had me pegged. I was often in my head and needed an explanation for everything.

"When reasoning or logic breaks down, you tremble. Sooner or later you again find some logic, some reason, and feel comfortable with it. Reality is beyond logic. You cannot capture truth by logic. If you can logically explain your life and all its experiences, then you have not lived life fully, you have not known life fully. If your experiences can all be put into slots of logic, then you have missed something very beautiful, something basic in life."

After everyone left the satsang, Guruji called me into his room. He was on his bed, lying on his side, listening to instrumental South Indian music. I had never liked Indian music, and hearing it through the tiny speaker of his cassette player didn't enhance my appreciation.

I looked at him and started wondering about the rose. But he had a question for me instead.

"So what is this digestive problem you have?" he asked.

I explained the symptoms and told him what the doctors had said. Guruji listened sympathetically, looking at me with wide-open eyes. He kept nodding his head as though he understood exactly what I was saying.

As I finished speaking, he sat up and turned off the music and closed his eyes. Within a few moments, the lights in the room appeared to dim and a soothing sensation spread through my abdomen. In a short time, I was in a deep meditative state, unable to move. For a moment, I had no idea where I was. As Guruji's eyes opened, the lights in the room began to brighten. He smiled at me and said in a low voice, "Go rest now, Michael. It is late."

When I woke up in the morning, I felt great. My chronic cramps and discomfort were completely gone. I had seen so many doctors who weren't able to help me. I didn't know what Guruji had done, but I was grateful for his help.

Those few days at Jeff's house were some of the most magical days of my life. I was happy for no reason. Michèle, Jeff, and I were like little kids at the North Pole with Santa Claus. Jeff and I took our cues from Michèle, who had already spent time around Guruji on the road.

"It's 10 a.m., Michèle," we'd say. "Do you think Guruji is out of meditation yet? Should we knock on his door and see?"

After knocking, the three of us would huddle around the door to his room, waiting for the high-pitched Indian voice to say, "Hmmm? Come." Once we received the green light, we would greet him like giggling school children.

Being with Guruji was simple and uncomplicated. Our only desire was to be in his presence, and we often just sat with him in a calm, enveloping silence. Sometimes he was like a child and I wanted to protect and take care of him. Other times he was the parent who guided with love and wisdom. Perhaps this blend of qualities is one of the reasons that people feel so safe around him.

Sometimes someone would come to the house and join us to discuss some knowledge or talk about plans to expand the organization. But no matter how serious the conversation, eventually we would all begin laughing uncontrollably and lose track of all rational thought. It was nourishing for my soul. I was lighthearted and carefree in his presence. Everyone who saw me would comment on how happy I looked, or how my face radiated with joy.

Most satisfying were the moments when I could do something for Guruji. At first they would be little things, like getting him some water, or dimming the lights when they were too bright for his eyes, or fluffing the pillow he slept on. I really liked it when he would ask me to run to the store and buy him something, like fresh carrot juice or an avocado. Serving him made me feel more connected, and was a way to express my gratitude.

Serving him became almost as pleasing as being with him. I started to use my creative talents and took on more responsibility. I organized his tours and itineraries, designed posters and flyers to promote his talks, and registered people for his courses. Each step was enjoyable and natural.

In those days, there were few devotees and not many demands on his time. And, as now, there was little need for him to sleep. After his public talks, a few of us spiritual "groupies" would meet back at Jeff's house for a private satsang in Guruji's room, lasting most nights until three in the morning. Although anyone could join us, we found ourselves a privileged few, and were continually amazed that no one else thought of entering his room.

Late one night, Guruji told us a story about his childhood.

"When I was a young boy going to school," he said, "I used to tell the other children that I needed to visit all my people who are waiting for me in England, America, Canada, Japan, etc. At first, they believed me and thought that I was going abroad. They asked me to bring them back some coins and stamps from the other countries. I said, 'Oh, sure, no problem, I will be meeting many people.'

"Then that summer was over and I hadn't gone anywhere. The children in school asked me what happened, and I said that I would be going in the autumn. The winter came and went and so did the summer. Still I didn't go anywhere. The other children began to tease me and doubted that I would ever travel outside of India. They wanted some proof, an address or something, but I didn't have any. I couldn't prove anything at that time. Then they branded me as a liar. You know how children can be, sometimes a little cruel. They kept teasing and teasing me.

"Then, one day, they put a sticker on the bathroom door that said 'London.' They said, 'Oh, you are going to London? We will go with you. We go to London every day.'"

He paused and looked at us sheepishly, adding, "I was so embarrassed."

Another childhood event seemed to hold a key to Guruji's later life. He told us that his grandmother was a big influence on him when he was a child, and it was obvious that he had a soft spot in his heart for her.

She was a pious woman who came from a royal family. Her husband had left her and their three children penniless after joining India's freedom movement and donating the family's wealth to Mahatma Gandhi. Guruji's father had to start working as a young teenager, walking several miles to work and school to support the family. Nevertheless, Guruji's grandmother always had great faith that everything would be all right.

Guruji admired her lighthearted disposition. She was a hefty woman (as Guruji put it), and sometimes she would come from her room very quickly, slip and fall, and land with a great thud, like a slapstick movie. She would simply sit where she landed and laugh. As children, Guruji and his sister found it great fun to watch, and admired her ability to remain happy and unaffected by the pain.

One day, when Guruji was a young boy, a funeral procession passed his house. The body was decorated with flowers and garlands. He asked his parents about it, but wanting to keep the idea of death from him, they simply said it was the "closed-eye deity." For a long time, he didn't know about death. Until one day, when he saw a funeral pyre being lit. Suddenly, everything felt meaningless and empty.

It didn't take long for him to understand that death came when people got old. Looking at his own family, he realized that his grandmother would probably go first. Determined to save her, he would sneak into her room every night and keep a vigil while she slept, making sure she continued breathing. He had previously had a dream that she had died and that he touched her and she came back to life. So, struggling to keep awake, he watched her breath closely all night, and woke her up if he wasn't sure she was breathing. He was eight years old when she finally died, but by that time, he had accepted death.

There would be other teachers and sages who would teach Guruji about the mystical power of the breath, but it was clear that his first thoughts about the secrets of the breath came from those nights he spent observing his grandmother.

The more time I spent around Guruji, the more I appreciated him. He was unpredictable, mischievous, and wise; the quintessence of kindness and compassion. Every moment was a time to grow, as he openly shared his wisdom and experience.

Perhaps for the Western mind, it is difficult to imagine a grown man becoming so devoted to a spiritual teacher. In the *Srimad Bhagavatam*, one of the ancient Indian texts, there are historic accounts of the many cowherd boys and girls, known as the *gopas* and *gopis* (devotees), who would drop everything to frolic with Krishna. Here I was, a modern-day gopa, enthralled with Guruji's bliss. The phenomenon was difficult to explain back then and even more difficult to write about now. On the surface, the days resembled something familiar, yet there was also something beyond logic and filled with joy.

Michèle once wrote to me about this period, saying, "It was a deeply innocent time and an extremely precious time, where we savored every second of every day. It was like new love, when you can't get enough of seeing, talking, thinking about, and being with the beloved. Every moment I was away from Guruji's physical presence was hardship and every moment with him was eternal, joy-filled bliss."

It feels inaccurate to say that I grew closer to Guruji over the years, since the connection was established so thoroughly from the beginning. But often I'd get a glimpse of him that deepened my feeling. I'd see the gracious way he interacted with people, or the intimate care he'd take with a devotee or someone in need who was meeting him for the first time. And, occasionally, I would come to learn about previous encounters he had with great souls and teachers, which would, again, expand my feeling of who he is.

Guruji has usually been cryptic about his past. I have never heard him give a comprehensive history, though I would sometimes probe like a detective in a crime novel, assembling the bits and pieces into a time line.

One event I learned about took place when Guruji was six years old. An elderly pundit named Samba Dixit had heard about a precocious child who meditated and chanted the *Bhagavad Gita,* and wanted to meet him. So, accompanied by his aunt, young Ravi Shankar went to the pundit's home.

Samba Dixit was a descendant of Muthuswami Dikshitar, a renowned late-18th-century South Indian saint, poet, and musician. Muthuswami had predicted that, in the future, two family artifacts would be reclaimed by a young man who would go on to lead a global spiritual revolution. These objects were a tiny emerald *Shiva lingam* (a sacred egg-shaped object embodying formless universal consciousness) and a small silver *naga* (a multi-headed cobra that symbolizes awakened spiritual energy and awareness).

Pundit Dixit invited the child to choose from a box that contained many bright shining deities and sacred objects. His young visitor instantly placed the emerald lingam and silver cobra together and picked them up. Pundit Dixit was astounded by the selection and proclaimed that Guruji was the one who would fulfill the prediction made more than a century earlier.

That same year, Guruji's father arranged for him to study the Vedas with Pundit Sudhakar Chaturvedi, a scholar, rare in that he was a master of all four Vedas. Years earlier, Chaturvedi had been Mahatma Gandhi's Sanskrit guru, as well as one of Gandhi's secretaries. Chaturvedi was imprisoned more than thirty times for his participation in Gandhi's independence movement. For many years after Gandhi's assassination, in 1948, Chaturvedi refused to accept another student. I'm not sure why, but Guruji was the first student he accepted after Gandhi's death.

Guruji's father would invite Chaturvedi to their home to give talks on Vedic knowledge, and Guruji enjoyed these sessions greatly. He admired Chaturvedi's conversational style of speaking and his use of humor and stories to convey knowledge, which are also qualities I admire in Guruji. Chaturvedi was born in 1897, but, remarkably, he is still alive as I am writing this!

Guruji's time with Maharishi followed soon after. It was a relatively brief but significant period. I found it interesting to learn that early in that time Maharishi presented Guruji to the revered saint, Anandamayi Ma, long regarded as one of India's mystic luminaries. Anandamayi Ma looked up as they entered the hall. "Ah, Baba," she said to Maharishi, "you've brought me the Ganga." (*Ganga* is both the River Ganges and the deity associated with the river.) The young Ravi Shankar felt shy and a bit confused, since Ganga is considered feminine. Was she referring to his long flowing hair and soft beardless face? "You've brought me the One," she said. "The one who will wash away the ignorance of the world."

Perhaps it was my own projection, but I imagined it was difficult for Guruji to leave Maharishi to start something new. "I was literally at a crossroads, waiting at a train station," he said. "I could board a train that would go (south) to Shimoga, or another that went to Delhi." If he chose to return north to Delhi, he would continue to work on projects for Maharishi but essentially be restricted to the TM movement. "I knew that if I took the train to Shimoga, something new and original would come up."

At a certain point, he also knew that Sudarshan Kriya would need to be made available to more people, and that courses would happen. But still he had a slight reluctance. "I just didn't think that we needed to start another organization," he explained. "I was already giving knowledge, and so many people appreciated and loved me.

"I decided to seek some advice from a 300-year-old saint, Devraha Baba, who lived above the Ganges River."

He so casually mentioned the man's age. Was he exaggerating? I knew that yogis had the ability to do many supernatural feats, but I didn't think that anyone could live to be 300 years old.

The saint lived in Varanasi (Benares), Hinduism's holiest city, and possibly the oldest city in India. As Guruji was traveling there on the long train ride from Delhi, a conductor approached him. Guruji had never talked to the conductor or told him the purpose of his trip, so he was surprised when the conductor started speaking as though they were old friends. "You've come into this life with a special purpose," the conductor told him. "Why do you want to go back without completing your purpose, or postpone it?"

He told Guruji that he'd had a vision: Coming out of the heart lotus was a young man with long hair and a beard who would be ushering in a new *yuga* (era), spreading knowledge, and having satsang with huge crowds of people all over the world. Guruji sensed that the train conductor was very evolved, but he couldn't understand why the conductor was telling him these things. The conductor even described what eventually became the Art of Living logo — in his vision, he had seen the sun surrounded by two swans.

By the time Guruji arrived at the Ganges, it was dusk. There was no moon that night, and it was getting darker. The man who ran the ferry refused to cross the river at first, saying it was too dark. But eventually he agreed to take him.

Devraha Baba lived alone, in a small hut along the Ganges that was elevated by poles. The 300-year-old saint had a disciple who lived in a small boat that was tied to one of the poles of the hermitage. He stayed there day and night like a watchman, bringing the old man fruits and vegetables, and anything else he needed.

"When I arrived," Guruji remembered, "Devraha Baba came out to greet me. He said, 'I'm so happy to see you have come.' I felt a little shy.

I was very young, and he was such an old man saying this to me, I thought he might be teasing me."

Devraha Baba gave Guruji a big melon, and said, "Water is flowing. It has to flow. If it stagnates, it will rot. So satsang should flow. Satsang is that force that allows the grace to flow in the world. Satsang is essential in the world so the world doesn't rot. You have to carry on the satsang everywhere in the world."

"I didn't even have to ask the question," said Guruji, "and still an answer came."

I was still struggling with the notion of a 300-year-old saint, when Guruji continued.

"Later, when I went back to South India, I met another saint, Kodi Swami, a 450-year-old man. He's a very nice being. People come from all over for his blessings, his *darshan*."

A 450-year-old saint? I thought Guruji was really pulling my leg now. But he wasn't. I later learned that Kodi Swami was a revered saint who had spent the last thirty years of his life in a small village near Pollachi, in the state of Tamil Nadu. He spoke a dialect that was no longer heard.

There was an 80-year-old devotee attending to Kodi Swami when Guruji arrived. (The devotee's father and grandfather had each served Kodi Swami in the same way.) When Guruji asked the 450-year-old saint for some knowledge, Kodi Swami just smiled and laughed. "All knowledge is already there," he said. "If Shiva comes and asks me for some knowledge, what knowledge can I give?"

As Devraha Baba had done, this saint told Guruji that he must do this work and bring out the Kriya and knowledge. He gave Guruji his blessings. "You should not stop," he told Guruji. "You should teach this all over the world."

Other factors were pushing Guruji to be on his own, as well. Guruji's father, Pitaji, was a respected leader in the community, and Maharishi had asked Pitaji to recruit students for a Vedic school for Brahmin boys that would open near Bangalore. The school was to offer traditional Vedic knowledge, along with direct experience of the Self through meditation. But soon after the school opened, the word came from Northern India that the students would be moved to Maharishi's ashram outside Delhi (the same place I stayed during the Vedic Science conference in 1980).

The South Indian children made the thirteen-hundred-mile trip north, but found it hard to adjust to the cold winter, change of diet, and the austere conditions at the new makeshift ashram that was so far from home. Many of them wanted to leave, and some of the parents threatened legal action for breaking the agreement. A lawsuit would not only affect Maharishi's reputation but also Pitaji's, since the parents had entrusted him with their children's welfare. To complicate matters, Maharishi could not be reached. Yet something had to be done.

Guruji saw that the situation could be remedied and the children could return home if he started the school again in Bangalore. "Everybody was baffled by my decision to take over the school," he said, "even my friends. 'He doesn't have any income. He doesn't work anywhere. He doesn't earn money, nor does he ask for donations. How is he going to manage this school?' People thought, 'Maybe he has gone a little bit crazy,'" he said with a laugh.

He seemed amazed at his own decision. It's difficult enough to bring up two children. Now he was taking over a school with 175 children. He would have to house them, feed them, and teach them, all free of cost, "like an orphanage," he said, "without any aid or any help from anywhere." The children stayed at his parents' house for six months. When their lessons were not going on, they could be found eating, bathing, or sleeping everywhere.

One day, after the boys had performed one of the traditional Vedic rituals, a gentleman approached Guruji and told him how touched he had been by the ceremony. He said he was leaving for New York and would be gone for some time. He handed the keys to Guruji and told him to "use the house as you like." The house, which was called Gurukripa (guru's grace), turned out to be huge, and the school was able to operate there for the rest of the year.

Today, young pundit boys continue to attend Ved Vignan Maha-vidyapeeth (the Institute of Vedic Knowledge), which is an accredited institution, and they live at the ashram campus near Bangalore.

Guruji had also been facing increasing challenges from certain individuals during this time. Despite his sweetness and calm presence, there were some who could not understand why Maharishi treated Guruji with such honor. Many of India's chief ministers, government officials, and swamis had also become fond of him, and many people were requesting Guruji's company and seeking his blessings. (At that time, Guruji was blossoming into enlightenment; or uncovering it, as it has been indicated.) Some who became jealous arranged for Guruji to be put in charge of the Vedic school in Noida, where he would be out of the public eye.

There was other mischief in this period, too. While staying in New Delhi, training Vedic pundits in meditation, his phone line was cut and a stop was put on his bank account. And, on a day when he expected many dignitaries for a banquet, someone dismissed the cook, leaving him with no food or any way to entertain his guests. But, amazingly, he managed to pull it off.

Guruji mentioned these things, almost like a fascinated observer, but noted that these obstacles brought many *siddhis* (abilities). He never complained to Maharishi, and never mentioned the things that were being done. However, Maharishi found out, and asked Guruji why he hadn't told him. Guru said, "I can't be useful to your work then. You have so much to attend to. I want to lessen your burden, not add to it."

Hearing him say this inspired me to serve Guruji even more.

After bringing the children back to Bangalore and starting to teach the Kriya, there was still some correspondence with Maharishi, and a phone call or two. But, as far as I know, they never saw each other again.

I relished my opportunities to spend such intimate time with Guruji and learn about some of his life.

In the summer of 1989, I was happy that everything was going so smoothly for me. But part of me wondered if it would continue to be this easy.

CHAPTER NINE

First AIDS Course

AFTER THOSE FEW FANTASTIC DAYS in Santa Barbara, we drove down the winding Pacific Coast Highway for a week of public talks that I had scheduled for Guruji in Los Angeles.

His first program was a talk at Marianne Williamson's AIDS support group in West Hollywood. I felt a little nervous about bringing Guruji to an event I knew little about. I knew that most of the participants in this AIDS support group would be gay men. This would be my first direct involvement with the gay community.

Getting lost on the way, we arrived at the meeting a few minutes late. The group was startled as they watched Guruji enter the room with his long, flowing hair, beard, and robes. Steve, Marianne's assistant, greeted Guruji with a token handshake and smile. Steve looked healthy, his eyes bright, and his angular face aglow. He informed Guruji that Marianne was out of town and unable to attend the meeting.

Turning to the group and laughing awkwardly, Steve told them that Marianne had mentioned that a "saint from India" would be coming to the meeting, but that he hadn't told anyone because he thought it was only a joke. The group looked solemn, not finding any humor in Steve's casual introduction.

There were sixty-five men and one woman crowded into the tiny room, sharing experiences in small groups. They weren't interested in this odd-looking man from India. They were involved in their own concerns about living with HIV or AIDS. I felt responsible for this meeting, but didn't know how to refocus everyone's attention on Guruji.

Nervous that Guruji would think I was incompetent, I glanced his way. But he looked unaffected, calm, and at ease. I was hoping he would do something to change the situation, but he just sat and smiled at the group with a loving gaze. Then I watched in amazement as his persona suddenly changed. He leaned forward in his chair and began to speak to the group as though he was a trained psychologist.

"Hello, my name is Ravi Shankar, and I am from Bangalore, India. I came here today to share some Eastern thoughts that might help you deal with having AIDS. Why don't you all introduce yourselves, and then we can speak about this knowledge."

He made everyone sit in a circle and speak for a few moments about themselves. The sadness and fear in their voices was apparent.

A young man named Don told the group that he had just found out he had AIDS a few days ago. Don looked depressed. His thin face made the dark circles under his eyes seem like endlessly deep holes. His hair was uncombed and greasy, and his face was covered with several days' growth of beard. After receiving the results of his blood test, he said he was so afraid of dying that he had not been able to eat or sleep since. He looked at Guruji with a forced smile.

Guruji nodded his head. "In life, one thing is definite — everyone is going to die. No one can escape this reality. The only difference is that some people may die a little sooner and some a little later. The doctor dies as well as the patient. The king dies as well as the servant. This is a place where everyone dies."

I scanned the room. Although Guruji was speaking about something I thought would be scary to them — death — the people seemed charmed. They were smiling and looked interested in what he was saying. I was relieved that they were finally paying attention to him and that the meeting I had set up was not a complete failure.

"No one knows how or when they are going to die," Guruji continued. "If you look at the situation in Third World countries, people live in extremely unsuitable conditions. There may be flood or famine, or even an epidemic. Monsoons may destroy their homes and the entire family can be uprooted, but still these people may smile and enjoy the life that they have.

"The intensity with which we live from moment to moment is essential. The only thing with HIV-positive people is that life may be short. Isn't it? The fear about this can disturb the whole system. So getting over the fear is an important process. The mind, free of fear, free of guilt, free of anger, and more clear, can have a healing effect on the body."

Don had been listening intently, and raised his hand. "This fear of death is paralyzing me," he said, almost urgently. "How can I get over the fear?"

"First," said Guruji calmly, "there is observation. Observe the fear. When fear comes, what happens to you? A sensation arises in the chest region of the body. Observe the sensation, and go deeply into it. You see, every emotion in the mind creates a corresponding sensation in the body. When you observe sensations in the body, they are released and disappear. The mind becomes clear."

His tone was intimate and caring, and he spoke to the whole group. "If observing the fear is too difficult, and isn't possible to do without some help, then another thing to do is to have a sense of belonging. You belong to God, to the universe, or to some power. Know, 'God is taking care of me, the Divine is taking care of me.' This sense of belonging is a simpler way to deal with fear.

"If this sense of belonging is also impossible," he continued, "then see the impermanence in everything. Everything is changing around you. You cannot hold on to anything. Things come and things go. Emotions change, behaviors change, the world is changing all around you. See the impermanence in everything. You will gain strength from this understanding and the fear will disappear.

"Fear is clinging to something," he explained, "holding on and not letting go. But there is nothing you can hold on to in this life. One day you have to bid good-bye to everything, absolutely everything, including your own body. This awareness brings an enormous strength in you."

The focus in the room became more intense; all eyes were glued on Guruji. And I thought about my own fears of death and mortality.

"Health can be regained by attending to the source of the mind," Guruji explained. "Pure consciousness is pure love, and love is the highest healer on the planet. It is your natural self. Love is not just an emotion, it is your very existence. It is what you are made of. To know this, you must be free of fear and anxiety."

Someone from the back of the room raised his hand and asked if there were any techniques that could help them experience this.

"One of the techniques I teach in the Art of Living Course is Sudarshan Kriya," he said. "During the Kriya, you are able to dive deep within and experience your inner self. Then you see how your Being permeates your body, emotions, and thoughts, and how it affects your health. After the Kriya, people feel more centered and free."

A middle-aged man named Bob interrupted. He asked simply, "Can this heal me?"

"The Sanskrit word for health, *swasthya,* actually means stabilized in one's Self," Guruji replied. "Health means being centered. When the mind is free of fear, free of guilt, free of anger, more centered, then it can heal the system of any ailment. There is a huge power in consciousness. When you are truly centered, nothing can disturb you. If you throw a small stone in a pond of water, there will be a great disturbance, whereas a lake needs a bigger stone to create disturbance. However, nothing can disturb the ocean. Mountains can fall into the ocean, but the ocean remains as it is."

The atmosphere in the room had changed. Everyone seemed more relaxed, and smiles had replaced the frowns. Guruji said we would have a special course in a few days for anyone who wanted to attend. Several people immediately said they wanted to come. Before the meeting concluded, someone asked Guruji to lead the group in a prayer and meditation.

Guruji smiled and asked them all to close their eyes. He began by chanting a few words in Sanskrit, and then led us through a guided meditation. In an instant, I was gone, lost in a bright golden void. It was a powerful meditation. As I opened my eyes, I could see that others in the group had gone into a deep state too, and it was some time before everyone was able to come out of the meditation and open their eyes.

Bob, who looked like a throwback to the sixties, with his tie-dyed T-shirt, faded blue jeans, and a silver peace medallion, appeared to be Guruji's biggest fan. He was the first to greet Guruji after the talk, and stayed by his side until he got in the car.

Before leaving, people lined up to greet Guruji, wanting to receive his blessings. One by one, each person embraced him. They were relating to him as a beacon of hope and a trusted friend. He arrived as a stranger but was leaving as a celebrity. Many said they were happy he had come and encouraged him to come to their next meeting.

Back then, Guruji was much more delicate. He was not accustomed to being hugged or touched by so many people. Maybe that is the reason he left the hall and walked to the car seeming drained and a bit woozy. (In contrast, within a few years, Guruji would be giving *darshan,* or blessings, to thousands of people, who would wait in long lines for a chance to receive his embrace.)

Seeing that he was tired, I wanted to help him in some way but didn't know what to do. I didn't ask any questions, and we quietly rode together. He sat with his eyes closed for most of the ride and then feebly asked me to stop at the beach for a few minutes. When we arrived at the beach, I helped him out of the car and watched him walk to the ocean. He pulled his dhoti up to his knees, dipped his feet in the cool water, and walked along the shore. Stopping to look at the sunset, Guruji began focusing his attention on his breath. His nostrils flared as he began breathing quick, rhythmic breaths. I assumed that he wanted to be alone, so I sat on the beach and watched him walk slowly along the shore. A few minutes later, he was running back toward me, splashing his feet in the ocean. He was back to his normal self, fully recharged and blissful.

"We can help these people," he said. "Set up a course and call all the people who expressed an interest in learning the Kriya." He wanted to teach them as soon as possible. "You will come with me, Michael, and help teach these people the Kriya."

Me help teach? I was ecstatic. I wanted to serve him in a greater capacity than I had been. He had already given me so much and now I wanted to take more responsibility. But how? None of us in those days imagined that anyone but him could actually teach the course.

"But Guruji," I said, "how can I help teach the Kriya? I haven't gone through any training. Won't I need some training?"

"Yes, yes, of course," he replied. "But there is plenty of time for that. We have a couple days. First set up the course."

We walked on the beach for a while. The sun had almost set and there was an orange halo in the sky. Guruji wasn't the least bit affected by the chill in the air. For a few moments, I started wishing I had a jacket. Then those thoughts dropped, and I was aware of how content and happy I was just to be with him.

All of a sudden, Guruji challenged me to a race back to the car. I ran with all my might, huffing and puffing, and was surprised to see Guruji passing me in his wooden sandals, as he ran with lightning speed to the car.

At home that evening, I was excited about the day's events and the prospect of helping Guruji teach the Kriya to the AIDS group. Afraid of making mistakes, I wanted to know everything that would be required to assist him. I repeatedly asked him to train me, but he kept putting me off, saying that there was still plenty of time. Eventually, I gave up, assuming I wasn't ready yet, or that he didn't really need my help.

I called the people from the AIDS support group who had expressed interest. The feedback I received from them was very positive. Everyone loved meeting Guruji. They were touched by his sincerity and were eager to learn the Sudarshan Kriya. Don was happy I called. He said he wasn't so afraid since meeting Guruji and would definitely be coming to learn the breathing technique.

Bob was awestruck. Over the phone, he told me that he had been waiting for years to meet a living master who would teach him a breathing kriya. "I have been searching for a master my whole life," he said. "And of all things, he just walks into my AIDS support group. This is unbelievable. That meditation that he did was out of this world — deep.

And his eyes, they're like puddles of love. Your guru is extraordinary. His compassion is so healing. It's an honor to be near him."

I woke up early on Thursday morning, excited that I would be accompanying Guruji to the first AIDS program. Before meeting him that morning, I did something that was not part of my routine — I stopped at a local grocery store to pick up a cup of coffee. When I entered the shop, the aroma of freshly baked croissants overwhelmed me, and I had a strong impulse to buy some as a treat for my guru. Soon, I had purchased a half-dozen croissants, two small containers of milk, coffee, and a newspaper, and was on my way to Michèle's house to pick up the master.

At the house, I overheard Michèle telling some of the other women who were taking care of Guruji that he needed to eat breakfast before leaving. I laughed to myself. They were always fussing over him.

"Oh, Punditji, you need to eat," Michèle said. "You had such a light dinner last night, and you won't be back until late. You can't leave without eating something."

"Michael has brought my breakfast," he said. "I'll be fine." And off we went.

As he entered the car, he looked at me with a mischievous grin. "Hmm? We have fresh croissants for breakfast?" he asked. "Did you also get the message to bring the milk? Good, good, good. We can eat while driving. Where is the bag?"

I wondered how he knew.

So there we were, munching on croissants and cruising down Wilshire Boulevard at nine in the morning, just Guruji and me. It felt so natural. "Can you pass me a napkin, Guruji?"

"OK. Did you get the newspaper? Oh, it's there on the back seat. Let me hold your coffee while you drive."

Could this be how it was for Krishna and his disciple Arjuna? My belly was full and my mind was elated as I drove with this divine being beside me.

As I parked the car, Guruji turned to me and said, "Michael, there is something you will need to know before we go inside. I will need to teach you something so you can assist with the Kriya."

Now he was going to train me!? Two minutes before the course!!?

"Remember," he said, looking at me deeply, "fire catches fire and breath catches breath. Got it?"

I looked back with confusion.

"Just be centered and relaxed. I am there with you and will always be with you when you are teaching. Good, good. Come. We will be late."

That's it? That's all I needed to know? He nodded his head as though he'd read my thoughts. We quickly left the car and walked to the course site. I had become accustomed to the fact that Guruji could be a man of few words, but I was dumbfounded to realize that this was all the training I would receive.

As I continued to develop and grow as a teacher, I found that this was typical of how Guruji communicated with me. I'm not sure how he instructed other teachers, but I never received much detail about teaching procedures or the mechanics of a technique. Whether I was leading advanced courses or teacher-training courses, Guruji gave me minimal instruction. My strength as a teacher did not come from great intellectual understanding, but rather from my connection to him. I have observed that for me and other Art of Living instructors, the greater the connection, and the more we step out of the way, the more the grace flows.

The eight people who showed up that morning to take the course were delighted to see Guruji again, and they were eager to learn the Kriya. Bob came in a few minutes late, clean-shaven, with a new white shirt and gray pleated slacks. He beamed with excitement as he offered Guruji a white rose and bowed in reverence.

Guruji gave a brief explanation of what we were going to do and then nodded at me to begin.

Surprisingly, I knew what I was doing. And I was completely relaxed, knowing that Guruji was there if I made any mistakes.

The Kriya was exceptionally powerful that day, and almost everyone had strong releases. Steve, Marianne's assistant, who was hosting the course in his home, was the first to share. "I feel so calm," he said. "I've been living with HIV for eighteen months now and every day I've been living with panic and fear. This is the first time in such a long while that I feel like my old self again." He smiled and tears of gratitude welled up in his eyes. "Thank you so much, Punditji. Thank you!"

Don's eyes were fixed on Guruji. He looked refreshed and calm. "I haven't been able to relax since I found out I had AIDS," he said. "It feels so different now, like I've slept for a week. Thank you for this gift."

Bob stood up when he spoke. "You know, I've been searching a long time. I've gone to many masters and been meditating for more than twenty years. But I've never experienced anything as powerful as this Kriya." Bob placed his hand in prayer position. "Thank you for sharing this beautiful gift." Bob walked over to Guruji and stood by his side. "I just want to be near you. You're just so sweet!"

Before we left the course that afternoon, Guruji picked up a copy of *Gay Life* he saw on a table. He asked Steve if he could borrow the magazine. He wanted to read the feature story that described how to handle the loss of a lover who dies of AIDS. Steve blushed at Guruji's request. For some reason, he hesitated, but was unable to refuse. I later realized that he was embarrassed because the magazine was filled with pictures of nude men and vivid sexual advertisements for gay partners. Guruji could see Steve's reluctance, but innocently put the magazine under his arm and promised to return it the next day when we came back for the second Kriya.

I felt as high as a kite as I drove Guruji home from the course. I remembered the way I'd reacted when Guruji told me I would become a teacher and instruct people in Sudarshan Kriya. Now I was grateful to be teaching and part of what Guruji was doing. It felt good to know that my actions that day had contributed to the welfare of other people, that I could make a difference in the world.

Guruji kept smiling at me as we drove down Santa Monica Boulevard. "Now, you are happy, Michael, aren't you?" I choked up with gratitude and couldn't speak, thrilled to be so close to him, to have him in my life, to feel I was contributing to people's lives.

The next morning, we were on our way back to West Hollywood to finish the rest of the course. Guruji sat beside me, reading the magazine he'd borrowed. Without any appearance of judgment, he flipped through the publication and examined the photos and advertisements. Homosexuality was illegal in India at the time and very much in the closet, and this was probably Guruji's first introduction to such an explicit magazine.

He grew perplexed as he tried to make sense of the personal ads. "What does 'GBM sks TWM for BS&M' mean?" he asked me.

"Well, I'm not sure, but I think it could mean 'gay black man seeks tall white male for bondage and sadomasochism,'" I replied.

Guruji laughed. "No, no. It can't be. People advertise for this?"

He kept on laughing, and for the next twenty minutes he kept asking me to decipher the ads.

After a while, Guruji closed his eyes and sat silently. Time seemed to pass slowly and I felt uncomfortable. I thought I might have stepped over some boundary or said something that angered or disgusted him. It was some time before he opened his eyes. Then, breaking his silence with a giggle, he said, "So, Michael you could put an ad that says, SSSJM seeks RPSJMFSM for R&M." He had such a big grin. "Isn't it, Michael? Short single spiritual Jewish man seeks rich petite single Jewish meditating female soul mate for romance and marriage." He laughed and laughed.

When we arrived for the second day of the course, we were greeted by friendly chatter and enthusiasm. There was a noticeable contrast in the participants, and many expressed their surprise at how great they felt. Steve's face looked relaxed. He told Guruji that he sang in the shower that morning — the first time he had done that since he was a teenager.

Another person said he felt as though a burden had been lifted from him. They were all eager to do the Kriya again.

The experiences during the second day's Kriya were even deeper than the day before. It was the only time I ever saw Guruji physically touch someone during Sudarshan Kriya. He got up from the sofa and kneeled down on the floor to help Bob as he went through a huge cathartic release. To settle Bob's nervous system, Guruji stroked his throat and chest with a rose he took from the vase on the table. Later, Guruji explained to me that Bob was finally able to release the grief he was holding on to from the death of his mother. She had passed away several years earlier.

By the end of the second day, they all looked so much brighter, happier, and more vibrant than when I had met them just a few days earlier. Guruji winked at me as he informed them that I had volunteered to conduct weekly follow-up Kriya sessions for them. They walked us to the door, and expressed their gratitude for what they had just learned.

I too was grateful. The high from simply being of service was exhilarating. There apparently was no escaping Guruji's plan for me to become an Art of Living teacher.

We were both quiet during the ride back to Michèle's house. I felt no need to speak. I was content and peaceful. There was now a new dimension to my life. I had been so caught up in the dramas of my life that I never imagined that helping others would bring such fulfillment.

"Guruji, I feel so happy and high. Will it always be like this? Will I feel this surge of energy when I teach people and you're not physically there? You know, I've been looking for this my whole life. Tell me, will it always be like this?"

Guruji smiled and made that familiar upward inflection that could mean almost anything —

"... Hmmm?"

CHAPTER TEN

Teacher Training

AFTER THE AIDS COURSE and a few public talks in Santa Monica, Guruji was going back to Santa Barbara to conduct a weeklong teacher-training program.

Even though I had experienced so much happiness serving others and helping Guruji teach, I was still nervous about becoming a teacher. I knew that, for me, teaching would not be a casual undertaking, it would become my life's work. I was reluctant and afraid to make that sort of commitment and wanted some time alone with Guruji to speak about my inner turmoil. I planned to drive him back to Santa Barbara so we could have some private time in the car.

I was helping the others pack their cars, readying the Guru's entourage for the drive up the coast, when John Osborne appeared out of nowhere. As he had done at the airport, he parked his car in the most advantageous position for enticing Guruji to ride with him.

A tall, well-spoken man with a boyish face, John was very dedicated to Guruji, and would eventually be the president of Guruji's U.S. foundation for many years. It was obvious that he wanted to serve Guruji, but I was aggravated that he had outmaneuvered me. How could he be so fast and do this to me again?

Frustrated, I sat alone in my car, sulking. As I was looking over at John's car, I realized that John was frantically removing luggage from his trunk, and suddenly he was coming toward me. He didn't have enough room for Guruji's things, and was desperate for me to take one of his bags in my car. I got out of my car and slammed the door. "No, John! I don't have any room in my car for your luggage. It's full." Guruji was behind me and overheard our conversation. As he walked in front of me, his eyes met mine. He was not pleased with my behavior. He got into John's car and I had no choice but to take John's bag.

I drove up the coast with John's suitcase, painfully aware of this childish rivalry. I was not only jealous that Guruji was riding in John's car, but also upset that he was spending the week at the Osbornes' new home, rather than Jeff's house, where I was one of the privileged few in those late-night sessions.

Guruji was the common bond in our group, and there was an underlying feeling of playfulness and support. However, the small-minded craving to be around Guruji could sometimes have an ugly and political side, excluding people and hurting feelings. Unfortunately, I sometimes excelled in this craving.

The Osborne home was in Montecito, near the ocean. It was beautifully decorated in an early American style that seemed to reflect the Osbornes' tastes. John, a graduate of Yale Divinity School and a former Trappist monk, was now an investment-fund manager. His wife, Catherine, was someone everyone assumed was well to do. She was astute in the art of etiquette, and gave the impression of coming from money. She was a wonderful hostess and thought of every detail when it came to making Guruji feel at home.

As the son of an Eastern European Jewish refugee, I was not used to having a potluck dinner served on fine porcelain china with polished sterling-silver utensils! Nevertheless, it was always inspiring to see how people of so many backgrounds would mix so easily around Guruji.

After Guruji settled in and rested awhile, he joined us for the evening satsang. Many new people were at the house that evening, and we hoped he would share some knowledge. After we sang awhile, Guruji opened his eyes, and we could tell he was ready to speak. He sat quietly for a few moments, and looked at the people who had gathered.

"Have you noticed what you do when you find something beautiful, or when you love something? You want to hold on to it and possess it. Trying to possess love robs the beauty in love and makes love ugly. Then, that same love gives you pain.

"Whenever you love somebody, you try to dictate terms to them. In a subtle way, you try to control them. Whatever you try to control, hold on to, or manipulate, turns ugly, because the little 'I' in us — *I, I, I,* — itself is ugly. When you possess something, your love is lost. Hasn't this been the case?"

Guruji looked at me briefly. I knew that was my pattern in every relationship I had. I smothered people trying to control them. Was I doing this in my relationship with Guruji as well?

"It starts in childhood with the relationship with mother," he continued. "'Love me and me alone.' It's a deep *sanskara* (past impression). We don't want to lose somebody we love. Love that has a fear of losing somebody or something doesn't blossom. It becomes ugly, and jealousy comes. We never love something that is big, that is enormous, because you have not become big and enormous. As long as you stay small, there is no joy, happiness, or peace. Joy is an expansion, becoming big in your heart. This can only happen in a situation where you are in so much love but you cannot possess it."

I knew Guruji was referring to the competition and politics that were beginning to surface in our group. People were competing over which car Guruji drove in, whose house he stayed in, which person cooked for him, and more. His timing was uncanny. I looked over at John, and he glanced at me somberly without a smile.

I knew why I was jealous of John's relationship with Guruji. I wanted the love I experienced with my guru to be exclusive. I was afraid that someone would be closer to him than I was. Whenever these feelings came up, I acted foolishly and did my best to push others away.

"You can love a guru, but you cannot possess a guru," Guruji said. "Having a guru does something good for you, because you have never loved something and not possessed it. In a guru, you can experience that love, but you cannot hold on to it. Your mind cannot possess it. Because you are not used to that type of love, your mind may undergo a little strain or frustration in the process. It's like 'sour grapes.' The tendency may be to run away and withdraw. But that doesn't lead you anywhere either. You came to swim, but instead you wet your feet and then went back, withdrew. You need to learn a new way, to love and still be centered. And that is what happens here.

"Loving the guru is the first step. God is so general, so universal, belonging to everybody, the whole creation all of the time. You don't love public places. However, through a guru there is a personal connection, and that bond is infinite. It's the bridge, because, before, you have known only personal connections.

"The guru breaks the pattern of possessing love," he said. "Whenever you seem to be dictating terms or becoming possessive, he will do the complete opposite — tighten the screw or loosen the screw, as it is needed. At the same time, a guru is not doing anything, it is just happening through him. It is happening through the Big Mind. There is no pre-conceived plan of action. Actions are spontaneous."

Guruji was describing my experience. We clearly had an intimate relationship, but it was contrary to anything I had experienced with anyone else. He was a mirror for me to see the limitations I had in my mind and heart, but unlike other relationships, I felt empowered and energized.

"Don't make the guru-disciple relationship into just another relationship," he continued, "like father, brother, sister, wife, or friend. It's not like any other relationship. Otherwise you will get into the same type of possessive attitude."

Someone who was meeting him for the first time sounded doubtful. "Does everyone need a guru to evolve?" he asked.

Guruji laughed and said, "There is no need for a guru if you don't need anybody in your life, any relationships. That is the path of the recluse — a monk's life, where everything is completely subdued in the mind, without longing, love, beauty, relationships, or even laughter — no social interactions. If any relationship is needed or essential for you, then an understanding of love is needed. In loving the guru, the guru does not get anything. It's only more of a botheration. He could be happily sitting in bliss. But once you become a guru, you have to look into everybody's calamities and remove them. It's just like shoveling winter snow. You remove it and then again in half an hour the snow is back, again you have to shovel it."

The satsang ended late that evening. As usual, a small group of us stayed behind hoping to get a few minutes more with our master. Guruji went back to his room and ate his dinner. And after an hour, he returned to the living room to speak with us. It was the first time I saw Guruji without his usual smile or lightness.

He looked right at me. "You think you know me," he said with a quiet firmness, "but you don't know me at all. Just sitting with me, being with me, doesn't mean that you are close. What is the Art of Living? It is being in service. If you could be in service to anybody, be there for them, then you are coming close to me."

I squirmed uncomfortably. It was the first time I had seen Guruji be so direct. "If someone asks you, 'Can you take some luggage in your car?' and you say, 'No, I have no room,' and then you say, 'Wait, wait let me see,' this is not service. Saying 'No' immediately causes a block for them somewhere. Afterwards, when you say, 'Yes, OK, I can take one more piece of luggage in the back,' you do it, but it has no effect.

"It would be better the other way around," he said. "First say, 'Yes.' Then if there is some difficulty, say, 'No, sorry, I can't do it.' Do you see the difference? It shows that you are willing. And it is that willingness that creates harmony. Being useful means having this inner 'Yes.'"

I felt really small. He could clearly see how selfish I was.

"Those taking the teacher training tomorrow should know that I want all our teachers to be in this inner state of 'Yes!' You should always be ready — 'All right, fine, I will do it.' It is your attitude, your willingness to be there to help. The attitude of showing 'No' first indicates fear inside. We are not conscious of this. It is not that this person is bad, or that person is good. Just be aware of this basic truth."

At that moment, I didn't think I would be able to rise to the occasion. Was I ready to be a teacher? Could I have a "Yes" mind? Was I mature enough to represent Guruji as one of his teachers?

"I am not telling you to be naive and let everybody misuse your generosity or whatever," he said. "No, that's also no good. What I am asking you is to come from that space of saying 'Yes.' Do you get what I'm saying?"

Guruji told us we would start teacher training early the next morning with *guru puja,* the ceremony of gratitude to the tradition of masters. Doing a puja meant something auspicious was going to happen.

It took a long time to fall asleep that night. I was still excited about teacher training, but upset and embarrassed by the way I'd acted with John's luggage. I relived the incident and Guruji's response several times. But after lying in bed for a while, I realized it wasn't about the luggage, it was about my mind, my ego.

The "Yes" mind was a new concept for me. Letting go of my small-minded self-centeredness was going to be a challenge.

Returning to Catherine and John's in the morning, I was struck by the major change they had made to their living room. It had been rearranged, as though a huge celebration was going to take place. Vases of roses from the garden were everywhere and incense was in the air. In the center of the room was a table with an exquisite picture representing the tradition of spiritual teachers, the *Guru Parampara.* It looked so regal with the delicate handmade garland they had draped around the picture.

Only eight of us arrived on time that morning for what was the most mystical puja I have ever experienced. After the ceremony, we all sat quietly and sank into deep meditation. In retrospect, I believe that Guruji was giving us *shaktipat* — transmitting the master's spiritual energy and grace, and empowering us to become teachers.

Although there were others who joined the teacher-training course that week, it was only the few of us who were present for the ceremony who were made teachers. These people are still among Guruji's strongest devotees.

I was glad to be on the course, but, at the time, it was just another excuse for me to be around Guruji. In the four days we were together, Guruji was constantly interrupted by phone calls and visitors. I was uncertain that, with such a short training program, we would actually be qualified to conduct courses (although it was a far longer training than the one I'd received to assist him!). Now Guruji refers to that course as "the emergency teacher training." He had no choice but to quickly duplicate himself for the knowledge to spread.

He wasn't rigid about having us memorize the contents or very detailed about how to teach this or that. He wanted us to know the course points well, but he seemed more concerned with how we lived our life. He wanted us to be compassionate and caring toward others, flexible and adaptable to all situations and circumstances; to be humble, grateful, and filled with love. The golden rule was to accept people as they are. "If you can commit yourself to total acceptance and not hate anyone, then it is worthwhile for you to start teaching," he told us.

"This is your commitment, to flow with the knowledge," he said on one of the days. "Teaching is not one aspect of your life, and then you're not living knowledge fully the rest of the time. It's like dyeing a cloth. You dye the cloth so totally and then it is completely dyed." It sounded wonderful, but I thought I had a long way to go.

Although our formal training was fairly brief, we were eventually able to see him teach dozens of courses. It was like an apprentice program. Looking back now, I feel so fortunate, for he rarely teaches the Art of Living Course himself these days.

When we completed our teacher-training in July of 1989, our group wasn't sure how to properly introduce the Art of Living Course to people. We thought that if we had an introductory videotape of Guruji, it would help. At first, he was reluctant to make the tape. In fact, he was averse to initiating any structured marketing program for spreading the knowledge. He insisted that word of mouth would be the most effective way to bring people to this path. I completely disagreed and did my best to convince him that we needed to execute a proper marketing and public relations plan.

Whenever the subject of marketing came up, Guruji made it a point to tell us that he operated in a much different manner. He was confident that his knowledge would spread naturally, and he wasn't interested in generating marketing hype. He told us over and over again that Art of Living would eventually touch the lives of millions around the world. Listening to him speak about the future growth of our organization, I was reminded of the passage in the Bible when God tells an elderly Abraham, who was childless at the time, that his seed would multiply and bring about a great nation. I'm not sure that Abraham really believed what God told him. With a group of only twenty close devotees, Guruji's vision was beyond my imagination. It was simply inconceivable that in only a few years, Art of Living courses would reach people in more than a hundred and fifty countries.

Determined to execute my plan, I recruited the help of other teachers to convince Guruji to make our first introductory videotape. He eventually agreed.

As the director, I wanted things as professional as possible. I hired an experienced video crew to come to Jeff Houk's house to film the session. I became a tyrant, pushing and shoving people around so the tape would come out as I wanted. I was even rude to Guruji, telling him that we were paying these men by the hour and that he needed to hurry up and come to the session as soon as he could. I was totally out of control!

Nearly everyone's buttons were pushed that day. However, Guruji didn't react in a negative way. In fact, it was just the opposite. Guruji saw my crudeness but I wasn't reprimanded or ostracized. Even though my behavior was rough, he was still encouraging me to be useful and contribute. I had not developed the skill and sensitivity to take into account how people were feeling, nor did I seem to have the natural instinct. At that point in my development, I was focused only on getting the job done and was unconcerned that my behavior was hurtful to other people. Worst of all, these negative tendencies seemed heightened around Guruji.

I don't know if Guruji was simply seeing beyond my flaws and limitations, but for me, being around the master was like being a bull in a china shop. There was such a contrast. He was so refined, delicate, and sensitive to others. If nothing else, Guruji provided an opportunity to grow just by observing how he moved in his life.

A week later, these incredible days came to an end, and Guruji returned to India. I wanted to start teaching courses as soon as I could. I thought of placing newspaper ads to promote the Art of Living. But I soon realized that the best way to organize more courses at that point was word of mouth — as Guruji had said. I pulled out my phone book and went through my list.

I decided to call Laurel, a woman I dated when I first came to Santa Monica. Petite, with emerald-green eyes and frizzy brown hair, Laurel had moved to Santa Monica to study gemology. She also dabbled in tarot cards, liked reading self-help books, and was interested in spirituality. I liked dating her, and had even thought of her as someone I could marry. But she wasn't able to commit to the relationship and retreated when things started getting more serious. We still stayed in touch and got together once in a while. I told her about my experiences with Guruji and the course but she was reluctant to register.

"It sounds like you've really made some big changes and I'm happy for you, but I don't think this is for me," Laurel said. And she wasn't hesitant to say why. "Do you realize that you're talking about Sri Sri like he's a saint? Don't you see that you're giving him your power and following him blindly? If it's working for you, that's great. But I'm not interested in following a guru."

I tried to explain that she didn't need to be involved in the same way I was. She could simply enjoy the benefits of the breathing techniques and the principles from the course. "I'm just on an adventure that is teaching me a lot about myself," I offered, trying to tone down my enthusiasm a few notches.

She told me she'd think about it, but it was clear that my glowing description of Guruji had frightened her off. I had been talking as if she would have the same feelings I did — even though she hadn't met him! I also forgot that I'd already become comfortable with the idea of a spiritual teacher from my time with Maharishi.

I knew there was a great value and safety in having a spiritual teacher who was part of a tradition. Guruji's teachings were based on an ancient tradition of yoga and wisdom — a tradition that many sages say has been passed down for hundreds of thousands of years. The path is individual, but seers who have traveled the path before have given signposts and shared what's worked and what hasn't. The grace of a tradition is also said to be passed down, with people today benefiting from the accumulated practice of previous generations.

Although *guru* is a word that simply means teacher, I knew that having a spiritual guru was often eyed with suspicion and still a fairly foreign concept in the West. I was continuing to discover what it meant myself. But I was not really seeing Guruji in a category. He was *my* friend, *my* teacher. I had come to see Guruji as someone who was entirely dedicated to eliminating human suffering on the planet. Besides sleeping just a few hours a day and taking meals, all of his time was spent uplifting others. He didn't have a personal agenda or a separate personal life. In that regard, you could say there was "no one at home." Those of us who gathered around him experienced something unique in his presence that was hard to describe. People blossomed. It was a common experience to enter his room and, while we were in there, no longer be bothered by the problems we had gone in to talk about. And while his content might depend on the receptivity of his audience, he was basically the same in public and private.

Although India, like other places, has its share of charlatans who project themselves as realized masters, the guru-disciple relationship is an integral part of the culture. People in Eastern traditions generally tend to accept the idea of a guru as normal and beneficial. The mother is seen as the first guru, and, as adults, many families have a relationship with a guru for guidance and help with their spiritual growth. A guru is usually considered essential for those who want to grow into self-realization/enlightenment, which is thought to be the height of what a human being is capable of — round-the-clock awareness of the unchanging, blissful Self. Living in that state, and seeing that unchanging basis of life in everything around, is considered rare. But the ability to bring others to that state is considered even more rare.

I said almost none of this to Laurel. I couldn't articulate it. I only knew I was experiencing something that was opening my heart, felt authentic, and was giving me a chance to be of service and grow. Guruji was providing tools for me to experience more mental and emotional freedom and become more natural, and he was skillfully helping me become aware of aspects of my personality that could benefit from refinement. He was starting to show me something that many people would probably not want to look at — the patterns of my own mind and where I was stuck in my ego. Guruji wasn't giving this type of attention to everyone, at least not so specifically. Maybe not everyone needed it. Or maybe I was simply open to it. But more significant to me was that I was discovering how much love I had inside.

After my phone call with Laurel, I decided it would probably be better if I wasn't so forthcoming about my personal relationship with Guruji. People needed to feel free to discover their own relationship with him, if that's what they wanted. It was already clear to me that the course was valuable either way.

A few months later, I received a call from Louis, an intelligent and energetic meditation teacher from my old neighborhood in Queens, New York, who was now living in California. He had heard from a friend who had taken the course that I was an Art of Living teacher. He said his friend had been meditating for years, but had never felt this good throughout the day. Louis was interested in having me conduct a workshop for him and some of his friends.

I was excited about having an opportunity to teach, but I was also apprehensive. How could I teach such an experienced meditation teacher? I had no experience and I lacked self-confidence as a teacher. He would clearly see that I didn't know anything. It would be a disaster! But Louis was persistent, saying he could get twenty people together.

Panicked, I called Jeff and asked him if he would teach the workshop with me. Jeff thought it would be fun and agreed. Since I had never taught a course before and our syllabus had only brief notes, I listened to audiotapes of Guruji teaching the Art of Living Course over and over again. Every day I studied and studied, memorizing his every word, inflection, and pause. I wasn't taking any chances.

Twice a week, Jeff and I had study sessions over the phone to help us prepare. We talked about knowledge and things we had learned about teaching the course, but mostly we laughed at the outrageous things we'd experienced around Guruji. I enjoyed these sessions with Jeff. We were both committed to sharing Guruji's knowledge and wanting to serve. He was becoming a really good friend and I was looking forward to teaching with him.

After three weeks of preparation, I felt ready to teach the first course in the United States without Guruji's physical presence. Twenty-two people showed up, most of them having practiced meditation for many years.

All my fears and apprehension faded away as I taught. Teaching was like a meditation, my mind was so completely present and involved in what I was saying and doing. Listening to myself speak, I was impressed with the knowledge that came out.

After the first session, Louis came up and thanked me. He said he was having such good experiences, and attributed it to my being such a good teacher. "You're very patient and kind," Louis said. "It's obvious that you love teaching this program and you're skilled as a teacher. You must have gotten a lot out of this yourself."

I smiled at Louis but couldn't speak. I was amazed by how effective Guruji's course was, and I was getting feedback that showed I might actually be making some progress in my life.

Relieved that everyone was enjoying the workshop, Jeff and I called Guruji in India to let him know that we were teaching our first course. He was like a mother hen. He wanted to know everything, especially whether everyone was in high spirits and having good experiences.

From the tone of his voice, I felt like he was proud of us. It was wonderful to share Guruji's knowledge with these people and feel I was making a difference. But on another level, it was rewarding to feel that I was pleasing Guruji, which I'm sure a psychologist would say was a relief from the way I'd felt around my dad. But by now I realized that, from his side, there was nothing that Guruji wanted or needed. His only objective was to help people be happier, more aware, and more peaceful. Some of the other teachers and volunteers helped him by making him rest or cooking for him, since he rarely seemed to consider his own needs. But for me, being a teacher seemed like the best way to help.

"Remember," Guruji told me and Jeff, "it's not what you say that is so important, it's your presence that matters most. What really transforms people is grace. As a teacher, you become an instrument for that grace to flow. Take good care of the people, and be sure that everyone is inspired to come back for the weekly Kriya sessions."

Besides encouraging people to do the practices daily, Guruji suggested weekly group follow-up sessions to reinforce the benefits from the course. Since there were so few teachers in those days, I conducted two follow-up sessions each week — one for Louis and his friends in Orange County and a second for the HIV/AIDS group in West Hollywood.

Thrilled with having just taught my first course, I wanted to share Guruji's knowledge even more. At the weekly follow-up sessions, I did my best to persuade those who had just attended the workshop to talk to their friends and set up introductory talks for me. I used every marketing trick in the book to perk up their enthusiasm so they would help, but I wasn't having much success, and, eventually, once again, my aggressive tactics repelled people.

One day, John Osborne called me to say he was hearing rumors that the AIDS group was so offended by my aggressive style that they planned to quit the Art of Living program if someone else didn't lead their sessions. When I spoke to Guruji on the phone to give him a status report on L.A. activities, I suggested that I drop out of the AIDS project and find someone more suitable to replace me. But he insisted that I continue and told me to do my best to build the group. I was sure it was a big mistake, but followed his direction.

The next day, I received a phone call from Bob, informing me that the AIDS group wanted to have a dinner meeting with me to strategize about the future of the Art of Living AIDS program. These guys want to have a strategy meeting with me? I didn't have a good feeling about the meeting. Yet I knew I had to attend.

The meeting was held at a vegetarian Chinese restaurant on Wilshire Boulevard in Santa Monica. At first, everyone was cordial and friendly, and seemed happy I was there. But once dinner was served, the group turned into a lynch mob. For two hours, I stared at my cold food as they tore into me.

"You are running our group like it is some sort of business."

"It is clear that you are homophobic and hate to be around us."

"You're a total control freak."

"I think you are looking for acceptance, and this is not the place for co-dependency."

"I think you need counseling."

"Why did Guruji put you in charge? You are so insensitive."

"We just don't like you, Michael, and don't want you to come to our meetings. If you come, we won't!"

I felt like crying. I was in shock. Why would Guruji have me work with this group? I was clearly the wrong person. There was a part of me that wanted to hold on to my position in the group, but I knew I had to let it go. Disheartened, I called Guruji again and told him about the meeting. "Continue and be strong," he advised me.

"Continue? But Guruji, these people clearly don't want or respect me," I whimpered. "How can I continue?" I felt like quitting. How could I go back to the group, let alone continue as a teacher?

Guruji was straightforward in his response. "If they don't respect you, so what! You respect yourself. That is enough. You cannot buy respect from anybody, Michael. I cannot sit here and tell you, 'You should respect me.' Do you see? This is a hopeless thing that you are looking for. If you don't respect yourself, then how can you expect others to respect you? And if you respect yourself, then what difference does it make? The whole world does not need to respect you. Let everyone stand and shout, 'Michael is a fool!' So what! Let the whole world humiliate you. How can you be humiliated if you do not want to be humiliated? If you are centered, you respect yourself and don't look for respect. Your yearning to be respected doesn't bring respect."

"But, Guruji," I interrupted.

He paid no attention and continued. "What is respect after all? Some floating opinion in someone's mind. What is the guarantee they will respect you forever? You respect me today. What is the guarantee that you will respect me tomorrow? So what if a person doesn't respect me? It is up to them. If a person has respect within them, they will always express it. They will bring it forth. If they don't have it for themselves, they will not give it to anyone else.

"Being on this path, Michael, you have to drop expecting people to respect you. Completely. Otherwise, there is no point in being with me. If you come here, you have to become like a diamond. Powerful. Otherwise, what is the point?"

His reaction surprised me. I had expected Guruji to reprimand me and lecture me on how I should change, or else to tell me that the people in the AIDS group were hopeless. But there was no mention of my behavior or theirs, just the tendency of my mind. He was more interested in turning me into a leader and making me strong. He was showing me that it was time to stop being the football of other people's opinions.

I knew Guruji wanted me to keep going to the AIDS group, and I saw the value in doing that for my own growth, but I didn't have the strength to face them.

CHAPTER ELEVEN

Surrender & Samadhi

It could only have been grace that propelled me to carry on as an Art of Living teacher after my humiliation by the AIDS group. The feedback I received was uncharted territory. Did everyone feel this way about me? Was I really that bad? Questioning over and over, I vacillated between blaming myself and blaming everyone else. Then, perhaps out of sheer exhaustion, my mind flipped over.

It became evident that if I were to grow spiritually, I needed to take responsibility for my actions and for how I projected myself. If I wanted to be around Guruji, I needed to be more like him. I needed to refine my personality and become more gentle and considerate of others.

As time passed, I again began to think of ways to expand Guruji's exposure in the U.S. One day, I saw a poster advertising the annual Whole Life Expo, a popular New Age event that presented the latest trends in personal development to thousands of spiritually minded seekers. I thought it would be a great idea for Guruji to be one of the featured speakers at the Expo.

I got together with Jeff Houk and Catherine (John Osborne's wife, who was now the chairperson of the new U.S. Art of Living Foundation), and we placed a call to India to discuss the idea with Guruji.

Guruji was reluctant. "I don't think that would be a dignified place for me to speak," he said. "The people who come to these types of things are not so dedicated. They are just coming to an event, shopping around for this and that. They won't be in that subtle space to get what I am saying."

I read him the names of the other speakers — Ram Dass, Bernie Siegel, Timothy Leary, Yogi Bhajan, Uri Geller, Deepak Chopra, etc.

But again, Guruji said no, and made it clear that he was not interested in attending an event like this. I tried a couple more times to persuade him, but he was still not interested.

Then out of the clear blue, he said, laughing, "Maybe I could come and wear my shawl with all the glitter and be the Glittering Guru."

"It's up to you, Guruji," I said calmly, trying to seem as if I had no attachment to his decision. "If you think it will be worthwhile, we can make the arrangements. Otherwise we can focus on other things."

"OK, yes, I will come," he said.

My mind became busy, planning and organizing for his visit. I contacted the organizers of the Expo. Most unknown and unpublished speakers were allotted forty-five minutes for their presentations. I convinced the management of the Expo that Guruji had a huge following and that all of his followers in Southern California would be coming to the Expo to hear him speak. So they gave him a two-hour, prime-time slot, on Sunday, from noon to 2 p.m.

To promote the event, I took out a full-page ad on the first page of the Expo's program guide. I was also able to persuade the editors of a local Indian magazine and a New Age newspaper to publish articles that promoted Guruji as a featured speaker at the Expo. Calls about his talk increased daily. I became confident that the event would be a huge success.

Lost in success, my awareness of becoming more gentle and considerate diminished, and eventually vanished. In a short time, arrogance prevailed. I was back to my old self, Mr. Know-It-All. Bossing around everyone who volunteered, I again became a tyrant.

I felt that besides bringing many people to the path, this event would make Los Angeles the Art of Living showcase for the whole country. L.A. was flooded with posters, halls were booked for additional programs, advertisements were placed, and the phone kept ringing. I thought I was a New Age marketing genius. I imagined that in the future, all Art of Living organizers would seek my guidance on how to promote Guruji properly.

Guruji was scheduled to spend a week in Northern California before arriving in Los Angeles.

As his arrival got closer, I felt increasingly compelled to travel with him. I'd found a new job, selling advertising for a local newspaper, but how could I sit at a desk while my guru was traveling around the country? When I asked my boss for three weeks off so I could take care of a "family emergency," he looked at me as though I had lost my mind.

"You just started this job two months ago," he said. "We can't let you have three weeks off now."

"Well," I asked, "can I take off time without pay?"

The negotiations went nowhere, and I felt no alternative but to quit yet another job.

Jeff and I drove up to San Francisco to greet Guruji and his sister, Bhanu, at the airport. This would be Bhanu's first visit to the United States. Jeff and I were so excited about seeing Guruji again that we forgot to bring what had become a traditional gift of flowers for him.

After parking the car, we rushed into the airport hoping to find a florist. Out of the corner of my eye, I noticed an unassuming, bearded Indian man, wrapped in a beige shawl, standing beside a short Indian woman. They were smiling and looking directly at us. It took a few moments to register that we had just walked past Guruji and his sister! He seemed so small and so much less powerful than usual. I almost didn't recognize him.

I have observed that Guruji often seems to change his energy field when he is in a public place. I think it is so he doesn't attract unnecessary attention. Once, in Boston, I drove him to a government office to sign some documents for his visa. As we approached our destination, it was as though someone had pulled the plug. Guruji became quite ordinary. The glow diminished from his face, and he even seemed to get smaller. I felt I needed to assist this feeble man into the office and help him take a seat. As he has said, being around a master is similar to being near a peacock. There are times when the peacock's feathers are fully displayed and other times when they are concealed.

Jeff and I greeted Guruji and were introduced to Bhanu. "Welcome to America, Bhanu," I said, as she smiled shyly. Her face was radiant and her eyes were soft and pure. I liked her the moment I met her and felt as though I was reuniting with a long-lost friend.

As we were leaving the airport, Janael McQueen ran toward us carrying a large bouquet of flowers and yelling, "Guruji! Guruji!" When she finally caught up with us, she said, "Oh, Jai Gurudev, Guruji. I have been looking all over for you. I thought I would miss you because I got lost on the way to the airport."

Guruji was pleased to see her. Janael was one of the women I met after Guruji's talk that first night in Santa Monica. She'd been introduced to Guruji the year before I was, and had traveled with him in Europe and India. She now taught the workshop in Northern California. Before meeting him, she was working as a therapist in Los Angeles, and had contemplated moving to Calcutta to join Mother Teresa and become one of her nuns. One of Janael's clients had persuaded her to see Guruji and take his course before moving to India and making such a dramatic change in her life. When she met him, it was love at first sight. Since then, she has been a close devotee and full-time teacher, traveling and sharing his knowledge.

We left the airport and drove across the bay to Marr and Joan's house, in Oakland, where Guruji and Bhanu would be staying. The Goodrums lived in a large old house on the top of a hill. The house had a huge porch, swimming pool, and a hot tub, which most of us who were traveling with Guruji appreciated but rarely took time to enjoy.

Joan was a kindhearted woman who taught kindergarten at a private school and was an expert at making the very best *chai* (Indian tea) for breakfast. Joan's husband, Marr, was an unconventional artist, who displayed his artwork all over the house and worked as a paralegal at a prestigious law firm in San Francisco. They were both easygoing and allowed us to take over their home.

Guruji's bedroom was in the basement. The room was huge, but he remained cross-legged on his bed most of the time.

Jeff and I shared a room in the house next door, and most of that week I was exhausted from lying awake each night, listening to Jeff snore like a freight train. I made several futile attempts to stop his snoring, but I couldn't wake him up. The worst thing about snorers is that they sleep very deeply and are impervious to the noise — and suffering — around them. They're also always the ones to fall asleep first. But this was the only thing I could find to complain about during those wonderful few days in Oakland.

We essentially had Guruji to ourselves. I was surprised that Marr and Joan went to work each morning. Didn't they know who was in their home? Even stranger to me, no one came to visit Guruji throughout the day. This left Bhanu, Janael, Jeff, and me alone with our master all day.

Bhanu was Guruji's younger sister and his first devotee. Married with two children, she didn't travel much at the time, and this was her first trip abroad. She was well educated, with a master's degree in Sanskrit, yet her natural innocence prevailed. She giggled a lot and seemed blissful most of the time. We all wanted to be around her as much as we could. She was so charming and kind. She had a pure and melodious singing voice, and she seemed happy to share tidbits about Guruji that we could never get from him.

She explained that Guruji was very special as a child. Instead of playing games like other children, Guruji would spend his time re-enacting the daily pujas and rituals that his grandmother performed. He enjoyed visiting temples, mosques, and churches, and then teaching her whatever new knowledge he learned. He'd always insist that food should be offered to God before eating, even chocolates. "Imagine being a child with sweets in your hands, ready to eat, and having to offer them first to God," she laughed. "I was so impatient, and the chocolates were so irresistible, I couldn't wait. I would quietly put them in my mouth, hoping he wouldn't see. But Guruji would catch me. He was so compassionate that most of the time he let me eat the chocolates, but other times he'd be more strict and would insist that I remove them."

On Saturday morning, Jeff and I left Oakland so we could prepare for Guruji's talk at the Los Angeles Whole Life Expo the next afternoon. Early Sunday morning we were at the Expo, carting a small sofa for him to sit on, rugs to cover the stage, and colorful flowers to make the stage look more festive.

The room started to fill early. By 11:45 a.m., the hall was filled to capacity, with approximately three hundred people. In those days, we usually attracted twenty to thirty people to Guruji's talks, so this was a phenomenal turnout.

"You did a great job, Michael," said Jeff, as he looked at the crowd that had gathered. "You are a real whiz at marketing and promotions. Guruji will be proud of you."

I kept reminding the other Art of Living volunteers to let me know the moment Guruji entered the building so I could make the appropriate introduction. It was already noon and time for the talk to start.

I could see that the audience was anxiously waiting to meet him. So, at a quarter past twelve, I went on the stage and gave a brief introduction to Sri Sri Ravi Shankar and the Art of Living Course. I assured the audience that he would be there shortly, and encouraged them to be patient and wait. However, I was getting nervous. Where could he be?

Five minutes later, Chris Reed walked through the door. He saw that Guruji wasn't there and came up to the stage area to reassure me. "I greeted him at the airport about an hour ago," Chris said. "Guruji said he was going to stop and freshen up and would be coming right to the event. Don't worry, he'll be here soon."

Just then, Divya came into the hall carrying her guitar case. Divya often traveled with Guruji, leading his audiences in tuneful bhajans and chants. "Guruji sent me to warm up the crowd," she said. "He will be here any minute."

She walked to the stage and began leading the audience in a version of *Om Namah Shivaya*.

I looked at my watch. It was half-past twelve. Now I began to worry. "Where is he?"

I left the hall and waited for him down in the lobby, as Divya entertained.

At a quarter to one, John and Catherine arrived, but no Guruji.

"Where is he?" I roared. "What is this? Some kind of a joke? People have been waiting for almost an hour! I thought you were going to drive him. If he isn't with you, then where is he!?" But John only gave me a pitying smile and said softly, "I'll make the announcement. He won't be coming."

"What!?" I screamed. "What happened? How could he do this?"

I was devastated. I felt my face flush and thought I was going to pass out. But I managed to say, "No, John, I'll make the announcement."

I walked slowly to the stage and told the crowd that Guruji would not be attending the Expo.

The hall cleared quickly, with many people complaining on their way out. One man shouted at me, "I could have watched Uri Geller in the other hall bending spoons with his mind. Instead I wasted my time waiting for your stupid guru!"

"Sorry," I whispered.

I was in shock. I felt nauseous and had a pounding headache.

As I stood there, a tall, stocky man named Dave Longnecker approached me. He had short, light-brown hair, wore a plaid flannel shirt and blue jeans, and spoke in a Midwestern accent. Dave wanted to know where he could meet the mysterious saint. "I think we missed the best part of the Expo," he chuckled. "Is there anywhere I can go to meet him?"

I couldn't speak. I was too raw. I wrote down a phone number for him to call and handed it to him as I flashed a limp smile.

My mind was racing. How could he do this to me? I had spent more than two thousand dollars of my own money. I felt so humiliated. I felt like a fool. I had even quit my job to be with him. How could I have been so stupid? I should just quit this whole thing. What type of guru plays such idiotic games with people's lives? Who knows what he might do to me next? I am going home now, and I am never going to have anything to do with this group again!

Then, suddenly, the anger subsided and the chatter stopped. I became deeply silent and calm, and a gentle energy flowed through my body. I was enveloped in a sea of love. The sensation was so intense I began to weep. I could feel Guruji's presence so strongly that I thought he was standing right next to me, and somehow I knew that Guruji's failure to appear at the Expo had been an act of love.

As I stood there with the tears running down my face, I felt someone gently take my arm and say sweetly, "Michael, I have something for you." I turned to see Bhanu, eyes full of compassion. She was holding a piece of candy that was wrapped in bright gold foil. "This is from Guruji. He sent it for you."

She unwrapped the candy and placed it in my mouth. It was sweet and soothing. "Come," she said. "Let's go. We will have some ice cream and then go see Guruji."

Divya, Bhanu, and I sat in an ice-cream parlor for over an hour. Though the rage had subsided, I was still feeling stunned and confused, and they didn't seem to mind waiting as I ate two banana splits before feeling centered enough to see Guruji.

"Come, come," said Guruji, when I knocked on the door to his room. "How did it go?" he asked, as I sat on the floor in front of his chair.

I didn't know how to act or what to do. I was still shaken, and didn't want to appear submissive or condone what had happened, so I pretended to be reserved and cool.

"It went fine," I replied nonchalantly. "We just had some ice cream and I brought some for you. Would you like me to bring it in?"

Ignoring my aloofness, he said, "I had all intentions of going to the Expo, but my body would not get up. You see, I am not like other masters. I don't care for a big following or big crowds. That's not why I'm here."

It became very still in the room, as he paused and looked directly into my eyes. "See, Michael, the light of the sun is greater than the light that comes from thousands of stars that are in the sky. If I can make just one sun, then I have done my job.

"You need to learn the lesson of non-doership," he explained. "When you offer something to the master, to the Divine, you offer it unconditionally, without a sense of doership. 'I did a good job.' 'I did a bad job.' You are not the doer. It is all happening through you. You are simply the witness — without ego, without doership. Otherwise, it is no offering. Do you see what I am saying?"

I understood and lowered my head to hide my tears. Guruji pulled me close and held my head in his lap, gently touching my head with a white rose. I felt like a baby in my mother's arms.

I realized that Guruji had nothing to gain by his actions. In fact, he had damaged his reputation with the Expo organizers and participants. He had insight into my personality, and I would reflect on this episode for years to come. Had he gone to the Expo, my arrogance might have been uncontainable.

I wondered why these lessons had to be so dramatic for me? I didn't see Jeff, Chris, or most of the others going through these experiences. From my perspective, it seemed easier for them. Was I such a hard-nut case? It was all so subtle, but I knew that Guruji wasn't interested in turning me into the perfect devotee. He just wanted me to become softer, more sensitive, and considerate of others — changes I didn't fully understand the need for at the time. Perhaps that's why he needed to use a sledgehammer.

As I sat up and got ready to leave the room, Guruji looked at me and said, "Tonight after satsang you will come with us to Apple Valley."

"No, Guruji, I can't. I have to do my laundry tonight. I haven't been home in days," I explained. I also needed a break from the "Guru Brigade." I just wanted some space for a day.

"Laundry can wait," he said. "Tonight we will drive to Raman Poola's house in Apple Valley. Make yourself ready so you can go."

"But I have no clothes," I said.

"It will be fine. You will have time for laundry tomorrow, when we get back," he insisted.

How could I say no? So that night, after satsang, eight of us piled into John Osborne's oversized car and were off to Apple Valley to visit the Poolas. There was a carnival atmosphere in the car as we drove down the freeway. Divya had a new cassette of her latest bhajans and debuted it on the car stereo. Guruji gently swayed his body and clapped his hands as he listened.

"Pass the *gulab jamuns* around, and there are *rasgullas,* too," he said, as the Indian sweets were handed around the car.

This festive mood was such a contrast to what I had experienced earlier that day. The Whole Life Expo had been erased from my mind. I was happy with my spiritual family.

Once we arrived at Raman's home, Guruji plopped himself down on a La-Z-Boy recliner and turned on the TV. He surfed the channels and stopped at a documentary on the Holocaust. We all sat until midnight, watching our guru gaze silently at the phenomena and horrors of World War II. At any other time, I might have considered this peculiar. But, somehow, it was an appropriate ending to this day.

In the morning, everyone gathered at 9 a.m. to watch Guruji's favorite TV show — *I Love Lucy.* After the show, he rushed us into the puja room. It was Monday, and we were going to do the *Rudram,* the traditional *Shiva puja* to the transcendental aspect of life.

I sat silently with my eyes closed and listened to Guruji chant the ancient Vedic hymns. The sounds of the chanting caused me to slip into deep meditation. My arms and legs were tingling all over, and my consciousness began to spiral inward. I was losing myself in a void. Then, all of a sudden, I stopped existing. I was gone — no body, or breath, or mind, or anything. Apparently, I was in this state for an hour and a half.

When I finally opened my eyes, no one was left in the room. They had all gone into the dining room to eat lunch. Guruji saw me stumbling in and said, "Michael is enjoying it here in Apple Valley. Yes?"

He motioned to one of the Indian women to serve me some warm food, and told me that I should sit and eat. The food definitely helped to ground me, but it took some time before I was able to focus. I wasn't sure what had happened to me, but I knew I had gone to a very deep place.

I felt calm and centered that afternoon as we drove back to Los Angeles for the series of talks Guruji was to give at a yoga studio in Santa Monica. We drove to Michèle's house in the nearby city of Venice, where Guruji was going to spend the next week.

I liked going to Michèle's house when Guruji was there. It was a place I associated with knowledge. Of course, there was the knowledge that Guruji shared through his words. But there was another type of knowledge that came from just being in his presence. Michèle was warm and supportive of me spending time around Guruji, and being at her house was always easy.

Michèle lived with her boyfriend, Daren, in a small two-bedroom house that was immaculate and mostly bare. They had no furniture in their living room, just a special chair that was reserved for Guruji. Daren had a propensity for order, but when Guruji was there he had no choice but to relinquish all control. People made his home their home, and the few things that were there inevitably got knocked over, including a candle, which spilled hot wax on the new white carpet.

With Guruji in town, their home was cramped and filled with activity. Unless Guruji was meditating or sleeping, the house was buzzing. Food was being prepared in the kitchen and vessels were everywhere. The aroma of curry lingered in the air for many days.

There was a sign that said "No Entry" on the door to the den, and, at first, I thought it might be a private altar, like the one I had seen at the Thakars' house. And it was. Sort of. When I peeked in, I saw two women ironing Guruji's clothes with utter devotion.

Many people were already there by the time we arrived and were sitting in the living room or in the backyard eating. Someone offered me a plate of food and I sat next to David and Terry, a couple who had driven down from Santa Barbara to be with Guruji for a few days. David was an acupuncturist and a natural-health practitioner who had taken one of the first courses that Guruji taught in U.S. He and Terry were committed to their spiritual path and practices, and were always around when Guruji was in town. As we ate together, David started needling me in a good-natured way about the Expo.

"I think it was the way you introduced him," he said, jokingly. "Guruji was probably there but left when he heard what you were saying about him." I smiled. When David and I were together, silliness prevailed. But I could feel his and Terry's compassion.

As the dishes were being cleared and the time to leave for the evening talk neared, Guruji came out to sit with everyone. I could feel the silent energy and peace that came into the room with him. The chaos stopped instantly, replaced by an atmosphere of eager anticipation and love, with all eyes fixed on Guruji.

A young woman approached Guruji and offered him a gift. He graciously accepted and commented on how beautifully it was wrapped. Guruji held up the present and marveled at the colors and design of the wrapping paper, as though he had never seen anything like this before. He carefully slid off the bow and removed the paper without tearing it, placing the paper neatly by his side. "Hmmm?" he said to Michèle. "You can save this, it's so nice."

I don't know what happened to all the wrapping paper Guruji asked us to save through the years. Although Guruji had a great love for trees and nature, I don't think saving the paper was about conservation. He also asked us to save the poems and greeting cards. To him, they were treasures that someone expressed from their heart. I thought of wallpapering a room for him with greeting cards and wrapping paper as a surprise, but I never did.

The present turned out to be a rag doll, and seeing Guruji's innocent face as he looked at the doll made me feel like a child. When we had previously asked him about his enlightenment, he'd answered with only one sentence, saying, "That's the day I became a rag doll." I guess that meant that he was free of inhibitions and fully surrendered to the Divine play. Everyone oohed and laughed when they saw the gift, which made Michèle giggle and then start laughing. I loved her laugh. It had a unique and contagious cadence. Within moments, the room was in hysterics, including Guruji.

The front door opened and Dave Longnecker, the man who'd approached me as I was leaving the Whole Life Expo, appeared. Glad to see him, and relieved that my efforts were not completely in vain, I got up to greet him. He had been determined to meet Guruji, and had made numerous phone calls to find him at this house. Dave seemed to feel at home right away, and he sat as close as he could to Guruji. Eventually, Dave would also become an Art of Living teacher and bring Guruji's knowledge to many places, including New Zealand.

After a while, the room settled down, and people started approaching Guruji one by one for guidance or to unload their emotional burdens.

I watched this procession of concerns in silence. Although there was little time, he didn't rush. For some, he was light and playful. For others, he gave knowledge and advice. For those who were unable to express themselves, he merely tapped them on the head with a flower, patted their back, or gave them some sweets.

In a corner of the room, a young mother and her two daughters watched from a distance. One of the young girls was only about six or seven, but seemed to be mentally handicapped. As Guruji was leaving the room to get ready for the evening program, the young girl cried out to him, "Please, Master! Help me! I am stuck in time. I can't go forward."

No one seemed to pay any attention to this girl, not even Guruji. Again, she cried out to him. But this time her voice sounded like an old woman, crying out in pain. "Only you can help me! Please, help me!"

As he walked by, he glanced at her from the corner of his eye. He extended his right hand to her for a moment and then continued to walk away. The moment that Guruji looked at her, I could see a stream of blue light flaring out of his nostrils and out from his finger tips, enveloping the young girl's head.

Startled, I looked around, wondering if anyone else had seen this remarkable sight, but everyone continued to ignore the girl.

Within a few minutes, Guruji emerged from his room, dressed for his evening talk. He motioned with a tilt of his head for me to ride with him in the car.

As we were driving, he said to me, "Ah, Michael, today you caught one of my secrets."

"Yes, Guruji, what was that all about? That young girl sounded like an old woman crying out to you like that."

"She was not in present time. Her mind was going backwards. She is not disabled like you think," he explained, "just some problem with her mind going back in time. But all that is gone. She will be all right now."

A few days later, I saw the young girl and her mother at one of the evening programs. I approached the mother and asked her if everything was OK.

"It's a miracle," she said. "I don't know what your guru did to my girl, but she is all right now. I didn't know what to do with her. I was thinking of sending her to an institution or something. But she is fine now. She is fine. I am so grateful!" The woman held on to my arm and began to cry.

As Guruji's visit to Los Angeles came to a close, more and more people arrived for the evening satsangs at Michèle's. They were joyful, candle-lit evenings, and Bhanu and Divya would lead us in bhajans.

During one of these evenings, I thought about a story from *Autobiography of a Yogi*. In the story, Paramahansa Yogananda, through his grace, puts one of his disciples into a state of transcendental bliss called *samadhi*. I kept thinking about how wonderful it would be if Guruji put me into this state. But I didn't think I was advanced enough and I'd never heard of Guruji doing that sort of thing. Yet, as we continued to sing bhajans, the thought of samadhi lingered.

Usually during the singing, I like to play the finger cymbals, keeping time with the music. But for some reason, that evening I wasn't attracted to playing percussion or singing. I just wanted to sit, listen to the bhajans, and observe my thoughts and my breath.

Within a short time, I began to experience the same energy that I had experienced in Apple Valley during the Shiva puja. Was this samadhi? My mind began to spiral inward and my body became immobile, like stone. It was happening again, but this was deeper. I completely disappeared. I was experiencing the bliss of eternity. I lost the sense of time, yet I was fully aware. I have no idea how long this lasted.

At some point, I felt Guruji's shawl brush against my face as he left the room, and I started to become aware of my surroundings. I could hear people speaking and laughing around me, and I realized that satsang was over.

It took some time for me to come back and be able to move my limbs. When I finally stood up, I went to Guruji's room. When I saw him, I started laughing uncontrollably. The other people in the room smiled, wondering what had gotten into me.

"I looked around the room tonight to see who wanted a taste of samadhi," Guruji explained. "Tonight it was only Michael who wanted the experience. So I had no choice but to give it to him. You will have this experience again and again," he said. "Have something to eat before you leave, Michael. Maybe someone can drive him home. It is getting late. Everybody go rest now."

I sat in the kitchen eating Indian food, some *idli* and *sambar* that one of the ladies from South India had brought. I was still feeling blissfully giddy as I ate. Everything was funny to me and nothing had any great significance. But my heart was filled with love and my awareness was crystal clear.

Somehow, I managed to drive myself home, and I finally went to bed around four in the morning.

The next day I woke up with a huge smile. A blissful feeling accompanied my various activities that day — until the afternoon, when, once again, John Osborne swooped Guruji away for the long ride up the Pacific coast to Santa Barbara. Guruji waved from the car and smiled, as I was left behind with Bhanu's and Guruji's luggage.

CHAPTER TWELVE

The Diamond Cutter

ONE YEAR LATER, at 6 a.m., the phone rang.

"Good morning, Michael, it's Michèle. I'm sitting with Guruji, and he said you should definitely bring the video camera with you to Vancouver."

"Sure," I said, half asleep and not thinking about what I was saying. "I'll see you later." I hung up the phone, closed my eyes, and went back to sleep.

It was July 1990, and later that morning we'd be going to Vancouver for a Guru Purnima celebration and advanced course with Guruji. For the past two weeks, I had been on tour with Guruji as he traveled up the West Coast with a small entourage of devotees, giving courses and a series of commentaries on the age-old *Bhakti Sutras,* aphorisms of love by the sage Narada.

Waking up late, and with little time before my flight, I scurried around my apartment getting ready to leave. In my rush to pack, and with my obsession for traveling light, I decided that it would be best to leave many things at home — including the video camera I had borrowed to record Guruji's talks. Although Guruji thought it would be good to bring the camera to record his talks, I had already been ambivalent about bringing it. I didn't want to lug the equipment to the airport, and Janael and others had complained that the bright lights and camera ruined the intimacy of the talks.

On the plane ride, Guruji was working out plans. "Michael, how would you like to go to Russia and teach there?" He explained that two teachers, Chris and Katherine, had been teaching Art of Living courses in the (then) communist countries of Poland and Russia and had already taught many people. Many others were asking for courses in Russia, and Guruji wanted me to go there with Judson, another Art of Living teacher.

At first, I was excited. Guruji must think highly of me that he would send me as his representative and have me teach internationally. But within a few moments, the excitement and honor wore off and fear set in. Despite growing up in New York, I had an aversion to cold and was afraid of the Russian winter. Couldn't he send me somewhere tropical? Sitting back in my seat, I was only half listening to Guruji now. I was preoccupied with how I would stay warm in the frigid winter.

We arrived in Vancouver just in time for Guruji to rest and meditate, and for those traveling with him to prepare for his public talk.

Guruji was continuing his talks on the *Bhakti Sutras*. Probably because they dwelled on devotion and love, these talks had an especially sweet feeling. That evening, he spoke about surrender. It was a concept I'd never really understood.

Right from his first words, it felt as though stillness was speaking. "Surrender all action to the Divine," he began. "Offer everything, all that you have done. Every moment and every action, offer it. When you offer every action from the past, you are free from guilt and are in the present moment.

"Your negative thoughts, emotions, and tendencies make you feel guilty and bad about yourself," he explained. "Your positive qualities bring arrogance and pride. Your whole life becomes a big weight. So when you go to a guru, a master, offer everything — your good feelings and your bad feelings, your anger and frustration, your arrogance and pride. When you offer, when you surrender, what remains is pure love. You become light, like a flower. All the weight is gone. Then you can live in the moment, totally. Without this, you cannot rejoice in the Self."

He also said something remarkable that made me think: "Offering every breath is Divine love."

I usually equated surrender with weakness, but for the first time I could see that the simple act of letting things go, of handing over my troubles and fears, could bring an inner strength and refinement. Guruji was again guiding us to the present moment. Over the years, I would come to realize that the Divine or the guru gets nothing from this sort of surrender. It is all for the devotee, so that anything that takes us out of the present can fade away without effort. Letting go like this could bring relief and make it easier to live with depth, in a relaxed and centered way.

I started thinking about Guruji himself in this light. It seemed that surrendering to the moment was actually what allowed him to exude confidence without arrogance, to know so much, yet remain innocent and open to learning or hearing suggestions.

As I was leaving the hall, I ran into a couple who had flown up from Los Angeles. Jeffrey and Pamela had taken the course at the beginning of the tour, in Santa Monica, and they had been to the talks and courses in each city since. Jeffrey was a talented writer and musician with brown, curly hair, who looked like Bob Dylan. Pamela was a healer, with a natural lightness and warmth. I liked being around them. They were bright souls who had been meditating for many years, and they were enthusiastic about their time with Guruji.

We started talking about the last several weeks, and Pamela smiled as she told me how much I beamed when I was with Guruji. "You look like a little kid when you're with him," she said.

Jeffrey agreed. "Whatever you do for the Art of Living," he said, "it seems that these times with Punditji are your reward, the thing that makes everything you do worthwhile." It was the first time I became aware that what I was feeling about Guruji was apparent to others.

But Jeffrey had a concern. "These talks we've been hearing are so great," he said. "I'm surprised that they're not being videotaped. I think many people will want to see them."

I gave him an assuring smile and agreed it was a good idea. But he could tell I was not going to do anything about it. "You could rent a camera tomorrow," he insisted. I nodded my head in agreement, but I didn't take his suggestion seriously, and we soon left the hall to join everyone else at the home of the family that was hosting Guruji.

We were treated to some wonderful Indian food and Guruji spent a few minutes with us. But soon he said he wanted to rest early, and sent everyone to bed. I was escorted to the house next door, where I was to spend the night.

A few hours later, around one in the morning, my host knocked on my door: "Michael, are you asleep? Guruji is on the phone. He wants to speak to you."

"Now?" I thought. This must be important. "OK, just a minute," I said and was on the phone a few moments later.

"Jai Gurudev," said Guruji. "So, Michael, how did you enjoy tonight's talk?"

"Oh," I said, half asleep and in my pajamas, "it was great, Guruji."

"And you are comfortable in your room?"

"Yes," I replied, still wondering what this was about.

"You looked tired at satsang," he said. "Are you feeling OK?"

"Yes, Guruji, I'm fine." But I wasn't fine. I was exhausted and wanted to hang up and go back to sleep.

"Michael, what happened to the video camera? How come you did not record tonight's talk?"

"Well, at the last minute I decided not to bring the camera. I thought the bright video lights would get in the way of the Guru Purnima celebration."

His voice sounded stern. "Didn't you ask me if you should bring the camera? And I told you to definitely bring it with you. Don't my words mean anything to you? Why do you ask me if you don't follow my words? What is the point of having a guru? So you can be the guru?"

I felt awful and couldn't respond.

"It is late now," he said, his voice soft again. "Go rest."

The conversation was over. He hung up the phone.

Go rest? How could I rest after that conversation? I lay in bed, but I was filled with remorse. How could I have been so stupid? I was dedicating my life to serving him, yet it was on my own terms.

I woke up early the next morning and sat outside his room, waiting for his door to open so I could apologize. When he finally opened his door, he greeted me with a big smile. "So, Michael, what is the program for today?"

I was confused. He didn't appear to be angry. Instead, he was smiling.

"Oh, Guruji, I'm so sorry about the camera and not listening to you," I blurted out.

My body started to tremble. I was afraid I was going to get a scolding. I remembered being a child and standing in front of my father. What would my punishment be? Would he still trust me and allow me to be close to him? I expected Guruji to growl at me, but instead he had a big smile and looked at me as though he had no idea what I was talking about. It felt awkward. I wasn't in trouble.

I wasn't used to this type of behavior. I was dazed, and, impulsively, I started to laugh out loud, but Guruji kept looking at me with a gentle smile. I realized I was still the abused child striving for appreciation and acceptance from my dad.

"Michael, drop the past. Go into the town today and rent a camera. We will want to record the talks during Guru Purnima. Many people will watch and be inspired."

My body continued to shake and tears welled up in my eyes. This was the strangest relationship. He had absolutely no attachment to the past and held no grudge. I was amazed at how he operated. He wasn't manipulating me or trying to make me feel guilty. He was showing me where my own mind was limiting me. He was helping me drop the past and feel safe to be myself.

It was times like these that I appreciated Guruji even more. Perhaps it was my trust in him that allowed him to take the liberty of showing me my unconscious or selfish behavior. He'd show me the pattern, and then I'd have a vision of how to move forward. I would always feel expanded after these events, partly from the personal attention and partly from the clarity, which helped me feel that I was growing.

I spent all of Sunday searching for a place that I could rent a video camera. Fortunately, one shop was open.

I arrived late in the evening for the advanced course, which had already started that day. Guruji gave me an affectionate smile from the stage as I entered the hall. At that moment, no one else existed — just him and me.

I felt light and free, and full of love, as I set up the camera that night, preparing for the Guru Purnima celebration that would begin the next day.

Guru Purnima is an auspicious day to be with one's master — a day of gratitude, and a day to ponder how much you have developed spiritually during the year. I consider myself lucky to have been able to spend the last twenty years with Guruji on Guru Purnima day. But the celebration of 1990 was the most extraordinary of all. It was off the chart.

Deep in a virgin forest on the edge of a remote lake, Guruji's commentary on the *Bhakti Sutras* ignited an unusual depth of love, devotion, and surrender. This seems to be the memory of everyone who was there that day.

The traditional *Guru puja* set the tone of love and deep feeling as the day began. There was a long group meditation, and Guruji was silent for some time. There was a stillness in the room, but a rich feeling too. As I stood behind the camera, adjusting the lens, I noticed that Guruji's brown eyes were soft, overflowing with love. He cleared his throat to break his silence.

"Hmmm?"

His familiar sound was melodic and sweet. As he spoke, it became clear why the camera had been important.

He told us there are three types of people who come to a master — a student, a disciple, and a devotee.

"A student goes to a teacher and learns something," he said tenderly. "You went to primary school, middle school, and secondary school.

You learned about the mind, you learned about computers, learned about mathematics. This is a student, one who collects information. But information is not knowledge, is not wisdom. Information cannot effect a big change.

"Then comes a disciple. A disciple is with the master for the sake of wisdom, for the sake of improving his life, for the sake of attaining enlightenment. He has a purpose, a cause. So he is not just collecting information, he is trying to look a little deeper. He is trying to bring a transformation in his life. A disciple is still centered on himself. So, according to their capacity, disciples grow, and one day they may get enlightened."

I listened closely, and thought about where I fit in. What was my motive in being with Guruji? Was I there only for my own development? Or was there more?

"And then there is a devotee. A devotee," Guruji said quietly, "is not there even for wisdom. He is simply rejoicing in love. He has fallen in deep love with the master, with the Infinity, with God. He doesn't care whether he gets enlightened or not. He doesn't care whether he learns a lot of knowledge or wisdom. But being immersed in Divine love every moment — that is enough for him or her. Students are all over, disciples are few, but devotees are rare."

Was *I* a devotee? This question would come to mind many times after this night.

He was expressing something not fully expressible in words. Going further, he said, "Attraction is everywhere, love is in some places, but devotion, again, is rare. A student comes to a master, teacher, guru, with tears in his eyes. There are so many problems. And when he leaves, tears still flow, but they are of gratitude, of love. It is so beautiful to cry in love. One who has cried even once in love, they know the taste of surrender, of devotion, and the entire creation rejoices. The entire creation is longing for one thing — transformed tears, from a salty tear to sweet tears."

Guruji talked about a great follower of Buddha, Sariputra. When Sariputra got enlightened, Buddha told him to go into the world to teach and carry on his work. "Now, Sariputra left Buddha," said Guruji softly, "but he was crying and crying. And people said, 'You are enlightened, why are you crying?'"

Guruji spoke with quiet emotion. "He said, 'Who cares for this enlightenment? It could have waited. I never asked for it. The joy of being at the feet of Buddha was so great, being a devotee was so great. Now I am missing this. I would have preferred that to enlightenment.'"

The personal way that Guruji was talking made it seem like he was describing his own experience, and it was triggering deep emotions in me too. Through the camera lens it looked like Guruji was on the brink of tears. It was an intimate glimpse into his heart, and several people in the room were wiping their eyes.

Guruji's voice got fainter as he continued.

"There is no separation," Guruji said. "There is no distance. That is a devotee. A devotee will never fall. He cannot fall. When Krishna was leaving his body, he spoke to Uddhava (his friend and devotee). It was the last thing he said. With tears rolling out of Krishna's eyes, he says, 'These gopis (devotees), they are so beautiful.' He says, 'I can't stand the amount of devotion they have. You go and tell these gopis, these devotees of mine, that only they can free me of their gratitude and of their love.' It's so beautiful," Guruji said, his voice cracking. "Krishna says to Uddhava, 'Go and tell them, I am not in heaven, I am not in temples, but where my devotees sing, I'm right there.' The Infinity longs for you as much as you long for it. It's waiting to receive you."

Guruji stopped speaking and clasped his hands in prayer, his eyes welling with tears of love.

I stepped away from the camera to wipe my eyes and saw that nearly everyone in the room was wiping their eyes or sobbing. The feeling of love was so strong. We were connected in a powerful and fundamental way, and waves of gratefulness started rising in me.

Later that evening, we took turns gliding across Loon Lake with Guruji on a wooden raft. It was romantic. The full July moon hung low in the sky, and a tinge of orange shined brightly on Guruji's face. Guruji's long hair blew in the cool breeze as he sat still and motionless.

On the shore, several devotees were singing bhajans as a flute played and stars sparkled against an endless canopy of sky. My mind felt bright and still. I felt at home in my own heart.

Years later, Lloyd Pflueger, who is now a religious-studies professor, would write to me about his memory of that day and the days around it. "Guru Purnima at Loon Lake was one of the most extraordinary experiences of my life. I didn't know I could feel so much love and gratitude. It was a transcendental episode — one of the highest moments in the Art of Living. This course was not so much about silencing the mind, but much deeper: opening the heart. Guruji taught us in several unexpected and skillful ways, but ultimately by example. He opened his own heart so widely that I felt we would all melt. He began to cry from the depth of his own feelings of gratitude. This brought most everyone who felt near to him to tears. For me, time and space melted away and there were just the tears of bliss. It was very intense crying, but it was all from gratitude. My body shook with the experience for days. Guruji moved the bhakti experience around in different modes — walking with him, swimming with him, singing with him, perceiving him with our eyes closed. My eyes were much wider when I left — because I could see everything with my heart."

After the advanced course, a few of us stayed behind in a small house in Vancouver for a final evening with Guruji before he departed for his trip across Canada.

After dinner, Guruji wanted to see the videotape of the Guru Purnima celebration that I'd recorded. But for some reason I couldn't get the video to work. I checked the connections and adjusted the various controls, but it just wouldn't play.

"Didn't the camera work properly, Michael? It would have been good to record that talk," Guruji said gently.

"Oh, yes, Guruji. I played the video and I know it worked. But for some reason I just can't get it to work now."

"If it is recorded, then why don't you play it? We'd all like to watch."

I started to sweat. I tried everything. My head was now behind the TV, tangled in wires. I started randomly pushing every button I could.

Then, in a muffled tone, I heard Guruji say, "Now all of you can critique each other so that you can become stronger as teachers. Let's start with Janael. You tell Michael what he does wrong, and then, Michael, you can tell Janael."

I could barely focus on what he was saying. After struggling to pull my head out from the wires and machines, I was met by Janael's bright eyes. They were beaming right at me.

"Well, Guruji, I don't know what to say." She hesitated for only a moment to bite her lip before continuing. "If I were to think of all the teachers in the Art of Living who could come into my area and teach the course while I travel with you in India, Michael Fischman would be my absolute last choice! He's rude, inconsiderate, obnoxious, and arrogant. He lacks communication skills, and people don't like him. I think he is dishonest and is only interested in obtaining a powerful position in the Foundation. I don't think he has a spiritual bone in his body! He is an egomaniacal, self-centered, spoiled brat. He's not interested in serving you or helping people. He's only interested in serving himself. And it will be people like him who will keep serious seekers away from you, Guruji," she declared. "I don't trust him at all."

I was numb. Her criticism had caught me off guard. Where was this coming from? We'd had a few misunderstandings, but nothing major. I thought she liked me. How could she say this in front of Guruji?

But Guruji showed no reaction. "Hmmm?" This time that familiar sound was irritating. "Good, good," he said. "You can continue." And he got up and walked down the stairs to his room.

I stood there, open-mouthed and indignant. After searching so long for my role in life, being criticized for not having the ability to teach was crushing. I took pride in being a good teacher. It had become my whole identity. The feedback I received from people who took the course was positive. They told me I was a great teacher. Guruji had chosen me to go to Russia. He must see that I had the ability to teach. So why was this woman attacking me?

The only thing I could do was defend myself. Within a few minutes Janael and I got into a heated argument. Everyone in the house could hear what we were saying. We were throwing words at each other without any concern for how it made the other feel. At one in the morning I was still fuming, but I was too exhausted to keep arguing. Throwing my hands in the air, I left Janael and went to my room.

My mind replayed the look on Guruji's face when Janael started bashing me. What did Guruji think of me? Did he agree with Janael? Was this all a set-up for me to look at myself? This would be my last night with Guruji for some time and I needed to speak to him.

I walked down the hallway and was glad to find his light on and the door open. He was packing his suitcase and listening to some music.

"Yes, Michael, what is happening? You and Janael had a good session?" he asked, with a mischievous smile.

"Guruji, she attacked me. I feel that I need to defend myself. I love teaching for you. If there is anything that I take seriously, it's teaching. I think I'm a good teacher. People have told me that. It can't be true what she is saying about me. You can't believe her," I said.

"First of all, know that I am your defense." He spoke softly and looked at me with understanding eyes. "When you are with me, when you are on this path, you don't need any defense. And second, know that all criticism is based on some truth. If someone criticizes you, know that they are basing it on their perception. So based on their perception, there is some truth to their criticism. We invite criticism. It helps us to grow. But we are not the football of other people's opinions. Listen to the criticism without reacting. Take what you think is valid and learn from that."

Ashamed, my eyes welled with tears. All my feelings were exposed.

I was so angry with Janael, but I was even angrier with myself. Down deep, I knew that some of the things she said about me were true. But it was unbearably painful to know that this was what others thought about me. I was afraid it was Guruji's opinion of me as well.

He could see my pain and looked at me compassionately. Shuffling some things around in his suitcase, Guruji said, "My suitcase is so crowded and heavy. I should take some things out and get rid of them." He picked up one of his silk shawls. "Hmmm, this is a bit old. Let me take it out of my suitcase." He draped the shawl around my shoulders and said, "Wear this when you meditate, and remember that I am always with you."

The next morning, I woke up early so I could see Guruji off at the airport. I was exhausted from staying up so late and arguing with Janael. Once again, I was in a state of confusion and lacked clarity about my future as a teacher.

But Guruji seemed unaffected. At the airport, he gave me the phone numbers of some people to contact in Russia. He said I should call them as soon as possible, work on getting a visa, and be prepared to teach overseas.

That night, back in Santa Monica, I crawled into bed, wishing I could sleep forever. But I couldn't. I was starting a new part-time job the next day.

I woke up feeling like I had a hangover. I needed to get ready for work, but I lay in bed thinking of alternate plans for my future. I hadn't made a move to start my morning Kriya and meditation. I entertained the possibility of stopping all my spiritual practices for a while. I continued with various visions of the future, until the phone rang, bringing me back to the present. It was Jeff Houk.

"I just spoke to Guruji on the phone," Jeff informed me. "He said that you should get your visa as soon as possible so you can assist Judson in Russia."

Now I was going to Russia as Judson's *assistant*, not as a teacher. This was humiliating. First Janael and now this. It was too much.

"Jeff, I'm not going to Russia and freeze to death just to assist Judson," I snapped. "Give me Guruji's phone number. I want to call him and find out what's going on for myself. If he doesn't think I'm qualified to be a teacher, I'll just quit. I'm not going as Judson's assistant!"

I called right away and was able to reach Guruji in New York. "Guruji, I just spoke to Jeff. Is it true that now you want me to go as Judson's assistant, to help him teach?"

"Yes, yes," he said. "It would be good for you to help Judson. He is very good and you can learn a lot from him and get stronger as a teacher." His voice was soothing and calm — a contrast to mine, which was irritated and shaking with anger and frustration. "Work on getting your visa," he said, "and call me when you're ready to go.... Jai Gurudev."

Jai Gurudev was the Guru's salutation. Like Maharishi, he used it to say good-bye and hello. Jai Gurudev — victory to the Guru, victory to the Big Mind. It was also Guruji's way of letting you know that the conversation was over.

I stared at the phone. I really didn't want to go to Russia. Not now. Not as an assistant. There wasn't any glory or prestige in being someone's assistant. I wanted to be on the front lines, not in the shadows. My ego and self-esteem were crushed.

I hoped to get another chance to speak to Guruji before he left the country. But what could I say to him? It wouldn't do any good to call him and defend myself or try to change his mind. He knew exactly who I was. I couldn't say, "No, really, Guruji, I'm not as bad as you think. I'm actually a beautiful human being who is completely selfless and needs nothing." I was stuck and didn't know what to do.

I tried to call him several times but the line was busy, so I gave up. I was late to work but didn't care. It was a meaningless job that I would end up quitting anyway. I sat in a cubbyhole making phone calls, selling ad space for a New Age publication. All I could think about was Guruji.

Late that afternoon, the phone rang at work. It was Guruji. How did he get my phone number? No one knew I was working for this company. I felt self-conscious speaking to him on the phone at my job.

He said he was getting ready to leave for the airport and wanted to tell me something before he left the country. "Michael, always remember one thing — a diamond cutter only cuts diamonds. Jai Gurudev!"

As uncomfortable as it was to speak to Guruji on the office phone, it was even more uncomfortable shedding tears of gratitude at my desk.

Oh, how adept Guruji was. This whole thing had been a *leela,* a play of consciousness, a cosmic set-up. He skillfully used each incident as an opportunity for me to see myself, to help me grow.

If he thought of me as a diamond, maybe I wasn't such a hopeless case after all. Guruji was simply doing his job. He was cutting a diamond.

CHAPTER THIRTEEN

Siddha, Buddha
& the Amazing Tiger Swami

STILL CONCERNED ABOUT FREEZING, I kept putting off arranging my travel to the former Soviet Union. But my overwhelming desire to serve Guruji eventually propelled me into action.

For the next several months, I was constantly on the phone, struggling with the Soviet Embassy to get a visa. In 1990, the communists restricted tourism and it was difficult to get a visa that would allow me to stay in the country for several months and be free to travel and stay with the workshop organizers. I repeatedly called my Russian contacts, hoping they could get the paperwork authorities required to issue visas for Judson and me to teach.

After several months, I was still waiting. Frustrated with the bureaucracy and lack of progress, I called Guruji in India, hoping he could perform some magic.

Guruji's ability to stay fluid and adapt to new situations is impressive. He can change course at a moment's notice. Now, he suggested a new itinerary — India.

"It would be good if you could come for a year and stay in Bangalore," he said. "We have many corporate courses coming up and you can teach them. We have very few teachers in India now, and I will be staying in Bangalore for the whole year, so it will be a good time for you to come. I am planning to have several international advanced courses starting in July, and we will be getting the ashram ready. See if you can get a one-year visa. It should be easier to get a visa to India. Look into that."

With all the visa difficulties I'd been having, I never really thought I would actually travel to Russia. But now I needed to make the shift to India.

India was definitely warmer. But I didn't want to go back to the land of dysentery. After my last trip to India, I'd promised myself I would never go back to a country that had cows, goats, and elephants roaming the city streets. I knew that I would be frustrated with the Third World conditions that lay ahead. I was not eager to leave the comforts and conveniences of home, and knew it would be a long time before I would be able to watch cable TV, taste Hâagen-Dazs ice cream, or eat pizza with extra cheese. But I applied for a visa.

Miraculously, within two days, I received a one-year visa, and I immediately booked a flight for the end of the week. I was so terrified of getting sick that before I left I took every possible vaccine the U.S. State Department suggested for tourists, including one for brain fever.

The night before my trip, I felt compelled to visit Charlie Lutes at his weekly Friday-night lecture in Los Angeles. When I walked in the door, Charlie was standing in his dark-gray suit, talking to some people before the lecture, looking, as usual, like a well-to-do businessman. He smiled at me and motioned for me to come over. He wanted to know what I'd been up to and why I hadn't been coming to his lectures. I explained my involvement with Guruji, and told him that I was leaving for India.

Charlie was well aware of Sri Sri Ravi Shankar but had never met him. He nodded his head reassuringly as I told him my plans.

"I went to India with Maharishi," Charlie said. "I helped him find the ashram we built in Rishikesh. In fact, when the Beatles were there ..." My mind drifted off as Charlie spoke. I was happy to see him. It was like being home again. I knew his stories so well I could recite them myself. Whenever he mentioned the Beatles, he told the story of how he would meditate late at night with John Lennon on a rooftop in Rishikesh. John admired his dedication to Maharishi and loved Charlie's esoteric stories. After we spoke awhile, Charlie indicated that he needed to start his lecture and walked to the podium at the front of the room.

After his talk, Charlie asked the audience if there were any questions, and I found myself standing up. I don't remember what I asked, but I know I was vague and enigmatic with my question. Charlie looked directly at me, indicating he understood exactly what I was asking. I was momentarily surprised, as a beam of white light surged from the center of his chest across the room, penetrating into my heart. It was so bright and visible, I was sure everyone else saw it too.

"You don't have this question about dharma any more," Charlie said. He raised his right hand in the air as though he were blessing me. "Your life is set now. You have a clear role to play in the world."

I felt extremely light and grateful. With Charlie's blessings, I knew I had embarked on the right path and that going to India was the right thing.

The next day, Chris drove me to the airport. He had gone to India a couple years earlier to be with Guruji at the ashram. At that time, Chris was fairly directionless and overly sensitive to everything. But he'd come back from India as what my father would have called a *mensch,* a Yiddish word that roughly means a good person, someone whose character you admire. He was now married to Judy, had started his own business, and had a beautiful one-and-a-half-year-old daughter named Chandra.

Chris wasn't going to India this time, though. "For some reason, I don't feel the need to spend as much physical time around Punditji as you do," he said, adjusting his wire-rimmed glasses. "The knowledge and the breathing techniques are so powerful and are really helping me handle the new business and baby. It feels like he's always with me." At the airport, Chris got out of the car and helped me with my bags. "Hey, have a great time," he said. "I know you like drama, so I'm sure you'll have lots of stories to tell when you get back."

A prophetic statement.

It was January 1991 when I arrived in Bangalore. I was amazed and relieved to find that Bangalore had a comfortable climate, similar to Southern California, with bright sunny skies, cool breezes, and little humidity. Rajshree Patel, a dear friend from Los Angeles, greeted me at the airport.

Rajshree, a beautiful Indian woman who was born in Uganda, had immigrated to the United States with her family when she was nine years old. After taking the Art of Living Course, she too fell in love with Guruji and had just taken a leave of absence from her career as a Los Angeles Assistant District Attorney to spend the year with Guruji.

Arriving in Bangalore a week before me, Rajshree already knew her way around town. We took a taxi from the airport and arrived at the house that I knew only from its mailing address on brochures and the back of Guruji's books: No. 19, 39 A Cross, 11th Main Road, 4th T Block, Jayanagar, Bangalore. This would be my mailing address for the next year. After a month, I could finally pronounce its name: Gyan Mandir (*g'yawn* mun-*dear*). Later, I learned it means Temple of Knowledge.

This was Guruji's city ashram, and was directly across from a small field with two milk cows and a lot of barking dogs. Guruji resided on the third floor, his bedroom adjacent to a large meditation hall that would become too small in only a couple years. Although it appeared an ordinary house from the outside, the influence of the master could be felt as soon as you stepped inside — confusion!

For the first six months, I never knew what to expect or what would happen next. There were British, American, Canadian, Polish, German, and French people staying or passing through. There were Art of Living courses, business courses, youth leadership programs, advanced courses, yagyas, satsangs, pujas, celebrations, and feasts — all under this one roof.

In the center of all this was our guru in all his glory, baffling minds and filling our hearts with grace and love.

At first, I was intimidated by India and the lifestyle. I was fanatical about hygiene and inspected everything I ate. I was so paranoid about intestinal parasites and dysentery that I lost twenty pounds in the first month. I longed to return to the land of grilled cheese and tomato sandwiches so I would never have to eat hot rice, curd rice, sweet yellow rice, flat rice, or even the ubiquitous plain boiled rice, again.

But over time, my stomach got used to the hot chili peppers, and even the plethora of rice dishes. I acquired a taste for all the South Indian delicacies — *idli* and *sambar, masala dosa, upma,* mango milkshakes, and, of course, that wonderful sweet, *gulab jamun* — fried golden-brown balls made of milk paste, cream, and flour, in a sugar syrup flavored with cardamom seeds and rosewater (or some variation thereof). Yum!

During my first week in Bangalore, Guruji took special care of me and made sure my transition to Indian life and culture went smoothly. I was extremely comfortable and happy. Rajshree and I had our meals a few blocks away, at Bhanu's house, and in the evening the people from the area would join us at Gyan Mandir for satsang.

Guruji had not spent much time in Bangalore in previous years, and at that time did not have a large following there. There were only a dozen people or so who came for the satsang. The midnight gossip sessions with Guruji were a highlight. Rajshree, Bhanu, a local devotee, and I would sit with Guruji on the roof of Gyan Mandir until one or two in the morning, laughing, singing, and gazing at the stars.

After doing our practices each morning, we were joined by a local family — two sisters, Shantha and Mohana, and their mother — who came to receive Guruji's darshan. We would all sit patiently outside Guruji's door on the third floor. Usually, the elder sister, Mohana, sang some devotional songs until Guruji was ready to join us. Then his door would open a crack. Guruji would peek his head out the door, and then his whole body would emerge.

That first glance from Guruji in the early morning was like nectar. His eyes glistened, as the morning sun glowed through the nearby curtains that flapped in the gentle breeze. There was no need to speak, no questions to ask. We were content just being there with him. Sometimes we sat for only a few minutes. At other times we were luckier, and the silence lasted for more than an hour. But eventually, the silence would be broken when one or the other of the sisters had to stand up to leave for work.

The other morning ritual was going through Guruji's mail. We would create three piles — an A, B, and C pile. "A" was for bills, legal or business matters for the ashram, and solicitations from vendors. "B" was for important correspondence with other organizations or institutions that were interested in having Guruji speak at their functions. And "C" was for cards and letters from devotees, expressing their concerns, gratitude, and love.

The only pile I ever saw Guruji attend to was the C pile. He made sure that we wrote back to each of them, sending his blessings. Many times the letters of gratitude were stories about some miracle that had occurred. Healings from cancer or depression, women who prayed to him and finally got pregnant, money appearing from nowhere just in the nick of time to avoid an eviction or some other catastrophe. Marriages were saved. More than one letter told of near accidents, with one person hearing Guruji's voice shout a warning after they had fallen asleep at the wheel, and another feeling his arms gently lower them to the ground after they flew from a speeding motorcycle.

It was inspiring to read these letters. So many lives had changed. At first it was difficult to make sense of the phenomena. There were hundreds of letters. And these were only from the people who took the time to write him. I knew that there had to be many more such miracles. It was beyond anything you could call coincidence.

The healings alone were mind blowing. There were improvements with asthma, substance abuse, paralysis, arthritis, sexual dysfunction, coronary problems; the list went on and on. Yet Guruji seemed unaffected and acted as if it was all normal. Perhaps just to satisfy me, he suggested that we do some research on Sudarshan Kriya. But many of these miracles were described as coming from people's faith and prayers, not just from the breathing practices.

During my first Art of Living days, I'd heard that Guruji decided early on to teach through spiritual transmission and pure consciousness rather than through miracles. I asked Guruji about the miraculous letters once. "It's not a big thing," he explained. "Miracles are part of nature. It's the small mind connecting with the larger mind, the consciousness, the universal energy. When there is faith and strong intention — a *sankalpa* — these things happen."

I began to fall in love with India and with the colorful rituals and exotic celebrations that are at the heart of Hindu and Vedic culture.

After my third week in India, Guruji told us that we would be celebrating the annual festival of *Maha Shivaratri,* the Great Night of Shiva. Shiva is the meditative and transformational aspect of nature, and it is thought that on this night, Shiva, as pure consciousness, is more available than on any other night of the year. To gain the maximum spiritual benefit, many celebrate the festival by staying awake and aware throughout the night.

Although the official celebration didn't begin until sundown, festivities started early in the morning, as the few devotees who were staying at Gyan Mandir at that point cleaned and decorated the house for the auspicious event. Following local custom, we hung mango leaves in the doorway and around the ceremonial puja area. A number of local Indian women who were devotees of Guruji came early to prepare *halwa* and *avalakkii* — sweet delicacies that would be given out after the ceremonies.

Wearing brand-new Indian silks, I sat in the packed meditation hall in a state of nervous anticipation. I worried that I wouldn't be able to sit through the entire ceremony. Without any cushions on the hard tile floor, I felt I would barely be able to sit cross-legged for more than a half hour.

At sundown, the pundits entered the hall, dressed in their finest saffron *dhotis* and shawls. They prepared themselves for the ceremonies by applying *kum-kum* (a red powder), sandalwood paste, and *bhasma* (sacred ashes) to their foreheads. Satish, Guruji's main pundit, made sure everything was in order for the puja. He lit the ghee lamps and arranged the flowers and fruit that would be offered in the ceremony. I became absorbed in the fragrant smell of the burning incense and the vibrant floral decorations that filled the meditation hall.

Then, seeming more to float than walk, Guruji entered the hall and sat cross-legged in his chair. Silently, he looked around the room, gazing into each pair of eyes as though he were blessing us. With a smile, he tied his long, thick hair above his head and closed his eyes, ready for the puja to begin. As he sat in deep meditation, the pundits began to ring small handbells and chant the *Rudram*, the traditional hymn to Shiva. The room felt holy.

At first, my legs were numb and my back began to cramp, but this discomfort was not at the forefront of my mind. As the night progressed, time and space dissolved. In a short while, I forgot about the hard floor and the pain in my body. I became lost in the rhythmic sounds of the ancient mantras. My breath became light and smooth and slowed dramatically. The breath was soon so soft that there was no noticeable movement of breath at all, my body sustained by something subtler than breath.

I sat in this non-moving state until midnight, when I felt some people walking around the room. After a few minutes, I joined the others in taking some *prasad* (blessed food). We sang bhajans until three in the morning, when Guruji took the twelve of us remaining in the hall for a walk under the stars.

We walked through the narrow back roads and alleyways of Jayanagar, a part of the city Guruji knew from childhood. We walked by several temples, and we also saw large groups of people observing the all-night tradition by standing in front of small TV sets, watching movies in Kannada, the local Indian language. I was amused to see that these people had a different interpretation of what it meant to "stay awake."

We walked until we came to a large temple where Guruji and Satish knew the priests. It was like attending a class reunion. Guruji was greeted and honored by several young pundits who had attended the school he had started when these pundits were still small boys.

Back at Gyan Mandir, we started a puja again at 5 a.m. I wasn't at all tired. In fact, I felt very alert. Through much of the night, I'd had the sensation that the top of my head had been cut off and light was pouring into my body. But something was different about this last puja. Again, I entered into that blissful breathless state, but this time my entire body and mind were pulsating with *shakti* (pure energy). Thoughts vanished, leaving only vastness and peace. After some time, I saw a beautiful being illuminated in iridescent blue light. It wasn't like watching a movie or seeing a painting, but I knew I was experiencing Shiva. It felt natural, pleasant, and consoling. In the fifteen years I'd been meditating, I had never had any visual experiences of lights or colors. Now, on this auspicious evening in the presence of my guru, I was seeing Shiva.

Then, for lack of another way to put it, I became Shiva; a veil that separated me from the Divine was lifted. There was no longer a distinction between the celestial and the mundane. It felt like the mantras were being offered to me and I was blessing the world. Negativity was being replaced by *sattva* (purity) throughout creation.

At some point, I sensed that the *aarti* flame was being offered and the puja was ending. I don't know how long I continued to sit there. I was beyond time, frozen in bliss.

Suddenly, someone gracelessly shook my arm and whispered, "Hey, Michael, you need to come down from the clouds and get ready to leave."

I had only an hour to come out of this experience and transform myself into an "executive swami" for my appointment with the director of personnel at one of Bangalore's largest corporations.

Colors of the early morning filled the horizon as we drove silently to India's premiere electronic engineering company. A gentle breeze was carrying the aroma of fresh coffee from open windows.

The road was bumpy, and dust was blowing into the car. I rolled up the window and sat back, remembering the feeling I'd had only a short while earlier, when my perception of Shiva had become clearer. My heart had grown in love beyond imagination. Later, when I asked Guruji why this had happened, he simply explained that it was a gift and that someday I would write about my experiences and inspire others.

But how could I explain what I had just gone through to someone like my father? He or others not familiar with the Vedic tradition would probably conclude that I'd converted to a different religion. But that wasn't the case. I still valued my religion. I was just adding another dimension. Here, in India with Guruji, spirituality felt vibrant and alive. When I listened to the ancient chants, I found it easy to go inward and experience the subtle flavors of consciousness; the essence of myself.

But now I was driving through Bangalore, the fastest-growing city in Asia. There was a thriving business community here, and Bangalore would soon become another Silicon Valley. In a fiercely competitive economy, chief executives in Bangalore — and the rest of India — were interested in any technology that would give them an edge.

Guruji had invited me to India to teach the Art of Living Course at corporations, and Bhanu's husband had made an appointment for Rajshree and me to present the workshop to the director of personnel at Bharat Electronics Limited (BEL). We were going there hoping to persuade him to offer this knowledge to his four thousand employees. But I wasn't sure if he or India's growing business community would be interested in personal development. What was the best way to present the Art of Living Course to a director of personnel in India? "Sudarshan Kriya will help your company produce more widgets"?

Stress management was a new concept for human resources managers in the Land of the Vedas. But they were very interested in speaking to an American with new ideas.

Rajshree and I walked into Krishna Rao's office with impish smiles on our faces, feeling ready to meet any challenge he might present.

Within a few minutes, we could see that talking about "experiencing one's Divine nature" and "smiling from the core of one's heart" were not the correct buzzwords for a hard-line executive with an electrical-engineering background. So we talked in terms of reduced stress and tension, increased productivity, improved health, freedom from fatigue, greater responsibility and community spirit, enhanced communication skills, and heightened enthusiasm. But he still wasn't interested.

It felt like we were in a Road Runner cartoon. Rajshree and I were Wile E. Coyote and the company director was Road Runner saying, *Beep, beep,* and running away each time we came up with a new point. After two hours that we thought had gone nowhere, Rajshree and I got ready to leave the office. As we thanked our host for his time, we were shocked when he asked us if we were free to conduct the course for a dozen people the following week. What changed his mind, we will never know.

Innocent faces and shy smiles greeted us as we entered the hall for our first corporate workshop. The course participants were eager to start the day and learn Sudarshan Kriya. It was exciting to bring spirituality to the workplace, though, to me, it seemed slightly odd for an American to be doing it in India.

The participants had great experiences during the Kriya. They shared them with enthusiasm, and they made an impression. "I felt as though I was floating," said one man. "Every part of my body was filled with an electrical current, and in the center of my head I could see a bright white light. My mind feels so fresh and filled with energy, I feel that I can take on any challenge." He was grateful that his company had provided an opportunity for him to have such a divine experience.

At the end of the workshop, the participants walked us to our car. They stood with their palms together in front of their hearts in *pranaam* (a traditional Indian greeting) and bowed at our feet. At first, people bowing surprised me. But I soon came to realize that the gesture of bowing was cultural. When they bowed, they were honoring the guru principle, they were bowing to the divine grace.

We eventually trained nearly four thousand employees at BEL. The Art of Living Course became BEL's official stress-management program and was mandatory for all employees. Since then, the Art of

Living corporate program evolved into what is now called the APEX Course — Achieving Personal Excellence — and it has been taught in major corporations and institutions around the world.

A few days later, at the end of February, another American arrived at Gyan Mandir. She was an attractive Hispanic woman, with dark skin, a flat stomach, small hazel-blue eyes, and an open smile. I was smitten. Her name was Margarita Emilia Lopez, but we knew her as Rita. A Colombian immigrant, Rita was a professor of political science at Cornell University. Now on sabbatical, she was traveling around India and had already visited several ashrams.

Rita moved into the room next to mine. She wasn't shy, and kept me up for hours, telling me stories about her adventures traveling through India. In the morning, she attended her first Art of Living Course, with Rajshree and me as her instructors.

An uneven number of participants were on the course, so I volunteered to fill in as her partner during one of the processes. Charmed by her beauty, I didn't pay much attention to the process. Afterwards, Rita extended her arms, indicating that she appreciated me and wanted a hug. But I couldn't respond. My right knee was completely locked.

As I forced myself to straighten my leg, I heard a rip in my knee. The pain was excruciating. Then, in less than a minute, my knee blew up like a balloon. Rita didn't seem to notice. She looked confused and walked away.

"Rajshree, help me!" I screamed. "See if there is a doctor somewhere. I'm in so much pain. I think I've done something horrible to my knee."

Rajshree rushed off to tell Guruji what had happened. In a few minutes, she returned. "Don't worry, Michael," she said. "Siddha and Buddha are upstairs with Guruji. They'll be down in a minute to help."

Siddha and Buddha were two eccentric elderly gentlemen with big bellies, who had long retired as medical doctors. They often came to Gyan Mandir to visit Guruji, entertaining him for hours as they spoke about the science of *ayurveda* — the Vedic approach to health.

I often wondered why Guruji spent so much time with them. To me they were two old screwballs, but Guruji treated them royally. He laughed uncontrollably whenever he sat with them, and had given them pet names that flattered their massive egos. Now I realize that however off I might find someone, Guruji will love that person all the same.

First, Dr. Siddha arrived. He looked at me with bewilderment as I clutched at my knee in agony.

"Yes, my dear American friend. What is the problem?" His pure white dentures clattered as he spoke. "I have been a chief medical doctor for more than forty years. I am at your service."

What type of doctor was he? Couldn't he see it was my knee?

"It's his knee," said Rajshree, pointing to my obviously puffed up knee. "It's swollen."

"Ahh, yes, yes, of course. Does it hurt if I pull it like this?"

"Yes!" I screamed, as he yanked my leg from side to side.

"I see. Now tell me, how are your teeth?"

"Fine!" I grunted.

"What about your mother's teeth?"

I nodded affirmatively.

"And your father's?"

"Rajshree, please," I protested. "Isn't there a real doctor somewhere who can help me? Please get someone. I'm in so much pain."

In a few minutes, Dr. Buddha arrived and looked at me sympathetically. I think Guruji called him Buddha because of his shining bald head and the perpetual smile on his face. "What is all the fuss about?" he asked. "Do you have a problem, my American friend?"

"It is his knee," said Dr. Siddha.

"Yes, of course. It is swollen. Does it hurt if I pull your leg like this?" Dr. Buddha asked.

"Yes!" I screamed. "Don't do that!"

"So tell me, how are your teeth?" he asked.

"Fine!!" I growled.

"And your mother's teeth?"

I held my head between my hands and began to cry. All the doctors in India must be crazy, I thought.

Then Guruji came down to see what all the shouting was about. Dr. Buddha greeted him with his professional diagnosis, declaring, "His knee is swollen, Guruji."

They all huddled around me and stared at my knee as though something was supposed to happen.

"It is much like a situation I experienced when I was the chief of surgery at the army medical hospital in Bombay," Dr. Buddha exclaimed. "There was a patient that came to the hospital with a growth protruding from his skull. Many of the surgeons said that it was a brain tumor and wanted to operate immediately. They conducted a biopsy and diagnosed it as malignant and did not think the man had any chance to survive. But I used my intuition to assess the situation. Immediately, I got a bowl of cold water and put it near the man's head and shouted, 'Jump! Jump!' And in no time, a frog jumped out of the man's head into the pot of water and the tumor was gone. It was completely gone and the man was able to walk home!"

Guruji and Dr. Siddha shook their heads in amazement, as though he had shown them a miracle. I couldn't believe my ears. Had they gone mad?

Guruji looked at me reassuringly and said, "Don't worry. Nothing is broken. Just put ice on it. It will take some time, but you'll be all right."

I thought my trip to India had come to an end, and it was time to go home to a hospital. But I rested in bed with ice on my knee.

In a few days, the pain subsided and I was strong enough to hop around Gyan Mandir. I still had a strong desire to leave India and return to the United States to see an orthopedic surgeon. But Guruji insisted I stay and that my knee would be fine.

After some months and numerous visits to a physical therapist, my knee was pretty well healed.

Guruji decided to take several of us with him on a trip he had planned to Northern India. It was an adventure.

We traveled first to the industrial town of Jamshedpur, where he conducted an advanced course for Tata Steel, one of the largest private companies in India.

After that, we moved on to Calcutta (now called Kolkata). It was quite a contrast to the five days of deep meditation and silence in Jamshedpur. We spent two nights in Calcutta, enjoying satsangs with a few local devotees.

On one of those nights, Guruji told us a story about Goli Waale Baba, an enlightened man who lived in the village of Kotla, not far from Maharishi's ashram in Noida. As a young man, Guruji often visited this saint, whom he affectionately referred to as Baba. Baba had been a military officer in the Indian cavalry and had been shot during a battle. As the bullet pierced his skin, it created a vibration in his body that caused him to go into enlightenment.

Baba spent the remainder of his life as a saint in a small village outside of New Delhi. His devotees were poor, uneducated people, who came to him for help with their problems. Often, these problems were quite trivial. They would come saying, "Baba, Baba, I have lost my watch!" or keys or shoes. And Baba would respond angrily. "I have so much knowledge to give you. Why do you waste my time with such stupid matters? Your watch is in your drawer. Now go!"

Baba himself was not well educated, and his home in the poor rural village was not very hygienic. In fact, it was always filled with flies.

"At that time," Guruji explained, "I still had one aversion — to flies. When I came to visit Baba and sat to talk to him, my body would be covered with flies. I felt so uncomfortable. I wasn't used to it. He could see that I had this aversion, and one day when I was covered with flies, he said to me, 'Just let them be.' And, with those few words, the last aversion left me. 'Just let them be.'"

Guruji rarely spoke about his past, and he almost always avoided questions about his state of consciousness. But that night seemed like a good opportunity to get more details.

I already knew that Guruji's shift had occurred in March 1982, after ten days of silence in a cabin at a farm on the banks of the Tunga River in Shimoga, Karnataka (several hours from Bangalore). Emerging from this period of silence, Guruji began to teach Sudarshan Kriya and the Art of Living.

"Guruji," I asked, "how did Sudarshan Kriya fit in with your enlightenment? They seem to have happened at the same time."

He explained that the transformation was happening even before he took silence. Guruji said that he had incarnated into this world by choice, and that he had maintained this awareness until he reached puberty, when a "veil" seemed to cover his consciousness so his development would be more "normal" and innocent. The veil began to lift before those ten days of silence, but it wasn't until he actually started teaching Sudarshan Kriya that he began to live his dharma and fully blossom into enlightenment. "Teaching the Kriya, living the dharma, and enlightenment were all simultaneous," he said. "Unless you are living that state, it is difficult to understand."

A few days later, we were off to Darjeeling, a small town (for India) of one hundred thousand in the foothills of the Himalayas, known for its tea. Guruji was taking our small group on a vacation.

The journey began with a fourteen-hour train ride from Calcutta. The train station in Calcutta was a nightmare to me. I was careful to stay near Guruji, and actually held on to his dhoti as we walked through the mobs of people rushing to catch trains. All over the station, countless families were encamped on the train platforms, sleeping and eating, as people hurried past them. Fathers, mothers, and children slept on the floor, covered only by a thin piece of cloth. I don't know how they were able to sleep with all the noise. For someone unaccustomed to such poverty, it was truly an awakening.

When our train arrived, we discovered that our hosts had been unable to purchase first-class tickets. They were sold out and we ended up having to travel third class. (A piece of advice to Westerners: Avoid traveling third class to or from Calcutta.) Our group was grumbling and complaining as we boarded the train. And after seeing our accommodations we were thoroughly miserable. I was sure I wouldn't be able to sleep on this train. It was crowded, noisy, and our sleeping berths were just metal frames without padding. There was a strong smell of urine, and thick cigarette smoke everywhere. I was so caught up in my own disturbance that I forgot I was traveling with Guruji.

Then, from the corner of our compartment, I heard Guruji quietly say the word, "Now!"

It was so powerful. We all settled down immediately.

"Now what is happening in your mind?" he said. "Just take a look and see all the agitation that is there. What is the purpose of being in this knowledge? Do you see what is going on in your mind right now? Where are you? Are you in the present moment? Are you here, now? Traveling third class has pushed all your buttons, and you have lost your very joy. The course is not just a weekend experience. It is training for a lifetime. Acceptance! Accept the present moment as it is. Now.... Now.... Now.

"You spend time with a master so you can learn through a living example," he said. "Am I not the same wherever I am — in a train or plane, with the rich or the poor? Don't look outside yourself for joy. Craving 'this' and an aversion to 'that' only causes misery in life. A small situation like this robs the smile from your hearts. Look at all the grumbling that is in your mind over something that cannot be changed. So what? We are sitting in third class. Where is the dispassion? Just drop everything and surrender it. Drop it, accept it, sing, and dance."

Then, without any concern or worry about what the other people on the train might think, we began to sing *Om Namah Shivaya*. Magically, all irritation stopped, nothing bothered me. Although Guruji's words were simple, they had gone straight to my heart. I felt waves of love as I watched Guruji sing and smile, his eyes twinkling.

After only a few moments of singing, the atmosphere in the train was transformed. Everyone was listening to us, and some other passengers joined in and sang. Out of noise and confusion came harmony. We sang for over an hour. The other passengers begged us to continue.

They offered food and drink, and even stopped smoking.

Even today, I'm still not sure why we went to Darjeeling. We spent only twenty-four hours there, we visited several temples, watched the sunrise and sunset, ate some food, and then left.

We were to fly back to Calcutta from a city called Siliguri, a six-hour car ride down a long, winding road. Two hours into the trip our car broke down. But instead of waiting for the driver to make repairs, Guruji grabbed my hand and said, "Let's walk."

For the next hour, the two of us walked by the light of the full moon, down a beautiful mountain road. He sang devotional songs by the famous 16th-century saint, Meera. Could there possibly be anything more enchanting than this? I laughed to myself, and decided I was certainly getting my money's worth from my trip to India.

Eventually the car was fixed and the driver picked us up on the mountain road. I was exhausted when we finally arrived late that night in Siliguri.

Before going to sleep, I spoke to Guruji about something that had been bothering me on the trip. It seemed as though the Indians were always in control, and whenever an American asked a question about our itinerary or what was planned, the Indians avoided answering us. I was frustrated and angry, and I expected Guruji to agree with me and do something to correct the situation.

To my surprise, he said it could not be so. I must be mistaken. I got irritated and felt hurt. Apparently, he was going to side with them because they were Indians. In an angry tone, I demanded a better answer.

Guruji just squinted, shielded his eyes with his hand, and asked me to turn off some of the lights. But the one shining right in his eyes wouldn't go out. I tried again and again but couldn't find the switch for that one light. I grew frustrated.

Guruji said, "Try again, you missed the switch."

"Impossible!" I thought. There were only four switches. I tried them all — twice. How could I miss? On the third attempt, I pushed them all again, and this time the light went out.

"You are wondering how you could miss the switch, aren't you?

Such a simple thing," said Guruji. I was mystified. "Now go and rest. We will talk more in the morning."

As I lay in bed that night, my eyes wouldn't close. How could I have missed the switch? My body was at rest, but my mind was buzzing. I kept hearing Guruji say over and over, "Try again, you missed the switch." But slowly, it dawned on me. The switch was inside me. My own judgments and resistance were preventing me from seeing things as they were. Life with awareness really was like walking on a razor's edge.

I woke up in the morning feeling lighter. Something within me had shifted.

After my morning meditation, I joined everyone for breakfast. When I asked one of the Indians what our plans were for the day, I received a complete detailed report. I realized that Guruji must have sympathized and spoken to them about being more communicative.

On the plane to Calcutta, I thanked Guruji for talking to the group and clearing up my little problem.

"I didn't talk to anyone," he said. "You just found the switch."

I ended up staying for a month in Calcutta, teaching corporate stress-management courses while Guruji conducted some programs in Delhi. I caught a bad case of dysentery that would stay with me for several months. In spite of the diarrhea, a constant low-grade fever, and a bad knee, I taught courses in many of the leading corporations in West Bengal — Hindustan Motors, Eastern Spinning Mills, and others.

These courses were great fun to teach. The participants were top executives for their companies, all brilliant people who challenged every word I said. It boosted my strength as a teacher and gave me a deeper understanding of the content of the Art of Living Course. Through the grace of Guruji and my new friends in Calcutta, I was quickly becoming the Great American Swami of Stress Management!

Calcutta is a city where extreme opposites coexist. Side by side, the very wealthy and the impoverished face the challenges of this noisy, crowded, and chaotic city.

While there, I stayed at Shashi and Sandeep's home. They belonged to India's new upper middle class. They were young, upwardly mobile, affluent Indians.

One evening, they took me to dinner at a place they called The Club. This was an exclusive and expensive nightspot for members and their guests only. It had originally been built for British military officers and dignitaries. Just inside the entrance was a fully equipped modern disco, complete with a singles bar and a dance floor jammed with good-looking young Indians. We sat in a quiet corner by the pool and ate a beautifully served and delicious meal.

Leaving around midnight, we drove through the dark streets of Calcutta. It was a dramatic contrast. Instead of the crowds of shoppers and business people that had filled those streets during the day, now there were poor and homeless people, bedded down on sidewalks for the night. Groups of five, ten, or twenty people lay close together, covered in rags, sound asleep. It reminded me of the extremes in India, and of how many people needed help.

After a few days, I was supposed to call Guruji to let him know the progress we had made in Calcutta. But how could I contact him? He was touring Delhi, moving on to Hardwar and Rishikesh, and then back to Delhi, going from house to house having satsangs. Not every home had a phone, and if they did, how could I find the number?

But Shashi was strong, independent and resourceful. And she usually achieved what she set her mind on. She was completely dedicated and had a single-minded focus on Guruji. She showed me her personal address book, arranged by city, listing all the possible places Guruji was likely to stay while on planet Earth. It was a highly prized possession and she wouldn't let the book out of her hands.

We turned to the "D" page. There were at least twelve contacts in Delhi where we might reach him.

At that time, it was difficult to make a long-distance call in India. There were no cell phones and many homes did not have long-distance service. We first tried placing a call with the local long-distance operator, but without any luck. After spending a considerable amount of time trying to get an open line, our only choice was to drive to the local telegraph office to place our call at an STD (Subscriber Trunk Dialing) office.

We drove for twenty minutes and came to the place I referred to as "Shashi's office." Most of the calls she placed to Guruji were from this telegraph station. It was a small, dimly lit room at the top of several flights of stairs. There were ten people ahead of us, and we waited an hour-and-a-half in the queue for our chance to use the phone.

There was no privacy in the telegraph office. The phone was on an open counter, in front of everyone else waiting in line. A dispatcher who sat behind a chicken-wire fence dialed the call. Although I didn't speak a word of Bengali, I could make out what was going on in most of the phone calls. One person was making plans to go to a wedding in Bombay (Mumbai). Another was discussing business with his partner in England.

It was hot and humid in this office. There was a musty smell, mixed with the odor of fried *masala* (a classic mixture of Indian spices) from the restaurant next door. Mosquitoes bit me on my toes and on the back of my sweaty neck. I couldn't help thinking of how convenient it was to make calls from my apartment in Santa Monica.

Finally, it was our turn.

We did not succeed on the first two attempts. First, we reached a wrong number, and then the line was busy. By now, it was past midnight. I was tired and ready to go to bed. But Shashi insisted we keep trying. On the next try, after a few words in Hindi, tears welled up in Shashi's eyes. "Jai Gurudev!" she said, gasping for breath. She clutched the phone close to her ear and had a huge smile on her face as she spoke to Guruji. I only wondered if she would remember that I was standing there and wanted to speak to him, too.

Guruji was glad we'd called and was very playful on the phone. He wasn't at all upset that we were calling so late. I spoke to him for about fifteen minutes. What I had to say was not as important as hearing his voice, filled with love and acceptance, while I was on my own in Calcutta.

A few weeks later, in April 1991, I returned to Bangalore. It was so wonderful to be back at Gyan Mandir. I'd longed to be with Guruji again.

When I entered the house, Rita greeted me with a warm hug and smile, as though she had been waiting for me. She was more charming than I had remembered. We chatted for a few minutes, but my attention was on seeing Guruji.

He was deep in meditation, when I entered the satsang hall. After a few moments, he briefly opened his eyes and smiled. Although there were many in the hall, I knew the smile was just for me.

Rajshree was back, too. While I was off teaching in Calcutta, Rajshree had traveled to Gujarat, Bombay, and Baroda. She was a real powerhouse. She taught hundreds of people, including some Bollywood celebrities and students from the Indian Institute of Technology, Bombay (India's premier university). Guruji was pleased with her, and said that many of her students would become pillars of the Art of Living in the years to come, which came true.

One late night, while sitting on the roof of Gyan Mandir, I asked Guruji if he was going to go into silence before the upcoming advanced courses. He gave me a big smile and ran into his room like a small child about to show off a new toy. In a moment, he peeked out of the room with a turban on his head. All his hair was tucked in the turban and he looked like a Sikh. He laughed and explained that someone had given him the turban in Delhi.

Then he told us he had already taken his silence while touring through Delhi. Without informing anyone, he decided to have someone drive him to a secluded Buddhist monastery. Disguised as a Sikh, he enrolled himself as a participant at the ashram to take silence.

"I just wanted to see how it would be to be on the other side," he explained, "being an aspirant, waiting in line for my food, and sharing my room with someone." For several days, Guruji stayed incognito at the Buddhist ashram. "I would get so hungry late at night," he told us. "They served so little food for dinner!"

After four or five days, he was ready to leave. When he told the head monk he was leaving, the monk encouraged him to stay longer, explaining that it takes some time to get used to the silence. He said that Guruji definitely had potential for deep experiences, and if he continued to meditate he could become a very good monk. Guruji thanked him for his advice, but left the ashram all the same. "They were so serious there," he observed. "Not much smiling or laughter."

Guruji had a car pick him up at the monastery to take him back to Delhi. The driver decided to take a short cut and drove the car through a small jungle area. Part way into the jungle, a fallen tree had blocked the road. The driver was afraid to move the tree because he had seen a tiger lurking in the area. Guruji tried to persuade the driver, but the driver refused to leave the car. So, after a short while, Guruji got out of the car and moved the tree. The driver was grateful and amazed.

On the way to Delhi, the driver brought Guruji to his village and recounted the story. He told his entire family and all his friends, "This Swamiji had no fear of tigers and had the strength of an elephant to lift huge trees with his bare hands." The village people insisted they do puja to Guruji and have a celebration. Guruji said that he was sure that for generations to come, this village would be telling stories of the Great Tiger Swami that had saved the driver's life.

There are numerous stories in India about various saints with all sorts of powers and abilities. That night I got an idea of how some of them might have come about.

After these stories, Guruji gave a look as if he had told too much. Then he asked, "What is the time?" Everyone groaned, knowing that was the signal for the satsang to end.

"Oh, Guruji," someone pleaded, "it's early. No one's even tired." Even though it was one in the morning.

"No, it's late. Go rest," he said. "Good, good, good."

Rajshree, Rita, and I considered ourselves impervious to his direction, so we stayed behind.

Guruji winked at us, and said, "Tomorrow, after lunch, I will be going to the ashram. So be ready to go."

CHAPTER FOURTEEN

The Heart of Desire

BEING TOLD THAT we were going to the ashram made me feel like a kid going to Disneyland. From the moment I arrived in Bangalore, I had wanted to experience the "real thing" — the ashram.

I'd heard so many wonderful things about our campus, I was eager to see it myself. I expected a magical, spiritual wonderland, with traditional temples hidden by tall coconut trees, saints sitting in deep meditation, pundits performing traditional rituals, wandering peacocks, and yogis twisted in complicated positions.

The reality was slightly different. Instead of a spiritual oasis, the ashram was more like a barren desert. The grounds were weedy and rocky, and the occasional trees only looked out of place. The only people we saw were some workers who sat along the road, resting in whatever shade they could find. There were no temples or majestic halls, just a few shabby half-built buildings. It would take a lot of work to turn this into the international spiritual retreat center that Guruji envisioned.

We arrived at the ashram after lunch, which was the hottest time of the day, so Guruji escaped the heat by going into a small building and taking a nap. An hour later, one of the workers brought us fresh coconut water and fresh papaya, which grew on the grounds.

After our snack, Guruji took a walk. He inspected the buildings under construction and spoke to the builders and engineers. The ashram needed to be ready in time for the international courses that were to take place that summer — only three months away!

Pitaji (Guruji's father) acquired the land in 1981, with the intention of establishing a Vedic school. The government had considered the topography unsuitable for agriculture and donated the land for use as an ashram. The ashram was originally referred to as the Panchagiri Ashram, the ashram of five hills. This land also became the site of Ved Vignan Mahavidyapeeth, the school that was created for the pundit boys Guruji brought back from Delhi during his time with Maharishi.

In addition to the Vedic school, Pitaji had also built a local school for the twenty surrounding villages. There were few children at first, but by 1992, the ashram was providing free education, school clothes, and other free services to about two hundred village children, with students achieving the highest test scores in the state. The vision of offering a spiritually based education in a nurturing environment eventually expanded into the Sri Sri Ravishankar Vidya Mandir Trust, which oversees more than a hundred schools from the pre-primary through specialty-degree levels.

While I was staying at Gyan Mandir that year, Guruji went to the ashram every day to oversee the construction. Dormitories and small houses, called *kutirs,* were being built, along with a large meditation and dining hall. Since the ashram was just being developed and there was no permanent staff, without Guruji's physical presence very little progress would have been made.

I had little experience in construction and engineering, so Guruji had me remain at Gyan Mandir for the most part, teaching courses in Bangalore and doing administrative tasks for the upcoming courses. Rita and I worked as a team, traveling around the city to purchase things that the ashram needed. We taught together, ate together, went to satsang together. At night, we went to sleep on the third floor of the city ashram, separated by only a thin wall. People teased us, and asked us when we were getting married. No one guessed I had fallen in love with her.

I believed that Guruji was playing matchmaker and had arranged for us to fall in love. I even concluded that it was probably the main reason he had brought me to India. I'd heard a rumor that he had done matchmaking with another couple, Chris and Katherine. They were sent to Russia and Poland together to teach the workshop, and while traveling they fell in love. Somehow, I believed and hoped that a similar plan was in place for Rita and me.

However, I was afraid to tell her how I felt. She had recently ended a long-term relationship with a man she wanted to marry and had begun a new relationship with someone named Tony. Tony was planning to come to the ashram during his vacation that summer. I wasn't sure where I fit in her heart and I didn't want to get hurt. All I knew was that as the days passed, we grew closer and closer. It seemed only natural to get some guidance and see if Guruji felt Rita would be right for me.

Late one night, I went to Guruji's room. A single candle was burning, and Guruji was sitting calmly on his bed, holding his prayer beads. He looked up at me with a smile.

"Guruji, may I speak to you?" I said shyly, not really sure how to put it. "I'm attracted to someone and I don't know if I should do something about it."

"Why do you need to do anything about it?" he asked.

His answer surprised me. "Well, I like her," I said. "And I hope she likes me. Shouldn't I tell her how I feel?"

"If you express your feelings, you will ruin it," he said. "You don't need to tell someone that you love them. If they are sensitive, they can feel it. Once you tell them your feelings, it changes everything."

"I haven't said anything yet," I said, "but I want the relationship to become more intimate."

"Real intimacy is when you feel you are already intimate," he counseled. "You don't try to prove it to somebody or try to become intimate. Love is like a seed. You have to plant it and keep it under the ground. When love is expressed too much, it is short-lived. Love somebody in such a way that they don't really know that you love them. Keep it a secret. Have you ever heard me tell anyone that I love them? No. It is kept within. See, what happens then, your love will flower in your actions. You'll make all the gestures in your actions. By saying it too much — 'Oh, I love you, I love you' — you destroy it."

"But, Guruji," I insisted, "you're different than me. You don't have personal relationships."

"I have a personal relationship with you, Michael. I have a personal relationship with everyone. I will never say, 'Oh, Michael, I love you.' But you can feel the love. In any word spoken, you can hear that love. That love has grown, it has blossomed. Do you understand?"

"I want to be in love," I said, trying to say it more bluntly.

"Your existence is love," he said. "You breathe and there is love. That is enlightened love. Real intimacy is knowing that you are already intimate, and relaxing about it, never trying to convince others that you are intimate, never trying to express yourself too much. Your anxiousness to make somebody know your intimacy destroys your intimacy. Do you see?"

"So what should I do?"

"Simply smile, Michael. You acknowledge, you smile, and allow them to become intimate by themselves. It's natural when you feel intimate that you want a response from the other side, you would like the other person to feel intimate too. Let them take some time. They need to breathe. Don't be in a hurry to express your intimacy. Then it becomes violence, you force your intimacy on someone.

"Just relax, Michael. You haven't come to India to get caught up in a relationship. You are here for another reason. Just take it for granted that you are intimate. They belong to you and you to them. Don't try to look into the other person to see if they are feeling intimately in love with you or not. Take it for granted, 'Yes, everybody loves me.' Do you know what will happen? Even if there is no love, if there is some doubt, all that will go away, all that will disappear. Do you understand? Good, good. What is the time now?" he asked, without waiting for an answer. "It must be late, so go rest."

A few days later, Rita told me that Guruji wanted her to go to Madras (Chennai) to help set up programs. She was leaving the next day and wouldn't be back for a month. So, for the time being, my feelings for her would remain secret. I would wait to see how I felt when she returned.

The next day, I went to the airport to see Rita off. I was sorry to see her go, but at the same time I felt lighter.

I spent the next month teaching almost every day. Many of the Bangalore corporations I contacted wanted me to conduct the course. During that time, a few other devotees came from abroad to be with Guruji. There were about twelve of us now at Gyan Mandir. Most of us taught in the Bangalore area during the day. Others would go to the ashram to help with construction and tree planting. It was getting closer to the summer deadline, when we expected to have hundreds of people arrive for the advanced course.

At the rate things were going, I didn't believe the ashram would be ready in time. "Just wait and watch the miracle," Guruji kept saying. And that is exactly what I thought would be needed.

It was already May, and they hadn't yet broken ground for the meditation hall. Most of the dormitories had only their foundations built, and there was still no decision on the location of the dining hall. And what about the bathrooms?

Application forms were coming in fast. With less than three months to go, we already had more than a hundred applications from around the world. Chris and Katherine were coming from Poland and planned to bring eighty people with them. Because of the economic conditions in Russia and Poland, Guruji decided to give scholarships to anyone from those countries who wanted to come. I had no idea where all these people were going to sleep and eat.

I suppose it was because I had so many doubts that Guruji put me in charge of housing. He asked me to come up with a housing plan that would accommodate all the course participants. My crash course in the Guru's School of Ashram Management began.

I was convinced that it was physically impossible to house all of these people. I started drawing multicolored illustrations, diagrams, pie charts, and bar graphs to prove it could not be done.

One day, we held a meeting to discuss plans and logistics. There were five of us at the meeting — Nalini from Canada, Ananda from Germany, Martine from France, and Janael and I from the U.S. All of us sat with Guruji, reviewing my charts and graphs. He liked the arrows and all the bright colors. But the topic he wanted to discuss was ... spoons.

"Should we purchase spoons for everyone," he asked, "or should people buy their own spoons? Spoons have a way of disappearing with two hundred people, and that is a lot of spoons. Maybe we should have people eat in the traditional way with their hands. And who will wash the spoons? Should people carry their spoons with them?"

For the next two-and-a-half hours, we sat in this crucial organizational meeting discussing spoons. My buttons were being pushed. I became serious.

"Guruji, we can work the spoon thing out, but where are people going to stay?"

He just smiled at me with total confidence and said, "It will all work out. It will happen, just like a miracle."

Two weeks later, Rita returned, and I was elated to see her. We went out to lunch at Pavithra's, our favorite restaurant in Bangalore, and talked for hours.

She looked tanned and fit but seemed tired. She told me that after a few days in Madras she'd started having doubts about being so involved with the Art of Living. She'd decided to take a break and visit the famous beach areas in Goa. She liked being in Goa and being away from Guruji and the ashram for a while. She went to parties and spent a lot of time at the beach. She told me that when her friend Tony arrived, she planned to go back there so the two of them could experience Goa's beauty together.

But I was barely listening. I was lost in fantasy. Her lips were full and the sunlight through the window made her eyes sparkle. I wanted to kiss her. And, without intending to, I blurted out my feelings.

She said she'd known all along how I felt and that she also had a fondness for me. But she was already involved with Tony. He would be coming to the ashram in a few months, and she didn't want to complicate her life. She just wanted to remain friends.

The more disinterested she was, the more appealing she became. I believed I could still win her over. I was relieved that I had told her how I felt. But now I didn't know what to do. I wished she had thrown her arms around me and said she wanted to marry me.

Even though I felt hurt, I loved her even more. To distract myself, I decided to focus on my work at the ashram and on teaching in the city. But that week, Rita came down with a high fever and a bad case of dysentery. She could barely hold down liquids and was becoming weaker each day.

Guruji called me into his room and told me to take care of her. "Have someone else teach the course for you this week," he said. "Someone needs to attend to Rita. I think you should take her to Dr. Shenoy, and you should stay with her until she gets better."

"Guruji," I protested, "maybe Nalini can take care of her. She isn't very busy now, and I think it would be better if it were a woman looking after her. I would like to continue teaching."

"If Nalini isn't busy, then have her teach. You take care of Rita."

What was he up to now? He knew how I felt about her. I was sure he'd sent her off to Madras so I could forget about her and become centered again. Did he think I was over her already? Had he changed his mind? Was he testing me? I knew that he wanted me to focus on teaching and helping with the ashram. Nevertheless, I was secretly glad to follow his instructions, and I took her to Dr. Shenoy that afternoon.

I stayed by her side for the next two weeks. I cooked for her, did her laundry, made her take her medicine, and even washed the vomit off her face.

As her health improved, her heart expanded. Her feelings changed from fondness to gratitude to, possibly, love. Rita opened her heart to me, and we were inseparable again. I wanted to believe she was in love with me, but I could tell there was still something holding her back.

Maybe if her feelings were more like mine I wouldn't have been so lost in this drama. But I was gone. My attention was now on her instead of the Guru.

During my first Art of Living Course, Guruji asked the group, "If God were to give you one wish, what would you ask for?" Inside, my answer was, "A relationship." It was my burning desire. I was thirty-seven years old and had never been married or lived with a woman. Though I'd had many girlfriends and flings, all of them had been short-lived. I wanted a permanent romantic relationship. I believed it would make me happy.

Rita was beautiful, brilliant, charming, devoted to the same master, and — unavailable. I desperately wanted her. I think I might have left the ashram and Guruji forever if Rita had agreed to go with me. My mind was feverish and completely unsettled.

When Rita and I were together, she would give me mixed messages. One time she said she loved me, but later she wasn't sure. Whichever way she pulled my strings, I would jump. I needed to speak to Guruji. I needed his help.

I found Guruji in his nightclothes, watering the houseplants outside his room on the third floor of Gyan Mandir.

"Guruji, I am having a very hard time. I need to speak to you."

"Yes, tell me," he said, as he continued watering. "What is it?"

"It's Rita. I'm in love with her. I didn't listen to your advice, and I shared my thoughts and feelings with her. Even though she says that she loves me, I don't think she feels the same way about me as I do about her. I can't get her out of my mind. All this makes me feel so distant from you."

Guruji put the watering pot down and turned his head. He had a soft and compassionate look, and his voice was quiet, but his answer was firm and direct.

"I don't think she has those feelings for you. It's not a good match for you. You wouldn't be good for each other. And when her friend Tony comes to the ashram in a few months, you will burn. Simply burn. She won't even know that you're there. You are just wasting your time with her. There is so much work that needs to be done. You have been given the ability to teach and you are wasting it. This is not the time to be focused on a relationship. You're getting drained and entangled in an illusion. You are with me at a very special time, when the stream is just beginning to flow. You will look back on this time and realize how special it was. You should begin writing about your experiences and put them into a book. Your stories will inspire others on the path. Focus your time on teaching and writing, not on Rita."

Deep inside I knew he was right, but my desires and frustrations were in charge that night. I felt as though I was missing something in my life and that having a relationship would make me feel more complete.

"Then why did you put the two of us together?" I demanded. "You have me sleeping in the room right next to hers. You made me take care of her when she was sick. You set the whole thing up!"

Guruji just smiled at me compassionately, picked up the watering pot, and attended to the plants. In a few moments, he looked up and asked softly, "What is it that you want?"

This was so intimate. I was embarrassed to tell him. Trying to hold back my feelings, the tears began rolling down my face. "I want a companion. I want to be with someone who loves me."

"I'm your companion, and I love you," he said.

"No, Guruji," I said through the tears. "I want to be in a relationship."

I was uncomfortable saying that. It felt so small to be demanding a relationship with a woman who didn't love me.

"Oh, you want to be in a relationship. Fine, go ahead. I can wait for you."

Couldn't I have Divine love and also be in a relationship? I felt so much pressure. I couldn't think straight. My desire for Rita had caused me to lose sight of why I had come to India. Being with Guruji and helping the world was no longer my priority. I was obsessed and determined to be in a relationship with Rita.

No matter how loving and caring Guruji was that night, I was consumed with the notion that I was being pushed to lead a monastic life. That's all I was hearing. He had encouraged other teachers to get married and have a family, why not me? I was so fixated on my desire that it didn't occur to me that Guruji might actually have understood my feelings or that he could be trying to save me from an emotional nightmare.

"Guruji!" I said. "Now I feel guilty about my desires! About wanting to be in a relationship!"

Frustrated and upset, I stormed out.

Lying in my bed that night, I kept churning over what Guruji had said. I was simply not able to understand what he was telling me. Or maybe I was blocking it. Conflicting emotions were arising in me and I didn't know what to do. Obsessed with desires, I felt horrible. My love for Guruji, which I cherished most, was moving into the background.

It was just before 9 a.m. when I went to the meditation hall for the morning darshan. Guruji was already there. He smiled at me as I entered, and gestured that he wanted to talk to me. I was fatigued from the lack of sleep and the thoughts rambling in my head. I could feel his care even before I got to him, but my wall was up, and my desires remained.

"Your desire for a relationship is just a combination of longing and your age," he said in an understanding way. "It is longing and sexual energy together that make you want to have a partner. I am not against you being in a relationship or getting married. But if you think having a wife or girlfriend or that anything outside of yourself will make you happy, you are mistaken. I just want you to be happy and to be free."

"You want me to become a monk, Guruji," I said. "I'm not ready for that."

"I don't want you to become a monk or act against your nature. I just want you to get the most out of your time here with me. Do you see that? You will look back and see how special it was to spend these days with me. I don't want you to regret wasting this time. You have so many talents to help people come to the path."

Again, he told me, "The experiences you have been given are so that other people can read and hear and be inspired by them. I'm telling you, don't waste your time with Rita. It is an illusion in your mind. Be with the knowledge now."

The idea of writing a book brought up fears of inadequacy and memories of my learning disabilities throughout school. I knew that the only way I could write a book would be through the power of Divine grace. But I wasn't feeling that now. I couldn't think about being creative or about anything Guruji had said. All I could think about was Rita.

As time passed, I became more involved with her. She assisted me when I taught, and we worked together preparing the ashram for the summer courses. I didn't understand what Guruji was doing or why he never tried to separate us.

My mind was clearly in two places at once. I loved Rita, and I loved Guruji. I wanted to have sex and be in a relationship. And I wanted to be a devotee and get enlightened. I knew many couples who were devoted to Guruji and the spiritual path, but based on my knowledge at the time, I didn't think it was possible to have it all. I was at a crossroads and was afraid to follow Guruji's direction. Although I had never found satisfaction in any love relationship, I couldn't imagine living out life as a single person or being celibate.

The next evening during satsang I asked Guruji, "Does one have to practice celibacy to progress on the spiritual path? To me, it seems unnatural. If everyone chose to be celibate, the human race would cease to exist. Not everyone can be like you, Guruji."

Speaking to the whole group, he said, "Celibacy is not a practice, it's a happening. Celibacy is when there is so much contentment that you are full of joy and bliss in every moment. Your whole energy is so high and full of bliss that you have no need for anything else. It's like having a peak experience every moment. You don't need to look outside yourself for fulfillment. Do you see what I am saying?"

While everyone was leaving the hall, I stayed behind and sat down in front of him. Guruji must have seen my confusion. He looked in my eyes and said, "I don't want you to be unnatural, take vows, or follow some strict rules. Yet, at some time or other you have to grow into that state of going beyond sex, and it is better to get off sex before your body becomes old, tired, and depleted.

"You are not a teenager anymore. You have experienced sex in life.

At some point you have to rise above your thoughts and your desires. Move beyond the body, don't get stuck. Wake up and see that life is much bigger, much vaster. Existence has much more to offer to you. In the ancient books it is said that the bliss and joy you get in meditation is equal to one hundred times the joy you get in sex."

He looked to see if I understood, but I felt tight inside. I thought these were concepts I couldn't put into practice. I felt inferior, less evolved, because I had sexual desires.

"There is nothing wrong or terrible about sex," he said. "It's a basic instinct you have been having for so many lifetimes. The oldest impression in the mind is sex. Don't feel, 'I'm no good because I get these thoughts,' or feel guilty or try to suppress them. When these thoughts come, the more you fight with them, the more you resist them, the more they will persist. By observing the energy and the sensations in the body, the energy changes naturally and moves upward," he said. "It's simple."

Simple for him, but not for me, and I wasn't sure that I could move beyond this. Was he telling me this so I wouldn't let my attraction for Rita overshadow my judgment? Or maybe he was just showing me another option?

"In Sanskrit, *brahmacharya* means married to God," Guruji explained. "Or, God has possessed you so much — He has so fully entered into every cell — that there is no space for anything else. Celibate means married to the Spirit. But again, I am repeating that it is not a practice, it's a happening. Having seen over and over again for lifetimes what sex is, you say, 'OK, let me move a step further and be immersed into That — into what is, immersed in love.'"

"Guruji, if celibacy is not happening in my life, would it be a good idea to learn and practice *tantra* techniques?"

"What do you get in sex?" he asked. "Joy, a thrill, some love and comfort. You know what happens in sex? An energy that is dormant in you opens up. A sensation rises all along your body for a few moments. Every cell of your body is in the present moment so totally. That is joyful. If the joy was just in the body, in the organs, it would remain all the time. It doesn't remain all the time. Your attraction dies out the moment your energy escapes or releases from the body. Attending to this energy, this is what real joy is. Focus on that rather than on an object that is outside.

"Sex gives you a glimpse of what the highest possibility of your life energy could be," he said, "how you could live in that vibrating, thrilling moment every minute, in love."

He was giving me a vision, yet I remained feverish. My desires prevented me from hearing fully. My body wanted one thing, my mind another, and my heart still another. Worst of all, the feeling of invincibility and security I had always felt around Guruji was now being overshadowed.

Fortunately, the projects at Gyan Mandir and the ashram kept me so busy, and talking to him had reduced the turmoil just enough, that I was able to keep trouble at a distance — for the moment.

CHAPTER FIFTEEN

A Fight at the Ashram

IN EARLY JUNE, Chris and Katherine arrived with nearly eighty people from Poland who planned to stay in Bangalore for several months during the advanced courses. Guruji had Rita and me stay at Gyan Mandir to host the Polish devotees and help them adjust to India. All the other international devotees living at Gyan Mandir moved to the ashram to make room for our new Polish friends.

Within a day, the house on 39 A Cross was bulging to capacity with hungry, tired, jet-lagged Polish devotees, who all seemed to need the one bathroom at the same time. We laid out all the mattresses we'd ordered, and every inch of space at Gyan Mandir was transformed into a huge dormitory.

That afternoon we held an orientation meeting. I had planned to welcome everyone and tell them what to expect while staying in India. But as I looked around at all the new faces packed into this small house, my throat choked and I could not speak. These people had no sign of fatigue or frustration from their long journey. Instead, they all looked like angels, with a luminous glow of gratitude and humility. Many of them had never been outside their homeland, and now they were in the land of the Vedas, looking forward to their upcoming time of silence, singing, and service, and to meeting, in person, the one who had added so much to their lives.

They stayed in this crowded house for a week before rooms were available for them at the ashram. There was never any problem — not even when we asked several of them to throw away the salamis they'd brought with them from Poland. Rajshree, back from teaching in Bombay, taught the women how to wrap their new saris. I took the men to the tailor to have *kurta pajamas* made. It all went so smoothly.

On the full-moon day in July, we were ready to start the advanced courses at the ashram with the traditional Guru Purnima celebration. It was time for all of us to leave the city and move to the ashram. I was attached to my room at Gyan Mandir. It had been my home for the last six months. It would also be the first time since she returned to Bangalore that Rita and I would be separated by more than a thin wall.

Life at the ashram kept me busy. There were two hundred people from all over the world who had come to spend time with Guruji. Miraculously, everything was working out, just as Guruji said it would. My friends from the U.S. were helping with the various ashram needs.

Jeff Houk came from Santa Barbara. I liked being around him and was glad that we continued to be close friends. Jeff was kind and sincere, and he was as crazy about Guruji as I was. He had a disarming quality that made me feel safe to open up and share personal things about my life. It was hot in Bangalore in the summer, and Jeff had a difficult time adjusting to the heat and to ashram life at first. But after a few weeks, he was on his feet and became the official ashram dishwasher — a change of pace from his corporate position at home.

Guruji had designated me as the course coordinator. I was busy, but I must say that my ego was jazzed with this position. I felt like a "somebody." With the responsibilities came the added bonus of having access to the Guru anytime I wanted. He called me into his room whenever we were going to make a decision about policy or structure at the ashram. I was busy, happy, and in my element.

During the evening satsang, Guruji gave beautiful discourses on Vedic knowledge. Jeff had brought a video camera to India, at Guruji's request, so we could record the series of talks he was planning. But something must have happened to it in transit because the camera did not work. We took it to a camera shop in town and were told that there was something wrong with the motor and that it couldn't be repaired in India. I assumed we would have to purchase another one.

Guruji looked somber when I told him that the camera was broken. "These talks we are going to give must be recorded for posterity," he said, and then closed his eyes, sitting silently for several minutes. The silence was deep and drew me into meditation. "Go and check the camera again," he said with a grin, as he opened his eyes. "I think it should be working now."

How could it be working now? The mechanic clearly said that it could not be repaired. But since Guruji instructed, I thought I would try it one more time. To my amazement, the camera worked.

That night, I began recording Guruji's commentary on the *Ashtavakra Gita,* an extraordinary and transforming series of talks that are treasured by people throughout the world.

After a couple months, the day I had been dreading arrived. For six months, I had deluded myself into believing that Rita had fallen in love with me. I did not want to deal with the reality of her feelings for Tony.

When Tony arrived, they jumped into each other's arms and embraced as lovers. Within a few days, Rita began to completely ignore me. It was finally clear to me that she truly loved Tony and merely thought of me as a close friend.

As Guruji predicted, I was burning with jealousy. She wouldn't even acknowledge me with a polite smile. My stomach was in knots, and I would see the two of them together everywhere. They meditated together, ate their meals together, were at satsang together, and worked in the garden together.

I was furious with her and disgusted with myself. I couldn't handle the anguish and excruciating pain I felt in the pit of my gut. I wanted to leave the ashram and return to the United States. I felt humiliated, defeated, and alone. I was burnt to a crisp. Guruji wouldn't comfort me or give me the opportunity to discuss the situation with him.

He would only give me a look that seemed to say, "I told you so."

Then, one day, without any notice, Rita and Tony were gone. I was shocked!

Tony's roommate told me they had gone to Goa. He explained that after Tony arrived, Rita decided they should leave. And she had no intention of coming back to Bangalore to see Guruji — or me — again.

I was devastated. I had invested my whole heart in her, and now I had nothing. I felt alone. I was angry at her for all the pain I was experiencing. I wanted vengeance, I wanted to hurt her in any way I could.

Sitting outside the meditation hall in a stupor of despair, I was approached by one of the young Indians close to Guruji. "Michael looks sad. You lost your girlfriend." He laughed at me. "You are stupid, Michael," he said, tormenting me. "Stupid!"

With each word he spoke I could feel the fire of anger rising in me. "You should have focused on Guruji," he said scolding me. "You are just stupid!" he shouted, pointing his finger at me to accentuate his point.

I was enraged. I felt animosity toward every woman who ever hurt me. After that, I don't fully remember what happened. I lost it. The next thing I knew, I had this young man pinned to the ground. Someone was going to pay for the pain I was experiencing. Looking straight into his eyes, I pulled my fist back in the air and landed it right on his face. I could feel the cartilage crushing as my fist hit his nose.

Immediately, a crowd of Indian workers gathered around us. One of the ashram workers pulled us apart. Within moments, Jeff was holding me back from hitting him again. "Look at you. You're like an animal! Stop fighting!" he yelled.

The workers that gathered were screaming and shouting at me. My opponent was still on the ground. I looked down at myself with disgust. My shirt was torn, and my arm had a huge gash where it scraped against the rocks. A puddle formed as the blood dripped down my arm. I was in pain. My body was shivering and shaking in shock and disbelief over what I had done. It was a miracle that I hadn't killed him. I was so ashamed, but I knew that I had to face Guruji before someone else told him what happened.

When I entered his room, Guruji was meeting with Chris and Katherine about the Polish devotees. He had already heard what happened. He glared at me as I stood in the doorway with my bloody arm and tears running down my face. I have never seen his face look the way it did that day.

"Look what you have done! You have brought violence to the ashram. You hit one of our boys — a white man hitting an Indian boy in front of all the Indian workers. I will have you pack your bags and leave! You are not fit to be my devotee. Just look at you. You are a disgrace. I have failed. Unconditional love has failed. I have been too easy with you. I have been giving you this knowledge like you were a prince. That is not what you need. I will need to make it hard for you now, and that is not my nature."

His words were coming at me with force, but without any negativity. It tormented me to hear him say he had failed when I was clearly the failure. I was ashamed of what had happened, and I was completely embarrassed to have Guruji see me at my worst. Now there were absolutely no secrets from him. I felt naked and fallen from grace. He asked Katherine to wash the wounds on my arm and ordered me to leave his room.

When I got back to my room, there was an inferno in my head. Thoughts raced through my mind at lightning speed. What had I done? What would become of me? I no longer knew who I was. I had never identified myself with violence. My past felt wretched and my future was a blank. I relived the incident over and over.

At first I blamed myself. Then I blamed Rita, then the path, the techniques, and Guruji's teachings. Finally, I blamed Guruji. He should have protected me and prevented this from happening. I wanted to run away from the ashram and hide somewhere. But where could I go? Leave this path and find a new master? I knew that I would take this same mind wherever I went. I was trapped. All I wanted was peace. But there was no peace. I was in hell, tormented by my own mind.

Someone knocked on my door and called out my name, but I didn't answer. I couldn't deal with anyone asking questions. I didn't want to talk about what had happened. I was ashamed and wanted to keep it a secret.

"Michael, it's me, Chetan. Guruji sent me. Please open the door."

Chetan was a young devotee from Salt Lake City, who had met Guruji near Rishikesh several years ago. Chetan was tall, broad-shouldered, and had the deepest piercing eyes. He was headstrong and mulish about advancing on the spiritual path, and strongly identified with peculiar concepts of what enlightenment was all about. Many people found him difficult to get along with, but I thought Chetan was a beautiful soul. He always inspired me. I opened the door and we looked at each other. He was so bright. He looked as though he had just been meditating.

"Look, something happened, I know," he said. "But I don't want to discuss it. It is not necessary. No one was right, no one was wrong. It was a happening. I don't want to be involved in the gossip. I came here to tell you that we are having a *yagya* tonight instead of satsang — a *Rudram Abhishekam* to clear the atmosphere of the violence that happened today. Guruji said that you should sit outside the yagya and not enter the puja area. Before it starts you are to wash everyone's shoes with soap and water and a rag. Do you understand?"

"I suppose he wants to humiliate me even more," I said. "Well, tell Guruji that I can take anything he dishes out. Fine! I'll wash shoes. I'm stronger than that."

"And, Michael, I love you, man. You are a good person. You have done so much while you've been here in India. Don't forget that. Don't destroy yourself because you made a mistake. It happens." Chetan gazed into my eyes with compassion and love. It was so kind of him. I will never forget his kindness.

I couldn't go to the dining hall and face everyone, so I didn't eat dinner that night. I went to the yagya and found Chetan waiting for me outside the meditation hall. "I'm glad you showed up," he said. "Here's a bucket of water and a rag. You're supposed to wash everyone's sandals and place them neatly outside the meditation hall."

I thought washing everyone's shoes was a ridiculous punishment, obviously meant to be symbolic. I didn't think it would have any effect on me. As people started coming to the hall and removing their shoes and sandals, I knelt down to wash them. People were laughing at me. They assumed it was some sort of joke. At that point, most people were unaware of the fight that had happened. They didn't know why we were having a yagya in the evening.

One of my close friends, Pierre, from Montreal, who liked to tease me, started poking fun at me, good-naturedly. "Oh, Michael," he said in his thick French-Canadian accent, "you are moving up in the world. Do a good job on my shoes and I will put a good word in for you with the Guru." These words pierced my heart and I began to cry.

I thought of Rita traveling to Goa with Tony and regretted involving Guruji and the ashram in my personal affairs. My hands shook and my heart pounded as I continued washing everyone's shoes.

Chetan told me that I was not allowed to enter the hall and that I was to sit outside. I sat close to a window near the stage so I could watch the pundits performing the ancient ceremony.

For the first time ever, I saw Guruji sit with his eyes open during puja. He looked uneasy. Thunder crashed in the sky and rain began to pour down. I was drenched, but I wouldn't move. I listened to the mixture of the sounds of the Vedic chants and the pouring rain as they washed my sins away. The yagya had been going on for over an hour when Chetan came to the window and said, "Guruji wants you to come in now, out of the rain."

Due to the storm, the power had gone out. The only light in the hall was a small kerosene lantern that illuminated Guruji's face. I entered the hall, walked close to the light, and sat behind him. He sat silently for a few minutes, and then slowly turned his head and looked into my eyes as he tossed me a small, sweet offering from the puja. That was all I needed — that one glance. In my heart I knew that it was impossible for him to be truly angry with me.

In this situation, he needed to show anger. He needed to punish me in order for me to learn a lesson. Yet there was still love, unconditional love, without judgment. I sat weeping as I ate the sweet *prasad*.

I thought about the person I hit and prayed that he was OK.

As I walked back to my room, my mind was lost in my drama. I didn't notice Guruji's father, Pitaji, walking toward me. He stopped me and gave me a hug, saying, "It's OK. Everyone makes a mistake." His words touched my heart and lightened the guilt I was feeling.

The next morning, Chetan came knocking at my door again. "I was in Guruji's room last night," he said. "He told me to tell you that you should take the advanced course that is starting today and hand over your responsibilities as ashram manager to Jeff Houk. Guruji said that you should sit in the back at satsang and listen to his lectures and find someone else to do the videotaping. You are free of all your responsibilities at the ashram. OK?" Chetan hesitated a moment. "And Michael, one more thing. Guruji doesn't want you to come to his house anymore."

That was the ultimate punishment. I was losing access to the Guru. And it killed me to hand everything over to Jeff. For many years after that day, I was on the outside edge of our organization and Jeff was on the inside. Jealousy and resentment do funny things. I wanted to hate Jeff, but how do you hate your best friend?

Out of sheer habit, and perhaps, partly, to test the situation, I went up to Guruji's house and knocked. Susannah, a devotee from Canada, opened the door a crack and peered out. When she saw who it was, she said, "Oh, Michael! You aren't supposed to be here. Guruji is busy now. Uhh ...." She was flustered. "Uhh ... he is not seeing anyone. We will call you later when he can see you." And she shut the door in my face.

Busy? Guruji had never been too busy to see me. It was the first time since I met him that I had walked away from his room without speaking to him. I waited for Guruji to call me. I waited and waited and waited. For four long, dark months Guruji completely ignored me and wouldn't acknowledge my existence. Not even a smile or a glance.

If I went up to his house when he was sitting on the porch and tried to join the other devotees, he would send everyone away or just get up and go inside. It was obvious that I was unwelcome. Not wishing to spoil everyone else's fun, I decided I would be better off keeping to myself. I would wait until he called me. It was a lonely, painful time. I longed to be back in his grace.

It was difficult to get my mind off the past. I spent most of my days by myself. My only activities were meditating, pulling weeds, killing mosquitoes, and then meditating some more. I prayed to Guruji each day to help me let go of the past and learn what I needed to learn.

Somehow, a spark of creativity dawned and I started to journal. I began to write down my experiences of the time I first arrived in India. I enjoyed the act of writing and found it satisfying. I thought that perhaps, as Guruji suggested, someone would be interested in my adventures, and I planned to submit some stories to the newsletter that the Art of Living organization distributed back home.

Then, one day, as I was absorbed in my writing, Chetan knocked on my door. He peeked into my room with bulging eyes and an impish grin. He cleared his throat, announcing the news as though he had come from the King's palace.

"Guruji is calling for you!" he declared.

Months had passed since I had walked the path to Guruji's house. Feelings of guilt simmered in me, as thoughts of the past came into my mind. I was nervous, knocking on his door.

Guruji was meeting with some dignitaries and didn't acknowledge me when I entered. I sat silently, contented, in the back of the room for several hours, watching the revolving door of people coming and going from his room. They all needed his attention. Many came with personal problems, some had questions about projects, but most just wanted a few minutes in his grace. He attended to each of them like a mother attending to her children.

After several hours, we were finally alone in his room.

Guruji looked at me with tenderness. "What are you doing all day, Michael? Are you sitting around feeling sorry for yourself? That will not help you grow at all." I felt that he was consciously lifting the unbearable weight of the last few months.

"You need a change," he said. "In a few days, I will be leaving the ashram and will be gone for some time. While I'm gone, it will be good for the teachers who are here from the U.S. to go out and teach around India. Rajshree can go to Bombay, Nalini and Martine can go north to Delhi, and you can go to Mangalore and teach there. It's by the ocean, west of Bangalore, near Kerala. Stay there for a while and teach."

"Guruji, I don't think I am fit to be teaching now. Besides, I have never traveled alone in India. And without any contacts, I don't know who I would teach."

"If you just sit around like this, you will get totally depressed. Stop thinking about Rita and brooding over the past," he said. "It's finished now. Go to Mangalore. You will do well there and teaching will be good for you."

In the morning, I went to his room with the other teachers who were going on the road to teach. I was feeling nervous about traveling outside the ashram. Before leaving, each of us gave him a flower and bowed at his feet as we received his blessings. After giving him a rose, I started bowing in a gesture of surrender, but my head didn't touch the ground. Only partly bowed, I was surprised to feel Guruji pushing my head the rest of the way to the floor. It didn't feel harsh, but it was very firm. An instant later, I understood what he was doing. To truly be of service to the world, to the Divine, I had to fully surrender, to fully let go of my small, limiting qualities. Just a token of surrender was now inadequate.

As Guruji once said: "Surrender means offering all that is – the bad as well as the good in you, which can bring pride. When you offer, what remains is pure love. You become light like a flower, all the weight is gone." I had come to India to be of service, but I had been serving myself. I was still obsessed with my desires, fears, and anxieties. Bowing down meant surrendering, not just physically, but mentally and emotionally, too.

The next day, I was on a train to Mangalore. My spirits were low, and I had little confidence that I would be able to organize a course and teach anyone. After arriving, I checked into a local hotel and ate some breakfast. I wasn't sure what to do next. With no contacts in Mangalore, I decided to look in the local phone book. I started calling large businesses that had multiple listings and spoke to the managing directors of the largest companies in Mangalore.

"Hello, I'm Michael Fischman from the United States. I teach a program in stress management and will only be in town for a few days. I would like to meet with you. I have some technology that can help you and your company."

I made four appointments for the next day. By the end of the week, I had three huge courses organized. And by the following week, I had more courses than I could handle. I was on a roll.

Teaching was my salvation. I felt empowered again and I could feel Guruji's presence with me. All the time I'd spent by myself at the ashram in introspection had made me stronger. I had more understanding of myself, and felt more compassion and sensitivity. I was experiencing a new depth to teaching and sharing knowledge. I knew firsthand that the process of letting go and dissolving the ego could be painful and uncomfortable for some people. I felt better able to empathize and help people.

At the end of the month, I returned to the ashram a hero. I had taught more than three hundred people in three weeks, which, at the time, was a lot. Guruji smiled when I told him of my success. That smile was all I wanted, and the chance to feel close again.

In the following months, I returned to Mangalore often, and taught many courses. A lush, tropical port city, it became my home away from my Indian home, and it seemed that everyone in Mangalore knew me and the work I was doing.

Most of the time, I traveled and taught on my own. A few times, other teachers traveled with me.

On one trip, Guruji sent Nalini to teach with me. Nalini was spunky, vivacious, and very bright, and she could always make me laugh. We had become close friends and I enjoyed teaching with her.

Nalini joined me in Mangalore to teach a course for the local port authority. We were housed in a charming guesthouse right on the beach. Each day, we would teach the course for four hours in the morning and return to the beach house in the afternoon. The house came complete with its own cook, who made elaborate meals for us, as we took long walks or meditated under the moonlight. In the evening, Nalini and I ate our meals on the beach, gazing at the stars and listening to the ocean waves crash along the shore. It was very romantic.

If I had not just gone through such a horrendous experience with Rita, I might have thought Guruji was playing matchmaker again. But few sparks of that sort were kindled; we were more like brother and sister.

In any case, I was definitely not looking for another relationship. I had scars around my heart that needed mending. On the other hand, I wasn't cutting off the possibility of a relationship in the future, and in the coming years I would, in fact, find myself in other relationships.

While I was caught up with Rita, I couldn't understand what Guruji was doing. Now that some time had passed, I could see that he was seeing the bigger picture. Rita obviously didn't love me and was not the one for me. My craving to be in a relationship and my desire to be with her had not let my mind rest, and eventually distorted my perception of reality.

In the past, I had wondered why so many masters and traditions spoke about the spiritual value of dispassion. I wanted to experience passion and enthusiasm and had seen them as incompatible with dispassion. I equated dispassion with being like a zombie — dead and disinterested. Now, I understood that dispassion wasn't about becoming an automaton. It was living without feverishness, living from a place of freedom, where you are fully present. It was the way I saw Guruji — dispassionate and filled with enthusiasm, awareness, and love.

Guruji once told us that the sign of Divine love is contentment. And that we generally don't look for love where it comes from, we look for it where it is not.

To illustrate his point, he told us one of his many humorous stories about the legendary Sufi mystic, Mullah Nasruddin. One day, Mullah was on the street looking for his key. A neighbor offered to help and asked Mullah where he was when he lost it. "Somewhere in the house," Mullah told him. The neighbor was surprised. "Then why are we looking out here?" And Mullah answered, "Because the light is better."

I had believed that the love, romance, and intimacy of a relationship would fill a void that was in my heart. But the same person I thought was the source of my happiness had eventually made me miserable. After this ordeal, I realized that, just like Mullah Nasruddin, I had been looking in the wrong place. The joy that was sparked was already in me.

It was Spirituality 101. Looking outside for joy is the big illusion.

Part Three

Chapter Sixteen

The Caribbean King

When I returned from my last teaching tour in Mangalore, the atmosphere at the ashram felt deserted. Most of the international guests had returned home, and only a few people remained.

The ashram had a slower rhythm, now that most of the hard work was done. The new meditation and dining halls had been built, most of the sleeping accommodations were complete, and rumor had it that we would even have a phone line installed in a few weeks.

With a break in the action, Guruji was like a teenager on holiday. Like a big family, we took day trips into the city in the yellow school van, visiting temples, drinking mango milkshakes, and seeing where Guruji spent his time growing up. He showed us the home of his early guru, Sudhakar Chaturvedi, the eminent Vedic scholar who had also been Mahatma Gandhi's mentor. Guruji affectionately referred to Chaturvedi as "Bangalorie," the name Mahatma Gandhi had bestowed on him.

Guruji also spent time leisurely walking around the ashram, sharing his vision for expansion.

One day, as the sun was just starting to set, and with only a handful of us now at the ashram, he told us that when he turned fifty, the ashram would be too small, and that more than two million people from all over the world would gather in Bangalore to meditate with him. As in California, I found his premonitions impossible to imagine.

Yet, most of the things that Guruji predicted in those days came true.

At first, Guruji's organization seemed to grow slowly. But at a certain point, his teachings took off, spreading quickly throughout the world. It seems that he was able to accomplish this in such a short time because of his leadership style. Instead of putting his attention on gaining followers, Guruji was interested in empowering people and making them leaders. He inspired through knowledge, and always encouraged an informal and personal connection.

At that time, most of us would have felt we had delusions of grandeur if we expected the Art of Living Foundation to become one of the largest volunteer-driven non-profit organizations in the world, or that thousands of its volunteers would mobilize to bring both physical and mental relief to victims of nearly every natural and man-made disaster, or that the Art of Living would be resolving conflicts in violent regions of the world. It would have seemed like a childish fantasy to imagine that Guruji would soon be a keynote speaker at the World Economic Forum and the U.N. Millennium World Peace Summit, or that he would address parliaments around the world, or earn the trust of opposing parties in long-standing conflicts, or be nominated for the Nobel Peace Prize multiple times. And walking through the dusty ashram on that late afternoon, I would never have thought that the ashram itself would become a lush oasis one day. Yet, all that would happen in only a few years.

In the coming days, I began to memorize the moments with Guruji and relish them. I had been in India a year, and I knew that this special period of my life would soon be ending. The most I could hope for was to extend my visa another few months, and then I would have to leave.

I had grown so accustomed to living in India and derived such pleasure from this unique spiritual culture that small things like the lack of hygiene, perpetual chaos, and occasional dysentery didn't bother me much any more. I loved waking up in a place where the atmosphere was charged with spirituality.

A few weeks before my stay in India came to an end, Guruji told me that it would be best for me to return to California and go back to work for a while. I was repulsed by the idea and couldn't imagine working at a regular job again. I told him I wanted to stay in India and dedicate my life to teaching full time. But Guruji thought it was best for me to return to America.

"Now, Michael, you've been with me in India for more than a year," he said. "It is time for you to return to California."

"Guruji, I don't think I'm ready to go back yet. I don't think I've grown enough. I wasted so much of my time."

"Of course you have grown," he said. "You can't be with me and not grow."

"I had so many experiences," I said, "but how do I know if it was real growth?"

"There are three yardsticks you can use to measure improvement in your life," he said, almost jovially. "First is your perception. Just look at how it has changed. In the past, you would attribute intentions to others' mistakes. You would hold other people responsible for your feelings and get angry with them.

"Your perception should go through the filter of knowledge. You can think, 'How would the master have handled this?' It opens up new avenues for you. How you perceive people and how you perceive yourself has changed, hasn't it? If your perception has changed, then you are making progress."

I was aware that the way I looked at things was different. But still, I wasn't sure if that meant I'd grown. It could have been simply the passage of time that affected my perception.

"Second is observation," he continued. "Now you are able to observe what is happening inside you — pleasant or unpleasant sensations. Your ability to observe has improved. You are less reactive now.

"Someone who is not on the path doesn't observe what is happening within them and will attach their frustrations to events that are happening outside them. Frustration is what? It is only energy moving in a particular channel in your body, and if you observe the sensations, it just shifts and moves away. Our *sadhana* (spiritual practice), all the things that we do, improves our observation."

Yes, this was definitely true. I had become sensitive to the sensations in my body. When I experienced strong emotions, my attention turned inward, and I observed the sensations, allowing them to subside or transform. I also noticed that most negative emotions didn't last as long as they used to.

"And third is expression," he said. "If you say people do not understand you, then you are not expressing yourself properly. If no one understands you, then you have not been talking their language. It's like you have been talking in Latin or Greek to an American crowd. You are love, no doubt, but you should express that love. Expressing love is not being goody-goody all the time. Being firm and tough is also love. If you don't agree with something and you need to take a stand, then disagree. But your firmness should come from caring," he said, "not from anger or frustration."

Yes, I had grown in this area, but it was still a challenge for me. I often felt that people kept their distance and judged me as insensitive and curt. But now there was a growing awareness (although sometimes too late) of how my words affected others. I hoped that I could still become more naturally sensitive and considerate.

"Look and see how these three things have changed in your life," he said. "Perception, observation, and expression. These three things should improve. As these things improve, life in this world, in society, becomes smoother. I won't say it will be smooth all the time. You will go through rough times. It is natural, it will happen. But it will be smoother. You are stronger now."

As I sat on the plane leaving India, I thought of Guruji's words. I reflected on everything I had gone through that year. There was no doubt, something had shifted.

Returning to Santa Monica, I felt out of place. I had grown accustomed to an Indian lifestyle and to ashram life, and found it difficult to adjust. More than anything, I missed Guruji's physical presence. I longed to be back with him.

Many mornings, I would cover myself with a blanket and stay in bed for a long time. I would remember my first days in India, sitting on the rooftop late at night with Guruji. I wondered if I would ever have another opportunity to spend so much time with him.

Eventually, my funds were running low, and I knew my only option was to find a job. I registered with several employment agencies, sent out dozens of resumes, and went on interviews almost every day.

After six weeks of job hunting, I received only one offer — marketing director for a Japanese firm that had a patent on a unique toilet bowl that eliminated odors with an inconceivably small fan. Was this the reason Guruji insisted that I come back to the U.S.? To be a toilet-bowl salesman?

Hoping that Guruji would have a good laugh and see the absurdity of me taking a job like this, I mailed him the full-color glossy brochures about this new, state-of-the-art toilet bowl. Maybe this would convince him that I was ready to return to India and teach full time.

A few days later, Jeff called to say that Guruji would be coming to the U.S. for three weeks. We would be celebrating Guru Purnima in California this year, and afterward Guruji would visit several nearby cities. The news gave me hope that things would change after he arrived.

That summer, after the Guru Purnima celebration in Aptos, California, I accompanied Guruji to the airport. While we waited for him to board the plane, Guruji took out a small world atlas that he carried in the black bag he always traveled with. He looked at me carefully, as he rested the map on his lap and took out a pen. "Michael, you and Nalini will go to Trinidad." I examined the map as Guruji drew a red circle around this tiny island in the Caribbean.

As he sketched my itinerary for the next year of my life, I knew this marked a new beginning for me as an Art of Living teacher. I would officially become a permanent full-time teacher.

"You can give up your apartment," Guruji said softly. "Now you'll be traveling and teaching full time. But I don't want you to look back and have regrets, thinking, 'If only I had money, if I had a job, then I would be happier.' Know that everything in life comes from the Divine. If you have a job and become prosperous, it is from the Divine. If you are successful at teaching, it is the Divine. Everything is provided by the Divine. On this path, you will never have to worry about anything. There will always be something to eat and a roof over your head. You will always be protected under this umbrella."

When Guruji first told me, years earlier, that I would be teaching around the world, the idea made me furious. I guess he was waiting for me to mature and desire this lifestyle for myself. Now, teaching full time was all I wanted.

Nalini and I made our plans, and in September 1992, we landed in Trinidad, the southernmost of the Caribbean Islands. It is so far south that you can see South America from its southern beaches.

There are 1.3 million people in Trinidad, with their roots in many parts of the world, including Africa, India, Europe, China, and the Middle East. About forty percent of the population is Indian. Someone must have put the bug in Guruji's ear: "Trinidad has lots of Indians. Art of Living will be successful there."

Nalini and I took pride in being the first full-time teachers in the West. We felt privileged to be on the front lines, focusing our lives on uplifting people with the wisdom and techniques we'd been given.

Although I knew that Trinidad was a tropical island, I was unprepared for the sweltering heat and humidity. We were just starting out as an organization, so we had a limited budget and had to find ways to economize. When we first arrived, we stayed with friends of friends in a small apartment without air conditioning. It was very uncomfortable. Constantly drenched in perspiration, I would shower five times a day.

When Guruji first mentioned Trinidad, I expected an exotic tropical paradise. But as we traveled around the country, I could see that paradise was far from where we were. Port of Spain, the capital of the country, was a small, dilapidated city in a tropical-island setting.

In the 1970s, oil was found off the coast of Trinidad. It was an era of rising oil prices, so drilling had quickly begun and refineries were built. But the government at the time was shortsighted and not concerned with developing and beautifying the country for tourism. The population was also content with short-term prosperity. Roads were built, houses were constructed, government contracts were signed, and bribes were taken. It is commonly believed that government officials took suitcases of money out of the country.

It was clear that the government was still recuperating from the poor planning and corruption that took place during the oil boom. Unemployment was high, and so was inflation. Cocaine and alcohol abuse were pulling the country down. With the crime rate high, every house had steel "burglar bars" on the windows and doors.

Trinidad's public transportation was fascinating. When I asked people how they were getting to the workshop, they either replied, "I have my car" or "I'm traveling." "I'm traveling" meant they were taking public transportation, one of the best deals on the island. There were government buses, taxis, and maxi-taxis. In those days, you could travel just about anywhere in the country for only fifty cents U.S.

Maxis were small buses or vans, with plush interiors and the most incredible sound systems. Usually, there were twelve to fourteen speakers in a maxi, with amplifiers and equalizers to boot. The treble and bass were both jacked all the way up and the mid-range turned all the way down. Blaring full blast from these speakers was *dub*, which, in Trinidad, is a musical style that is heavy on drums, bass, and effects.

I'm convinced that no one in the Caribbean, or on Earth for that matter, could understand the words to this type of music. I'm sure that if scientific studies were done it would show that dub is harmful to human beings and other living organisms. My hypothesis is that the sound of the heavy bass desynchronizes the hemispheric brainwave patterns, causing a decrease in mind-body coordination. It was awful.

A few days after arriving, we were off — but where and how? Our hosts did not really understand what we were doing in Trinidad. They didn't know many people and were reluctant to help. With no leads, we went door to door, on cold call after cold call. Each appointment was the same. Trinidadians (or "Trinis," as they call themselves) are very polite and friendly, but there was not much interest in something new. Most people asked for local references. They were apprehensive about being the first to take our course. We were referred from one person to the next, and then the next. We met Hindu leaders, Baptist ministers, managing directors, psychologists, New Age practitioners, and meditators. But there was still no interest.

Nalini and I traveled all over the country, in humidity and ninety-eight-degree heat, with the deafening noise of the maxi-taxis pounding in our heads and perspiration dripping from every pore. It was truly like a sauna. Even though I wore a clean, pressed shirt and tie, it irked me that I always looked ragged by the time I got to our meetings with business and community leaders.

After ten days of hard work, we had only two participants signed up for a workshop that was four days away. We were exhausted and frustrated.

Perhaps it was the heat and lack of success that caused Nalini and me to argue. We argued about the smallest things. Adding to the pressure, our hosts asked us to find another place to live. They told us they had family members coming for a visit, but we didn't believe them. They clearly wanted us out.

Finding another place to live was extremely difficult on our meager budget. After paying for our accommodations in a dilapidated guesthouse, we were totally broke. We could barely afford to buy curry and *roti* (flat bread).

With the workshop only a few days away, we knew it would take a miracle to pull it off. Despite my Whole Life Expo experience, I still believed in marketing and felt that I could create an ad that would have an impact.

That Friday evening we had twenty-six people for the first workshop on the island. Within a month, we had taught three courses and eighty-two people. It was finally happening. People loved the course and were elated with their experiences.

When we called Guruji to share our news, we could hear from his voice that he was pleased. As we expected, he asked us to stay a little longer and keep the momentum going.

Through word of mouth, Art of Living gained popularity, and

Nalini and I were soon teaching courses every week. We rented a wonderful house on Scott Street, in St. Augustine, which served as a center for us to teach and live. Although it was a little expensive, this house was a haven for us and helped the transition into the Caribbean lifestyle. It was a big, modern house, with plush carpeting, stereo, TV, and most importantly — AIR CONDITIONING.

Once we were confident in our ability as teachers and saw that things were developing positively in Trinidad, we decided to expand. Nalini went to Costa Rica and I traveled around the Caribbean. I taught courses every week for the next six months, island hopping from Trinidad to St. Lucia to Dominica.

One day, while speaking to Guruji about my progress, he said it was time for him to visit the Caribbean. I was elated. Finally, all the people who had been taught would get a chance to meet Guruji, and I couldn't wait to see him. He would be staying with me at our center in Trinidad. Once again, I would get a chance to spend quality time with him. But after I hung up, reality set in.

I had a huge task ahead of me — Guruji would be coming in less than six weeks. With no time to waste, I immediately started preparing.

The next evening, I held a planning meeting at the house on Scott Street. I was pleased when a dozen strong volunteers attended. They were appreciative of my work in the Caribbean and wanted to see the Art of Living expand there. And they seemed excited about the opportunity to meet Guruji.

But as we started to plan, they could only express their doubts and resistance. They said that there were too many obstacles. Another swami, who already had a large following in Trinidad, would be visiting the country at that time, and there was a Chutney Fest scheduled during those days, as well. (*Chutney* is an Indian/Caribbean dance-music style that is popular in Trinidad & Tobago.)

"Your guru is unknown here in Trinidad," said a psychologist who was one of our strongest volunteers. "No one will go to see him. They'll all be going to Swamiji or to the Chutney Fest. It's better you tell him not to come now."

I was shocked. I expected more from her. She was always someone I could count on. I couldn't understand why she had such little faith that it would work out.

As the meeting progressed, I became increasingly frustrated. I wanted these volunteers to be as excited about his visit as I was. I couldn't call Guruji and tell him not to come.

"Look, let's not worry about all these obstacles," I said. "If we put our full effort into his visit, we can make it happen. Let's work together. I worked for a huge advertising agency in New York, and I'm sure, if you all follow my direction, Guruji's visit will be a big success."

"Not so fast, man," a thin, older gentleman said in a husky voice. "You think you know everything, but you don't know Trinidad. You're not the Caribbean King! We have our own ways here. Just because you were a hotshot advertising executive in New York doesn't mean that you know how things get done here in Trinidad. Whatever schemes you have just won't work here!"

They all shook their heads in agreement and mumbled some Trinidadian expression under their breath. Even though they all spoke English, their accent was so heavy and foreign to me that I often couldn't understand what they said.

I couldn't hide my feelings. They could see how aggravated I was. They had looked up to me as someone who was always calm and collected. But now that I had displayed my emotions, they were losing respect for me. In my enthusiasm to inspire them, and desperate for support, I pushed them too hard. I had inadvertently caused more harm than good. I could see that I was repeating a pattern. It was clear that the third sign of growth that Guruji mentioned — expression — still needed work. I wanted to inspire them to help and serve, but I didn't know how.

Normally, after a function or meeting, many of the volunteers would hang around for hours, listening to my guru stories, drinking herbal tea, and eating cookies. But that evening, everyone left in a hurry. There was an eerie feeling of emptiness in the house on Scott Street that night.

Most of the people who attended that organizational meeting

stopped coming to *satsang,* the weekly follow-up Kriya sessions. And all but one volunteer simply refused to help with Guruji's visit. Then, for the first time in Trinidad, I had to cancel a course because there were not enough people to teach.

I didn't want to call Guruji and tell him not to come. Worse, I didn't want to tell him that the devotees were disenchanted and had turned against me. I was disheartened and didn't know what to do. I blamed myself. I thought that this was happening because of my inadequacies, my lack of skill. I felt isolated and miserable.

I missed Nalini and wished she were there. Being alone, there was no one to commiserate or share my frustrations with. I'd had enough of Trinidad's heat, humidity, and Third World conditions. I was discouraged and just plain wanted to go home. But where could I go? I had given up my apartment and I had no job or income. I felt trapped. I thought about going to our new ashram in Canada for a while, just to get away from everything. Maybe doing more meditation would help me grow.

As the days passed, my energy dropped and my doubts became rampant. I wasn't making any progress on Guruji's visit. So, finally, there was nothing else to do but call him and cancel his visit.

"Maybe this is not the right time for you to come to Trinidad, Guruji," I told him. "There are so many problems here, and I don't think I can get people to work together and help me. And, Guruji, I think I should take a break from teaching. It's clear to me that I don't have the skills to be a leader. I don't think I'm cut out for this type of work."

There was silence on the phone. I thought the connection was lost. Then I heard that familiar sound, "Hmmm?"

"If people are unhappy around you, if they challenge and oppose you, you definitely feel it. It hits you. But holding on to it and identifying yourself with your fleeting feelings is stupidity — especially for someone like you, a teacher on this path. It's time for you to stop dwelling on your feelings. One moment you are up, the next moment you are down. When unpleasant feelings come, be like a rock! Let them come. How long will they stay?"

I had no response; I was caught off guard. I didn't really think he would say to stop teaching, but I thought he would sympathize with the situation and tell me to leave Trinidad for a while. I could tell by his voice that he wasn't angry, he was just being direct.

"What is so great about your feelings?" Guruji asked. "I'm not saying you should run away from your feelings, but if you sit and dwell on them all the time — 'Oh, poor me! I am bad! Nobody likes me. I am frustrated. I feel good. I feel bad.' — you create a hell for yourself. Who cares for your feelings? Feelings are just some energy that lasts a moment and passes; they just come and go."

He was right. I was feeling sorry for myself, and blaming myself, the path, the people around me, and even the culture. It was an old habit and I needed to move on — but how?

"If you're miserable now, you probably made other people miserable in the past, and now it's your turn. Difficult times came to Rama, to Jesus, even to Buddha. Do you see what I'm saying, Michael? Some roughness will come in life — then handle it. Smile through it. Whatever roughness you face is really nothing. What can happen to you in life? Somebody is coming to shoot you with a gun? I tell you such things will not happen. You are protected. The roughness you are feeling is just the minutest percentage, only the amount essential for your growth. That is why it is there. The moment you are centered, it won't come at all.

"Go by your dedication, your commitment to a cause on this planet. That will draw out the valor, vigor, peace, stability, and focus from within you. Otherwise, you feel good one moment and bad the next, and the cycle will only continue.

"Running away from the situation won't make it disappear," he said. " 'Oh! I'll go to the Himalayas and meditate for three to five years, then things will be different.' What will you do? Five years later you will get into the same mess, or an even bigger mess. Stop worrying about, 'Who will help me? How will I get the resources?' Why should nature give you more when you are stuck with your little mind?

"The greater your commitment, the greater nature will support that commitment with more energy and greater help. And the means will come to you automatically. That's the beauty of life, the magnanimity of life, the way to expand in life."

After I put down the phone, I sat on the sofa with my legs crossed and felt very still. I welcomed that stillness as I would welcome an old friend. It was comforting and intimate. It was something I associated with grace and Guruji. I closed my eyes and the stillness became so pervasive that the hum of the air conditioner and the birds chirping outside my window eventually faded into the background and disappeared. I sat for a long time. There were few thoughts, only feelings of gratitude that Guruji had taken the time to help me in such a personal way.

But now I had to get moving, there was so much to do.

Throughout the day, I kept thinking about what Guruji had said. Guruji knew me like no one else. He knew my capabilities and my limitations. All these situations were opportunities for me to rise to my potential. There was no choice. I needed to move forward and grow.

Whether I was teaching in the Caribbean or living at the ashram, the lesson was the same — no one but me was responsible for my feelings. I realized that I had this pattern of attaching my feelings to events or situations outside of myself. It was always because of "them" that I was miserable or unsuccessful — or even feeling good.

Even if it was uncomfortable, I had to take responsibility for my own feelings, and stop blaming other people for them. Many times, Guruji spoke about how essential it was to have this skill. I had to identify with the ocean inside me, not the little waves or storms. I had to be bigger than the events, and totally accept the feelings or sensations that came up in any moment.

No matter what obstacles came my way, I was determined to stay one-pointed and not get caught up in the drama.

There is a Trinidadian expression (which is more charming when spoken with a Trinidadian accent) that says, "De deeper de darkness, de nearer de dawn." Things could only get better.

I was now putting my full effort into Guruji's visit. As the time of his arrival approached, my sense of commitment grew. I spent sixteen hours a day completely focused on the master and sharing his knowledge. I was like a warrior. I refused to give in to negative thoughts, feelings, or doubts. Not that I pushed them away, but when negativity came up I didn't blame other people, I observed the sensations, watching the negative thoughts like passing clouds. Even though there was so much to do, I did the Kriya regularly and spent even more time in meditation. And I wasn't resisting and fighting the way things were.

Guruji was my portal to surrendering to the moment. I could feel his presence; the stillness was with me nearly all the time. It was as though I was enveloped in grace. I was so focused on Guruji that after a while I felt almost like I'd become him. All the petty chatter in my mind stopped. I could barely find where Michael was. For some time, I felt the small self becoming the Big Self. I felt invincible and knew Guruji's visit would be a success.

After a while, my enthusiasm started to catch on and the group began helping again. There was magic in the air. We managed to pull off a major public-relations coup. Being in a small country, I was able to do many things that would not have been possible in the U.S. I was interviewed on many radio and TV shows, and had articles about Guruji's upcoming visit in all the papers. We conducted an intensive direct-mail campaign, sending invitations to all of the key officials. A devotee who owned Royal Castle, the largest fried-chicken chain on the island, sponsored daily full-page ads in the major papers for the week leading up to Guruji's visit. On the night of his arrival, the evening news featured a story about Guruji and mentioned his upcoming talks. In essence, we had made Guruji a celebrity.

We were all very ready for our master's arrival. I was filled with so much energy and excitement, I couldn't sleep. I knew Guruji would be pleased with all the work we had done. My heart was full and my body exhausted.

I decided to go to the airport alone and have all the devotees wait at the house to surprise him when he arrived. As we drove quietly in the car, Guruji seemed to be thinking, "I came to see the people. Where are they?" But as soon as we opened the door to the house, Guruji saw the bright shiny faces that had been anxiously waiting.

Guruji lit up the house on Scott Street. It became a mystical wonderland. There was so much love in the hearts of these people who were meeting him for the first time. They'd been listening to my stories about him for almost a year. Now, they were finally able to experience Guruji firsthand.

At the talks that followed, more than four thousand people met Guruji. Many of the talks were so crowded that hundreds of people stood in the streets just to hear a faint whisper of his knowledge. During the day, we had public satsangs and hundreds of people came to greet Guruji. People were clearly ecstatic, inspired by his words and moved by his simplicity and care. It was amazing to see how one man could create so much joy.

Guruji spent four days in Trinidad and two days in St. Lucia before flying to the United States. Without a doubt, his tour was a success. In fact, it was the first time he had ever addressed such huge crowds. He never acknowledged that I had done a good job, but I knew he was pleased.

In a week, I would again see Guruji, this time at our ashram in Quebec, for the annual Guru Purnima celebration.

But before that, it was time to visit my father.

Chapter Seventeen

Coming Home

My father was now eighty-two and lived in Century Village, a huge retirement complex in Deerfield Beach, Florida. Dad looked well for his age, and although he suffered from a bad back and severe arthritis, his sun-tanned complexion gave him a glow that made him look several years younger than he was.

He lived in a small one-bedroom condominium that was cluttered with family photos. We had to purchase two shelving units just to accommodate all the pictures. They were everywhere — photos of my sister and me as kids, high-school graduation, my bar mitzvah, my sister's wedding, and my sister's kids; the grandchildren, Mark, Adam, and Seth.

As I looked around his house, I noticed that there was one thing missing — there was no current picture of me. Nothing that represented the man I had become. Photographically, my life had ended in high school, bringing back old feelings of being unworthy and no good.

Whenever I visited my father, I felt as though I was an imposter, a fraud. I had chosen so foreign a path, it was beyond anything my dad could comprehend. Like most fathers, my dad wanted his son to be successful — which, to him, meant married with children and sound financial investments.

I had some remaining fear of my father's judgment and still sought his approval. I didn't want him to worry about me, and I was too intimidated to tell him that I had given up material security to travel the world and teach on behalf of an Indian guru. And it would only have filled him with anxiety and fear if he learned that his son didn't have a conventional job with traditional benefits and a retirement plan.

I told him that I taught a stress-management program for a nonprofit foundation, and traveled around the world opening franchises for the organization. I was always vague when I spoke about my life and job. I think he had the impression that I worked for some secret government agency like the CIA, an impression I partly encouraged.

"How much do you earn? What is the potential for advancement? What type of retirement plan do you have with this company, and who is the beneficiary on your savings account? How long do you have to continue traveling around living out of your suitcase? When will you get married, settle down, and start a family? I want to have *naches* (joy) from you — grandchildren!"

No matter how hard I tried to avoid his interrogations, I would get caught in his web. I would deliberately deceive him to avoid a confrontation, but we would get into an argument anyway.

We both wanted the same thing — closeness, intimacy, love. He was hurt that I was hiding the truth, and I didn't feel safe to reveal it. It was exhausting. I hated being deceitful and felt guilty about hiding the truth about my life. But what was my alternative? I knew he would not be able to accept my lifestyle or understand it. He would only worry endlessly.

Our visit ended in a mess. I left my dad's house a few days early to check into a hotel and get some rest. I was wiped out from arguing with him and from working so much in Trinidad. I slept for two days.

I was still bothered about my relationship with my father as I traveled to the Canadian ashram to be with Guruji. When I arrived, Guruji greeted me and sensed that I was troubled.

"How did the visit with your dad go?" he asked sympathetically.

"Oh, Guruji, I feel like an impostor. I hate lying to my dad. In all these years, I have never told him about you or the work I am doing. Living like a monk and following a guru is so foreign to Jewish culture that I don't think my dad would understand — he would be worried to death about my future. I just want to be honest with him and have our relationship be smooth."

"Sometimes it is best to tell people what they can hear," Guruji said.

"But, Guruji, don't you think it would be better if I just told my dad the truth?"

"I'm not against you telling your father anything. But do you think if you tell him what your life is about it will bring an end to this problem? If your dad doesn't know what makes him happy, how could he know what makes you happy? I don't want you to mislead your father. I don't need you to continue teaching full time if you feel a conflict. I just want you to be happy and do whatever brings you the greatest joy."

I'd been fortunate to spend so much intimate time with Guruji, but as he gently looked into my eyes, I felt a closeness that I hadn't experienced before. He wasn't interested in me as one of his field soldiers, he was concerned about my life and what was best for me. And he knew how my father intimidated me.

I'm sure that, to an extent, my relationship with Guruji mirrored my need for paternal approval and acceptance. I wanted to be a success in both my father's and my guru's eyes.

"Guruji," I asked, "did you ever have problems with your parents not understanding you?" I couldn't imagine Guruji having difficulty with his parents, but I asked anyway.

"Well...." He paused and smiled playfully. "When I was a child, an astrologer told Amma (Guruji's mother), 'Since your son was born on *Shankar Jayanti,* he is going to leave and won't take care of you.' So my mother was always a bit worried about me," Guruji explained. Shankar Jayanti is the birthday of Adi Shankara, the founder of the Shankaracharya tradition and a proponent of *advaita*/non-duality.

"When I sat for meditation," he said, "Amma would often scold me and hurry me up. 'Enough, enough,' she would say. 'You are taking too long! You take one-and-a-half hours when it should only take a few minutes.' For me, meditation would take a long time. I would do one mantra and then look at the sky, thinking about Brahma, Vishnu, and all the *devas,* expecting a response."

Guruji laughed at himself as he told the story. I loved his stories. Though he was always personal, it was rare for him to share details about his personal life.

Guruji was in a particularly talkative mood that day and continued to share. "My school teachers would tell Amma, 'Your son acts so peculiar, he doesn't behave like a normal person. He discusses philosophy, meditates, and wants to do puja all the time.' Hearing this, Amma would get very worried and hide all my puja items. I would come back from school and cry, and refuse to eat until all my things were given back to me. She would hide them somewhere up in the attic, and I would have to climb up and find them. 'You should study,' she would say. 'You don't study at all.'"

Then Guruji's father, Pitaji, would console her. Pitaji dabbled in astrology, and would tell her, "Don't worry, he has very good stars. He is a great soul and will do very good things."

"To please Amma," he continued, "I went to St. Joseph's College and completed my degree. Then she wanted me to get a job. She forced me to go for an interview with a bank. But I didn't see myself taking a job. So I threatened her: 'If you want me to take a job, I will join the Merchant Navy and leave home.' I knew that Amma wouldn't go for that.

"But somehow I went on that job interview. This company gave me the train fare to Delhi to meet with them. I wound up interviewing them instead of the other way around. When I told them that I had been teaching meditation, they got so interested they wanted to learn more. I spoke to them about meditation, but I was not attracted to take their job. After the interview, I wound up spending one or two days in Rishikesh, and then I returned home. Afterward, I kept getting postcards from these people, inviting me to join their company.

"When I returned home from being with Maharishi," Guruji continued, "my hair was longer and I had grown a beard. Amma didn't like it.

She was not used to seeing men with beards. The style in South India was to be clean-shaven, with short hair. I explained to her that when I went to teach classes without the beard, people would think I was just a young boy. Nobody would listen to me as a teacher. 'What can we learn from him?' they would think. I had to put on the uniform of a guru and grow a beard to look a little more mature. Amma was not too happy about this, and still she wanted me to shave the beard. But after a while she got used to it."

I laughed, and felt consoled by his stories. I was always impressed by how much Guruji honored and cherished his mother (in later years, he would name the grand assembly hall at the ashram after her), but knowing that he'd had some challenges with her when he was young made the situation with my dad more bearable.

Then, out of the blue, without changing his tone or his pace of speech, Guruji asked, "Michael, how would you like to go to Australia? There is an advanced course scheduled to start in a few days, and we need to send a teacher."

My personal time was over, and within a couple days, I would be off. For the moment, I could forget about my problems with my father. But I knew that eventually I would have to resolve that situation.

The flight didn't start out well. The flight attendant could find no record of the vegetarian meals I'd ordered. So, for the next sixteen hours, I sat hungry on the plane, accepting the present moment as inevitable and inedible. I did learn, however, that by not eating during the flight, I had virtually no jet lag when I arrived.

It was now April 1993. Life in Australia was much easier for me than Trinidad. I wasn't wilting from the heat and humidity, and I felt more mentally balanced without maxi-taxis. However, there were some similarities. Both countries drove on the "wrong" side of the road, were obsessed with cricket, and were a bit slow, at first, to attend the courses.

But with perseverance and commitment, things started rolling, and within a few months, many "blokes" and "sheilas" were enjoying the benefits of Sri Sri Ravi Shankar's knowledge.

I traveled weekly between Sidney, Melbourne, and Perth, teaching Art of Living courses. Sharing and caring for people was my daily ritual, my highest priority. I felt grace and at peace with myself. I thoroughly enjoyed what I was doing. Having taught for three years, I finally found my own voice and became more polished as a public speaker. Most of my students repeated the course and encouraged their friends and relatives to attend whenever I was in their town. Doctors, psychologists, and body workers who attended the course were referring people based on the changes they saw in their patients and clients, as well as the improvements they saw in their own physical and mental health. The transformation I was seeing in people was immediate and, in most cases, long lasting. People were more enthusiastic and happy.

One person who stands out from that time is a woman named Betty, who had lost her husband a dozen years earlier and had never recovered emotionally. She hadn't left her home for eighteen months, and the psychiatrist who recommended her had diagnosed her as agoraphobic, having an abnormal fear of crowds and public places. Medication didn't work and she was willing to try anything.

I remember her looking like a homeless woman, hunched over in the back of the room with a forlorn face. Her personal hygiene was appalling, and she smelled so bad that no one came near her. For some reason, she trusted me, followed all my instructions, and came back daily. After her first experience with Sudarshan Kriya, she seemed more natural and relaxed. She waved good-bye to me when she left the session.

No one recognized her when she returned to the class the next day. She had showered, brushed her hair, and changed her clothes for the first time in weeks. She still didn't speak to people but she now had a constant smile on her face. By the end of the course, she was taking baby steps, interacting briefly but regularly with other people in the class.

Betty was committed to doing the Kriya daily. When I returned three weeks later for a follow-up session, Betty was waiting for me. She wore a beautiful dress and greeted me with a bouquet of flowers. She told me that her whole life had changed. She had gone to the library a few times and also started cleaning her home. I could tell she still had traces of her illness but she was clearly on her way. Within three months, she was volunteering at a senior center once a week and thinking about getting a job.

In September 1993, Guruji arrived for a four-city tour, which included some time to see kangaroos. It was hard work preparing for the tour, but it was easier this time than before. I better understood how to support and inspire the local volunteers and we worked well together. It was also fulfilling to see Betty at the events.

There was a lot of media interest in this visit, including a writer who interviewed Guruji for the *Sydney Morning Herald*. The reporter had a weekly column that appeared in the Sunday Life & Style section. Each week, he would ask the same twelve questions to a VIP who was visiting. The interview went well, until the columnist asked the sixth question.

"Tell me, Sri Sri, if you could change anything about yourself, what would it be?"

Guruji looked at the reporter, smiled, and said lightly, "Hmmm? Nothing."

The reporter was caught off guard. "Well, maybe you didn't understand the question. There must be something about yourself that you would change."

"No, nothing." Guruji replied very innocently.

The reporter seemed to get irritated, "You really wouldn't change anything? Not one thing?"

"Hmmm?" was all that Guruji said.

Flustered, the reporter dropped question six and moved ahead with the interview.

After a while, he came back to the question, saying, "Sri Sri, there must be something about yourself that you would change if you could. Everyone I've interviewed for the last four years has had an answer."

This time, Guruji looked as if he was sorry he had to disappoint the reporter. "I don't see anything wrong with me," he said almost timidly. "I wouldn't change anything if I could."

For Guruji, there were no issues, no regrets. Nothing needed to be changed. How extraordinary! It was such a gift to be around Guruji and experience firsthand how simple and natural enlightenment really is.

After Guruji left Australia, the article came out. It became a collector's edition. It was the first time since the column began that there were only eleven questions. The writer omitted question six without any explanation.

Near the end of my stay in Australia, an older Israeli woman attended a course I taught in Byron Bay. She was very affected by the course. Her son had been shot to death at a border crossing while serving in the Israeli army, and since then, she had suffered from anxiety and panic attacks that would leave her incapacitated for days. Sudarshan Kriya was bringing her tremendous relief and she was inspired to help. She had many contacts in Tel Aviv and wanted to sponsor me to teach there.

I had always wanted to be the first person to bring Art of Living to Israel. Israel had great significance for my family and me when I was growing up. Since my life now centered on bringing peace and contentment to individuals, regardless of their religion or culture, I wanted to bring Sudarshan Kriya and the knowledge of the Self not only to Jews, but to all the people in the Middle East.

I saw Guruji's teaching as something that could bring diverse people together. It was not in conflict with any religion. I had already taught leaders and practitioners of many faiths, including Hindus, Jains, Sikhs, Christians, Muslims, and Jews — and all had enjoyed and benefited from the program. Believing that Art of Living could make a difference, I called Guruji and asked if it was a good idea for me to go.

I knew that he wanted the knowledge to spread in the Middle East, but for some reason he hesitated. Perhaps he saw some obstacles and was being protective. After questioning me for a little while, he said it would be fine to go. But he insisted that I should stay only for a short time, just a few weeks.

I arrived in Israel in October 1994, two days before suicide bombers blew up a bus on Dizengoff Street, the main shopping area in Tel Aviv.

The terrorist attack took place on the eve of the signing of the Israel-Jordan Treaty of Peace, and my host, like everyone else in Israel, was glued to his television for the latest reports. At that time, it was the deadliest suicide bombing in Israeli history. I could sense the fear in the air, and felt the wave of panic that would arise in people every time the screeching sirens of fire engines or ambulances drove through the streets.

Yet, on another level, I was very much at peace in the Jewish homeland. It was a secure feeling, like having a family around.

I was scheduled to teach a few workshops in Tel Aviv. I was interested in seeing how Israelis would respond to Guruji's knowledge. In a country that is under the constant threat of terrorist attacks, I think that many Israelis unknowingly suffer from post-traumatic stress disorder. At least that seemed to be the case on the courses I taught.

At first, I found the Israelis difficult to handle. They challenged every word I said. But their experiences during Sudarshan Kriya and the rest of the course were extraordinary. Almost everyone felt lighter and more free. It was amazing to see the transformation in just one or two days.

After teaching several courses in Tel Aviv, I decided to take some time off to be a tourist. I wanted to visit the holy shrines of my forefathers, the most sacred being the Western Wall, in Jerusalem. Also known as the Wailing Wall, it is the surviving portion of Judaism's holy Second Temple, which was built fifteen hundred years ago after Solomon's Temple was attacked and destroyed.

Taking a night bus to Jerusalem from Tel Aviv, it was an eye opener to see hundreds of young men and women in military uniform patrolling the public bus depots and boarding buses with commando assault rifles. By early morning, I was in the ancient walled section of Jerusalem known as the Old City.

Standing before the Western Wall, I remembered the stories that my father told me of his life in Eastern Europe, before the Nazis destroyed his family and his home. For years, I had denied and abandoned my Jewishness and identified myself with Eastern mysticism. Now I was in the homeland of my ancestors.

It was a crowded area, with everyone focused on touching this ancient structure, which is especially sacred for its proximity to a place in the Temple where it is said that the Divine Presence has never departed. The Western Wall has become a symbol of mourning for the temple's destruction, and of hope that someday, when the true Messiah comes, the temple will be restored.

As I inched my way closer to the wall, emotions welled up in me. With one hand clinging to the wall and the other clenched at my heart, I began to weep. I thought of my mother's parents, who had gone through the pogroms, the anti-Jewish massacres in Russia, and of how my father's family had been destroyed in the Holocaust. I cried for the millions of Jews who had been persecuted throughout history. Spontaneously, my body began rocking back and forth in the same way that Jews have always rocked their bodies when they *daven* (pray).

It was after dark when I finally left the Western Wall. Walking on a cobblestone path that led out of the Old City, I was stopped by Israeli soldiers. They had set up a barricade due to a bomb scare, and I was delayed for more than an hour. Once again, I was reminded that Israelis live with that kind of fear and danger every day.

The next morning, I returned to the ancient city and visited several Jewish, Christian, and Muslim shrines. In the early afternoon, I sat at a cafe, drinking mint tea and eating baklava as I checked my guidebook. Since it was Saturday, the Jewish Sabbath, many of the shops and attractions were closed. However, King Solomon's tomb was open and appeared to be only a short distance away. A taxi driver, who said he knew exactly where the tomb was, took me on a long, chaotic, two-hour cab ride, finally leaving me off somewhere that he said was close to the tomb.

Lost, I stopped a young *Chassidic* man (a type of Orthodox Jew) and asked him if he knew the way to the tomb. I didn't really expect him to respond, since it is common even for Chassids who understand English to speak only Hebrew or Yiddish. So I was pleasantly surprised when he said, "Yes, I know where King Solomon's tomb is. I will take you there."

My new friend, Rabbi Avraham Novick, told me he used to go by the name Dancing Coyote. He had been an acid-dropping hippie, and a regular at Grateful Dead concerts. He eventually traveled to Israel and slept in the crevices of the Sinai Desert's mountains, where he says he heard the call of God in a rainstorm. He decided to leave his former lifestyle and pledge his allegiance to the *Torah,* the law of God as revealed to Moses and the holiest of Jewish writings (the Torah is the first five books of the Holy Bible, which in English are called Genesis, Exodus, Leviticus, Numbers, and Deuteronomy).

As we walked, he asked me where I was from and why I had come to Israel. I told him I was there to teach yoga and visit Jerusalem. We stood in front of the tomb together, and he told me that there was someone he wanted me to meet — Gutman Locks, a *Kabbalist* rabbi who had spent time in India with many great masters before coming to Israel. My companion assured me that I would enjoy speaking to Gutman Locks.

He tucked his arm through mine and led me through the Old City to the rabbi's home.

After knocking on the door, we were greeted by a tall Chassidic man whose face was covered with a thick salt-and-pepper beard that hung below his neck. He wore a white shirt with sleeves rolled half way up his arms and black pants that were supported by suspenders. *Tzitzis,* (braided prayer threads) dangled at his waist. He wore a black *yarmulke* (skull cap), and had long, uncut sidelocks and sideburns, called *peyes,* that were rolled behind his ears. He looked happy to see us and made a welcoming gesture with his hand.

"Yes, come in, come in. Good *Shabbos,*" he said greeting us with a smile.

"Please have a seat." He showed me which chair to sit in and offered me tea. "Tell me about yourself. Is your mother Jewish?"

"Yes," I replied, knowing very well what he was up to — he wanted to identify my roots. The Jewish religion is based on the maternal lineage; you are considered Jewish if your birth mother is Jewish.

Gutman Locks had a brilliant intellect and a sharp wit. His face looked worn, yet his eyes sparkled. He had spent many years in India with various saints, learning about Eastern mysticism. In the 1960s, he received knowledge and guidance from Sathya Sai Baba, a renowned avatar from South India, and Swami Muktananda, a realized master from the Siddha lineage. With their direction and blessings, he spent twelve or more hours a day meditating in a cave near Mangalore.

He said he acquired spiritual powers after some time and began to bless people. With his new abilities and heightened awareness, Gutman Locks took on the role of guru and set up an ashram in a small apartment on the Upper West Side of Manhattan. As I drank my tea, he told me his story.

"All I had to do was walk into a room and raise my arm into the air and people would go into ecstasy. I became so sensitive that after blessing people, I would take on and experience all of their emotional and physical pain. To clear myself, I meditated for eighteen to twenty hours a day. Then I would come out and give darshan again, repeat the same clearing process with eighteen to twenty hours of meditation, and again give darshan. I was getting exhausted. It became too much for me. Once you acquire these powers, no one tells you how to use them."

His search for fulfillment finally brought him to Judaism. He began learning Hebrew and lived strictly by Jewish law. Before long, he had started the process of becoming a rabbi.

Our conversation then turned to me. I told him why I had come to Israel, and immediately he started to quiz me.

"So why are you a non-practicing Jew? You came to Israel to teach idol worship?" he both asked and told me, in a Jewish fashion that was familiar to me. "You're no longer a Jew, you're a 'Hinjew.' You were not born a Hindu. You were born Jewish to be Jewish, not to be with a guru. Your dharma is to be a Jew and to practice Jewish law, to fulfill the 613 *mitzvot* (the good deeds prescribed in the Torah). Krishna told Arjuna in the *Bhagavad Gita* to fight and uphold dharma. If your master is a real master, he will agree that your dharma is to be a Jew."

Gutman knew just what to say to a person like me to persuade him to come back to his Jewish roots. He knew the vocabulary and where all my buttons were.

I was definitely on the hot seat. I began to explain, "But I was never attracted to Judaism. I never felt the presence of God in the synagogue."

"I understand," he said. "Nevertheless, you are wasting your time following a guru. What you are being taught is not a reality. It is a dualistic approach. There are always two on your path, not one. There is the disciple who aspires to be like the master, but he never becomes the master. He is kept separate. Your master is above everyone. He sits on a couch with garlands and flowers all around him. Of all the people who follow gurus, who gets enlightened? Very few, or maybe no one at all."

Gutman looked at me intently, and it seemed like the thought had annoyed him. I wondered how many had gotten enlightened as Jews, but I felt too intimidated to talk and I simply let him continue.

"In Judaism, the *Shema* is our most sacred prayer — *Shema Yisrael Adonoy Elohanu Adonoy Echad*. 'Hear O Israel, the Lord our God, the Lord is One.' Do you understand what that means? On the surface it appears to mean that there is only one God. Yes, but if you see more deeply, it means that there is only One. Monotheism means that everything is God. You are involved in the path of idolatry. Your guru becomes your icon for God. Jewish law says, 'Thou shall not have any other Gods before me.' Do you see? By having this icon for God, you are putting the guru before God."

I was intimidated by his directness, and clearly out of my league. I felt defensive and didn't know what to say first. I didn't see my relationship with Guruji as idol worship. He was my mentor, my inspiration, my dearest friend. He was a pathway to God and an example of what the Divine is capable of.

Many people considered Mother Teresa to be a living saint. She had a worldwide following, and was eventually venerated by the Catholic Church. And there was Padre Pio, a Capuchin friar from Italy, who was regarded by many as a holy man and became world famous for his stigmata. I also thought of the role of the rebbe as a spiritual leader in Chassidic Judaism. A growing number of Jews believed that

Mendel Schneersohn, the prominent Lubavitch Rebbe, who lived in Brooklyn, was the manifest Messiah. In fact, a few years ago, my brother-in-law went to the Rebbe's grave to pray for his family's health and prosperity. Was that idol worship too? Where do you draw the line? Whether in sports, music, movies, business, or spirituality, heroes and mentors are there to inspire and honor. Even the Torah is kept in a special ark in the synagogue. Is the Torah an idol for God? Or is it honored because it represents God's grace?

I was trying to find a way to express these thoughts, but it suddenly felt like an odd thing to defend. "How can there be only one way to God?" I said. "It's so personal."

"No. You are misunderstanding me. I am not saying that Judaism is the only way to God. I am saying that each individual needs to follow a path of truth. Truth is following your dharma. Your dharma is to be Jewish. Why were you born a Jew? To live life as a Jew."

What he said made some sense intellectually, but emotionally it felt so limited. Is everyone's dharma only what they were born to? Would he stop someone from converting to Judaism? Should a slave remain a slave?

He could see that I was thinking things that I didn't know how to put into words, and he smiled sympathetically. Then he placed a sugar cube between his teeth and sipped his hot tea from a glass. My grandfather used to sip his tea in the same Old European way. Despite his intensity, there was something I liked about this rabbi. He had a warm presence, and I felt comfortable and at home.

Standing up, he said, "I need to go out for a while. In the meantime, you can meditate. I will show you where to sit. By the time you are done, I will be back, and then we can talk again. Come with me, I'll show you where to meditate."

He grabbed his long, black coat and fur hat as he led me to the door. We walked about a quarter mile along a cobblestone corridor in the Old City. Finally, we stopped in front of a pale-blue metal door that looked like a janitor's closet. Inside, there was a sliver of light coming from a broken window, which barely lit the barren, cave-like room.

There was no covering on the floor, just earth. In the center, there was a deep pit that had been railed off.

"You should meditate here, but be careful not to go past the railing or you might fall in," the rabbi instructed. "Please, I would like you to do a *pareve* (neutral) meditation, without your Hindu mantra. Meditate without practicing Hinduism. You can focus on your breath or watch your thoughts if you like. Anyway, in a short time you will go very deep. When you finish meditating, come back to my apartment and we'll talk more."

He closed the door and left me sitting on the ground with my legs crossed and eyes closed. I considered my path to be spiritual rather than Hindu or religious, but I definitely wanted to be innocent and see what the rabbi had to show me.

I brought my attention to my breath. Slowly sipping the air through my nostrils, my breath ceased and my mind dissolved in a deep state of transcendental bliss. I lost all awareness of body and time.

A couple hours later, I began to be aware of my body and breath, and I remembered I was sitting on the floor of this ancient room. It was such a powerful meditation. "Wow!" I thought. "Who is this rabbi?"

A few minutes later, still in a settled state, I managed to get up and walk back to his apartment.

"Please, come in," he greeted me. "How was your meditation? Deep?"

"Yes!" I said. "Very!"

"You just experienced the power of Jerusalem. That room has been set aside as an archeological site. That railed-off section is an ancient water pit. Since the floor that you were sitting on has never been paved, you experienced the power of the land without obstructions. And the round roof, built centuries ago, magnifies the energy in the same way a geodesic dome does. It is the energy of Jerusalem that allowed your meditation to be so deep. There are many more places like that around the Old City. That's one of the reasons I live here. When you are ready, I'll show you how to pray."

I thought about the day's events as I walked back to my hotel. I was impressed with my new rabbi friend. He obviously knew something, and I wanted to spend more time with him.

In the morning, I went to Yad Vashem, the Holocaust Museum. It was a deeply affecting experience. In Israel, I thought of my father constantly, so for me the museum was more than a collection of historical relics. It brought to life the hell that he and other Jews had experienced during the war.

In the afternoon, I decided to walk back to the rabbi's apartment to visit him again. I found him walking in the Jewish Quarter, speaking Japanese to an Asian woman who wanted to convert to Judaism. He later told me that he had lived in Japan with a judo master, studying and teaching martial arts. Besides speaking fluent Japanese, he held a black belt in judo.

We walked back to his place and went up the stairs to his apartment. As we drank some tea, he showed me a book that he had written years ago. It was filled with beautiful poetry of longing. Each minute that passed revealed some new impressive facet of this man.

Gutman showed me some old photos of himself as a guru in Manhattan. His face looked radiant as he sat on his dais before his followers. In one of the photographs, I recognized Alan Ginsberg, John Lennon, and Ram Dass. "They were sitting in my living room waiting to receive darshan," he explained.

Again, he tried converting me into a practicing Jew. He told me of his experiences with the masters that he'd studied with in India. He claimed that they lacked integrity and that their personal lives were very different from what they presented to their followers. He spoke of abuse of power as well as financial and sexual scandals. It sounded like he felt betrayed on some level, and it made me wish that he could have spent time around Guruji.

"I can see that you are a natural teacher, Michael. I feel you are destined to become a rabbi, to educate Jews in Jewish law. You weren't put on this planet to be subservient to a master. If you weren't Jewish, I would be speaking to you differently, your dharma would be different.

You would be free to follow any guru you choose. But you were born of the chosen people. Your dharma is to become a rabbi, and …" His words were falling on deaf ears. I understood what he was saying, but I rejected his narrow perspective.

For the last couple days, I had allowed myself to be influenced by Gutman's persuasive viewpoint. He had appealed to my Jewish roots and forced me to re-examine my commitment to my spiritual path. Gutman was definitely a powerful, charming, and insightful teacher. He had a keen understanding of both Eastern and Western paths to God, and he very convincingly presented his point of view. But when I looked into his sparkling eyes, they lacked Guruji's tenderness, his love. There was fear and guilt in his teaching.

I was grateful to him for his keen insights, but now it was obvious to me that Guruji was more than my spiritual teacher. He was someone who consoled my heart and helped me find meaning and purpose. He was there to lift me up and inspire me with wisdom and he helped me see the joy and enthusiasm in life and in myself. I couldn't imagine my life without him.

At that moment, I realized that I wasn't with Guruji to get anything. I just loved him and wanted to serve.

Then it hit me. This was the answer to the question I had asked myself on Guru Purnima so many years ago. I wasn't a student or a disciple. I was a devotee.

When I returned to my hotel room that night, there was a message from Jeff Houk. I was stunned that he had tracked me down. Absolutely no one back home knew that I was in Jerusalem. Another mystery.

The message indicated that he had spoken to Guruji, who said I should come to India immediately. So the next morning, I boarded a bus and returned to Tel Aviv to teach a workshop I had set up earlier, and within a few days I was on my way to India.

The familiar smell of petrol and the blaring horns of the trucks and aggressive taxi drivers greeted me as I exited the airport in Bangalore.

There was a banner on one of the ashram school buses that said, "Welcome Delegates to the International Conference on Art of Living."

Several Indian volunteers had come to the airport to greet those who were arriving from abroad. A young man approached me, saying, "Jai Gurudev! I am Vikram. Welcome to India. Tell me where are you from? Will this be your first advanced course?"

How could I explain where I was from? I had been living out of my suitcase for so long that I was no longer an American, or a transplanted New Yorker, or even a Californian. I was from nowhere and everywhere. I smiled at Vikram and accompanied him to the bus. As we drove through the crowded streets of Bangalore, I looked out at the familiar sights.

The bus stopped at Gyan Mandir. We were told that a huge satsang was going to take place in the center of town that evening. We were to rest for a few hours and would then get a ride into town.

Entering Gyan Mandir brought back many memories for me. I went to my old room and thought about Rita. All those cravings I'd had … they were gone now.

The satsang was a gala event. There must have been a thousand people. Most were local Indians. Sitting in the back of the hall, I watched Guruji's face on a big screen near the stage. I could see by the crowd that Guruji's popularity had grown. There was no longer a need for American teachers to spread his knowledge in India.

The satsang ended late that night, and we didn't arrive at the ashram until one in the morning. Exhausted from traveling, I couldn't wait to take a shower and get to bed. A young Indian man helped me with my luggage and guided me on the long walk to my room in the new dormitory. It was so dark that I was grateful he was guiding me. But I wasn't at all pleased that we were going to the farthest building from Guruji's house.

When we walked into the dormitory, I wondered where I was going to sleep. "Sorry, Mr. Michael, but we have run out of beds," he said. "Tonight you can use this straw mat and pillow. Hopefully we will have some sheets tomorrow."

Irritated, I could feel the sensations rising in my body. My mind began to race. Doesn't he know who I am? I've been teaching this knowledge around the world. I'm one of the founding members. I helped build this ashram! Sleep on the cold, hard floor? This is the thanks I get?

I was deeply offended. My mind was agitated, and I could feel the anger rising as my body grew rigid.

Then, suddenly, I woke up and caught myself. "So what!" I thought. "Right now I'm on the floor and there isn't anything I can do about it." It was actually something we taught in the course — acceptance. In a few moments, my mind began to settle down and the sensations in my body began to subside. It was like having an itchy mosquito bite but not scratching. The irritation was there, yet I was able to relax and observe it, and in a short time I fell into a deep sleep.

In the morning, I woke up with an aching body, but it didn't bother me. I was surprisingly cheerful. I hadn't had a chance to meet with Guruji yet. So, after a quick shower, and a meditation that was filled with the anticipation of seeing Guruji, I was off to his house.

He was standing outside in his garden and watched me walk toward him. With a smile on his face and eyes wide, Guruji extended his arms and pulled me close. Giving me a warm hug, Guruji said, "So, Mikey, what's happening? Are you happy to be back at the ashram?"

I thought it was funny that he called me Mikey. Guruji had never called me that before. He had always called me Michael. Having him call me Mikey was endearing. It made me feel childlike and simple. I laughed, wondering if this was how Hindu monks felt when they got *diksha* (initiation) and received a new name from their master.

There was a feeling of fun as he grabbed me by the hand and walked me into his room. I was amazed how, after only a minute, all my questions had vanished. I had wanted him to ask me how things went in Australia and Israel, and I had hoped we would discuss my experiences with Gutman Locks, but there wasn't an opportunity.

Instead, Guruji opened a bag of potato chips and shared some with me. He made some small talk, and then wanted to know how my father was doing and if he was happy that I'd gone to Israel.

I hadn't thought about the conflicts in my relationship with my dad for a long while. Miraculously, things felt noticeably smoother now. Since I'd told Guruji about the situation, Dad and I hadn't had an argument during any of our several phone conversations.

While sitting next to Guruji in his room, my mind eventually became blank. He sat for a while, silently looking at me, and then he closed his eyes. In a few moments, I slipped into meditation.

I relished the silence. It was like coming home. I felt as though I were sitting in Guruji's heart. I felt no separation, only peace, and a deep understanding that, in silence, there is no duality — only one Big Mind. There was nothing to do, just be.

CHAPTER EIGHTEEN

The Way of Grace

As Sri Sri Ravi Shankar has become more widely known as a spiritual leader and humanitarian, I don't get to see him as frequently. But still, now and then, I've been able to spend some extended time with him.

In 2003, Guruji invited me to travel with him on his first visit to Israel. I was thrilled to accompany him as he walked through Jerusalem's Old City.

His visit to Israel was sponsored by the Simon Wiesenthal Center, which was promoting a Holocaust Memorial exhibit that had been touring the globe. For the first time ever, an educational program about the Holocaust was displayed in New Delhi, India. Guruji had supported this project and had helped promote the exhibit in India.

As it was an official visit, numerous meetings were organized for Guruji with major government and religious leaders of the country, including Israeli president Moshe Katsav; Rabbi Yisrael Meir Lau, the Ashkenazi Chief Rabbi of Israel; and Shimon Peres, the Nobel Peace Prize winner and former Israeli prime minister.

Our days were packed from early morning to late evening. Each meeting provided an opportunity for the Israeli media and the Wiesenthal Center to get photographs of Guruji with these Israeli dignitaries. Surprisingly, during each meeting, Guruji introduced me to the

dignitaries and encouraged the photographers to take additional photos so that I would be included. The other Art of Living members who
were on the tour kept teasing me, saying, "Guruji must think you're a
real VIP. He wants you in every photo." I didn't understand the royal
treatment I was getting but I certainly enjoyed it.

While in Jerusalem, thoughts about Guruji's past incarnations kept
coming to mind. Among ardent devotees in the Art of Living, there
was sometimes talk about who Guruji was in his previous incarnations.
But they were only rumors. Guruji never made any claims, nor would
he confirm any speculations. The most popular rumors were that he
was Krishna, Jesus, and Shankara. I had heard this type of thing many
times but never gave it much importance. In the TM movement, there
was talk about Maharishi being John the Baptist, and disciples of other
masters hear similar things about their master. So I attributed this to
nothing more than good gossip. But as we walked with Guruji through
the Old City, it felt so familiar. I wondered if I had walked there with
him before.

One day, we visited the Church of the Holy Sepulcher, the church
that venerates the place where Jesus was crucified. As I walked around
the church, I cried, identifying with the pain the Apostles must have
felt as they watched their beloved master hang on the cross. Inside
the church, Guruji and I stood shoulder to shoulder in front of the
tomb where Christ is said to have been buried and resurrected from
the dead. Guruji kneeled down before the tomb in this sacred place,
brought his palms together, and bowed his head. There was no need
for words.

Later, our hosts provided a superb opportunity for Guruji to experience the Old City during *Shabbat,* the Sabbath. At twilight, several
rabbis escorted us to the Western Wall so that Guruji could join the
thousands of Jews there for the Friday-evening prayer service. Men
were on one side, women on the other.

Again, I was beside him as he made his way through the hordes of
people, getting closer and closer to the Western Wall. I think it was
the *yarmulke,* the Jewish cap that covered Guruji's head, that made

the congregation wonder. Dressed in his usual elegant, flowing-white Indian clothes, and with his long hair and beard, Guruji's presence was confusing to the Chassidic and Orthodox rabbis who gathered to pray. They stopped our hosts for details. "Who is he?" "Is he Jewish?" "Is he a great rabbi?"

As he proceeded toward the Wailing Wall, Guruji greeted everyone who stared at him by nodding his head and smiling.

Finally, standing before the Wall, Guruji reached out and touched it and then closed his eyes. His body began to rock as though he were *davening*, the slight movement people make during traditional Jewish prayer.

Suddenly, out of nowhere, a small flock of children gathered. They pointed at him, declaring in Hebrew, *"Mashiach! Mashiach!"* (Messiah! Messiah!) Guruji turned his head, smiling, blessing them with his eyes. Hoards of Jewish children ran after him, laughing and singing, as we made our way across the courtyard to the Temple Mount, which is known to Muslims as the Noble Sanctuary and Dome of the Rock.

The Temple Mount is the holiest site in Judaism. Jewish legend holds that it was from here that the world expanded into its present form, and from here that God gathered the dust he used to create the first person, Adam. It is a shrine that stands where King Solomon built the First Temple and is the place that Jewish tradition says will be the site of the third and final Temple. The area is also the place where Islam says that the Prophet Muhammad, accompanied by the Archangel Gabriel, made the Night Journey to the Throne of God. And it is the site where Abraham offered his son in sacrifice. It is the most contested religious site in the world, holy to Muslims, Christians, and Jews.

We stood silently at the site. Then Guruji stood alone for a while, gazing at the night sky. It was a full lunar eclipse and the stars were shimmering brightly. I felt so lucky to be with Guruji at these holy shrines.

Before leaving Israel, he made sure that I had copies of all the photos we took with the various dignitaries.

"Show them to your father," he said. "He will be able to relate to these pictures of you with all these important Jewish people. He'll be proud of you."

I felt so loved and touched that he had orchestrated this for me.

My flight to the U.S. stopped in Miami, so I had a chance to visit my dad and show him the pictures. It was the first time I had ever shown him a photo of Guruji, and I was apprehensive about his reaction.

As Guruji predicted, my dad expressed pride as he viewed these photos.

"Who is this man in all the pictures with the long hair and beard?" my dad asked.

"He's my boss, Dad. We call him Sri Sri," I said.

"Oh, he looks nice. He looks to be for Israel. Is he?"

How to explain that Guruji supports everyone? "Yes, Dad, he is."

My dad smiled and seemed to be content, knowing that my boss was supportive of Israel.

After visiting my father, I was off to Washington, to teach an important APEX course. It would be the first time I would be teaching at the World Bank.

After checking into my hotel, Guruji phoned me. I was surprised that he was calling. I knew he was in India on a five-city tour where thousands of people would be meeting him. I assumed that he was calling to give me some special instructions for the course I was teaching.

He made small talk with me, and then asked, "Mikey, did you show the photos to your father?"

In the midst of his busy schedule, with thousands of people clamoring for his attention, Guruji was interested in knowing how my dad reacted to some photos. There was nothing else on his mind. He had only called to find out which photos my dad liked best. I was astonished!

Later that year, I was back in Florida visiting my father, helping him with some doctor appointments. My dad took out the photos from my trip to Israel and marveled at them.

"Michael, can you please buy a frame for this one? I would like to hang it on the wall. It is a nice photo. You look so happy standing next to your boss and Shimon Peres."

I was speechless. Was he serious? For me, this was a miracle.

For so many years I was afraid to tell my dad about Guruji, and now he wanted to display his photo in his home. I held back the tears and hoped that Dad didn't see them welling up in my eyes.

Today, a photo of Guruji hangs among the family photos in my dad's living room.

Epilogue

My plane landed smoothly at the Bangalore airport. It was February 2006, and I was excited to be back in India. In a few days, the Art of Living Foundation would be hosting its Silver Jubilee celebration.

Bangalore was no longer the quaint city I had come to know in the early nineties. It had become a major metropolis and was now a leading producer of software and other information technology. But the city was not all that had grown. The Art of Living and the perception I had of myself and the world around me had both expanded and changed since my first Art of Living Course in 1988. For seventeen years, I lived out of a suitcase, traveling the world and teaching Sudarshan Kriya. For much of that time, the Art of Living was a small, growing organization, so I'd had to depend on the generosity of the people who opened their homes to me — and I had to trust that there would always be a place to stay. This kind of receiving, trust, and flexibility had all been new.

When I took that first Hollow and Empty advanced course, there was absolutely nothing that would have made me guess that I would now be leading those silent retreats myself, or that I would end up training hundreds of people to teach the Art of Living Course. As a college dropout and the son of a delicatessen owner, it was a great leap of faith for me to teach Guruji's knowledge at such organizations as IBM, Shell Oil, and the World Bank.

Over that time, an appreciation for the common bond we share as human beings also grew. In 2001, I spent a year traveling through the Arab countries of the Persian Gulf, bringing Guruji's gifts to sheiks, imams, sultans, and their royal families. I felt a great affinity for Islam, and even took lessons in the Koran from the Grand Mufti of Oman.

Much of the emotional drama and turbulence I'd experienced during my early years had subsided, and I became more comfortable with the ambiguities of life. I became less stiff and controlling, and more in the moment. The years of service and long meditation had cultivated an appreciation for the silent space between thoughts, and the senseless mental chatter had gradually decreased. I was now more accepting of myself and was able to enjoy my own company. But the most delightful change was that I was now feeling Guruji's love with me almost all the time.

Once, while traveling with Guruji, he told us that the ancient rishis described five things that happen when one is in the presence of an enlightened master. Knowledge flourishes, sorrow diminishes, joy wells up without any reason, abundance dawns, and talents manifest. I know this was true for me, and for thousands like me who have had the good fortune to be around Guruji or enter this path.

I did ask Guruji once about people who aren't able to spend much time with him. Silent for a moment, he shook his head, indicating that I wasn't getting the full picture. He had just visited Russia for the first time in six years, but people had reported many extraordinary experiences during those years. The same was true in Argentina, China, and other countries that he visited only rarely. It was another reminder that Guruji is more than his physical body. I realized that Guruji must have other ways to connect with people.

After I got my luggage, a huge poster of Sri Sri Ravi Shankar greeted me in the arrival lounge. The Art of Living Foundation had grown beyond anything I could have imagined. Guruji had become the equivalent of a rock star in India, where hundreds of thousands of people were attending his public talks and satsangs. More than twenty million people had participated in Art of Living programs in India alone.

It was daunting and a bit overwhelming to see hundreds of people waiting outside Guruji's door at the ashram for a chance to be close and receive his blessings. In fact, I had to fight my way through the crowds just to get to my room.

The most unpleasant part of Guruji's new popularity was being stopped by security people as I tried to get into his house to visit with him. In the early nineties, only a few Americans and Europeans were teaching and spending time with Guruji in India. Now there were approximately ten thousand teachers in India, and many more volunteers engaged in the various courses and service activities. The growth that had taken place was not just happening in India. This explosion was becoming a global phenomenon.

Within a few days, I found myself at an event that drew 2.5 million people from more than a hundred countries to celebrate the Art of Living Foundation's twenty-fifth anniversary and Guruji's fiftieth birthday. Cultural, religious, and political leaders from many nations and traditions shared their appreciation for the work that Guruji and the Foundation were doing to strengthen individuals and uplift human values, including the role they were playing in bringing peace and relief to troubled areas around the world.

During the celebration, I had a chance to meet many old friends who had been at the Bangalore ashram back in 1991. Some had gotten married and had children, and a few of them had started successful businesses. Most had become volunteer Art of Living teachers, with several directing specialized service projects.

It was inspiring to meet people from all over the world. Volunteers from India, Africa, and South America took pride in telling me their stories of bringing housing, drinking water, education, and greater peace to many villages. In India alone, youth leaders had adopted and uplifted more than thirty thousand villages.

I even talked with someone who'd assisted me in organizing that first AIDS course I helped Guruji teach. He had a scientific background and had pressed us to conduct research on the medical benefits of Sudarshan Kriya. I was against it at the time, thinking it would turn our spiritual program into a superficial scientific laboratory. But my fears had been unfounded. Now, research on Sudarshan Kriya and the other Art of Living breathing techniques has been published in scientific journals around the world, and has only verified the many changes I have witnessed in course participants over the years.

It felt rewarding to have played a role in all of this. But, overall, it felt like the whole thing had taken place by some sort of grace. As far as I remember, my family never used the word grace, in the spiritual sense, when I was growing up. But I had come to see it as the word for unseen blessings; the support that comes from being in tune with nature, with something bigger than myself. I was finally understanding what Guruji had been saying all along, that feeling gratitude brings more grace, which brings more gratitude. While the mechanisms of grace are still a great mystery to me, such grace had become a dependable feature of life around Guruji.

Despite all these changes, and in the midst of this enormous event, it was clear that one thing had not changed at all — Guruji. Well, maybe he had changed a little. His beard now had sprinkles of gray and his hair had thinned a bit. But Guruji was the same. After so many years of watching him in various situations, Guruji had never been one person in public and a different person in private. His innocent nature, sense of caring, and unlimited compassion have remained unchanged. And, from my experience, I knew that even with so many people, if someone in the world really needed to contact Guruji, they still could.

After the colossal Silver Jubilee celebration in India, the U.S. Art of Living Foundation held its own twenty-fifth-year gala, in March 2007, at the prestigious Kennedy Center in Washington, D.C. Sharing the stage with Guruji were members of Congress, the country's future vice president, educators, artists, scientists, business leaders — and me, the Foundation's president.

Epilogue

Although I had been a professional public speaker for nearly twenty years, and had taught numerous business leaders, politicians, and celebrities, I was reluctant to speak at this event. I started comparing myself to the prominent members of society who would be on stage and in the audience, and my old habit of judging myself resurfaced. Feelings of unworthiness rushed in. How could I introduce Guruji in front of all these famous people?

Sitting in a planning session with Guruji and the event organizers, I gave every excuse I could think of to get out of this chore. Guruji did not need to use any mystical powers to sense my nervousness and see how reluctant I was to speak. In a kind tone, he insisted, "Mikey, as president of the Foundation it's your role to welcome the distinguished guests and introduce me."

There was no way I could refuse. I consoled myself with the near certainty that no one would remember a word I said after Guruji took the podium. Diligently, I forged ahead and wrote the shortest possible welcoming speech I could.

The night before the gala, three of us joined Guruji in his room — me, my good friend Jeff Houk, and John Osborne, who had also become a good friend. Guruji started talking about the old days. That night, as he repeated many stories I had heard years earlier, he seemed to be going out of his way to tell them in significant detail. As I listened, I wondered if he did this to help me refine what I had written for this book.

When our evening was ending, and everyone was leaving his room, Guruji pulled me aside. I stood close to him, and he looked straight into my eyes. With total love and appreciation, he whispered, "Mikey, tomorrow, as president, *you* get the honor of representing the Foundation and all the work that's been done."

With those words echoing in my head, I went to my room and got into bed. More important than what he had said was the look of unconditional love in his eyes, which continued to linger in my heart. It was sweet, like the fragrance of a freshly cut rose offered to a beloved. It was the same look I'd seen when he glanced at me from the window of a car as he drove around the campus of MIU, so many years ago.

The next evening, I was backstage at the gala, dressed in my new black suit, white shirt, and red-striped tie, waiting to introduce Guruji. All those fears of not being good enough had vanished. They were already a distant memory I could no longer relate to.

When the master of ceremonies called me onto the stage, I was surprised to hear a thunderous round of applause and cheers. As I looked out at the audience, I felt a tidal wave of love and appreciation. It was like a blessing. Everything I'd given was coming back a thousand-fold, as though the Divine was smiling at me for the part I had played, too.

Then, in a moment of inner stillness, I realized that all the events that had taken place were just the play of consciousness, a *leela*; a game that happened in a dream, to help me — and others — grow. Along the way, I had learned some lessons about handling my emotions, being more loving and accepting, and not blaming others or myself. But beyond any lessons has been the growing experience of an unchanging silent Self, and a constant love that exists outside of any problems or limitations I have known.

As I finished reading the brief introduction I had prepared, Guruji walked onto the stage. He winked at me as he made his way to the podium. I felt that my heart would burst, there was so much grace.

Filled with gratitude, I faded into the background, as the crowd gave Guruji a standing ovation.

Wake up and see,
life is a game.
Whatever happened until now,
isn't it like a dream?
You had dinner this evening,
meditated in the morning,
and went to bed last night.
And if you look into your memory,
there were good events, bad events,
you had profit, you had loss.
But right at this moment,
it's all gone."

— SRI SRI RAVI SHANKAR

Jai Gurudev

Sol, Sharyn, Michael, and Claire Fischman, 1958

Sol at the deli, 1952

Swami Brahmananda Saraswati

A young Guruji (second from left) and Maharishi (center), at MIU, 1979

Sri Sri with Goli Waale Baba (the Bullet Saint)

Sri Sri, after the ten days of silence in Shimoga, 1982. His father, Pitaji, is at right.

In Calcutta, 1991

In third class with Guruji on the train to Darjeeling, 1991

Summer at the ashram, 1991 — top left: Guruji on Guru Purnima; top right: Michael
and team recording the *Ashtavakra* knowledge series; above: Guruji's ashram house.

Bhanumathi Narasimhan
(Sri Sri's sister, Bhanu)
at the ashram, 1991

A day trip into Bangalore with Guruji on the ashram bus, 1991

Guruji at the
international facility
in Quebec, 2001

The photo with Sri Sri and Shimon Peres, 2003

His Holiness Sri Sri Ravi Shankar

Acknowledgments

When writing this book, I sometimes drew on transcripts of talks by Sri Sri Ravi Shankar, choosing transcripts that matched my memory of what he said. I am grateful to the Art of Living Foundation for giving me permission to use this material.

I would like to thank everyone who helped make this book a reality.

I'm grateful to all the people who hosted me in their homes as I traveled throughout the world teaching Art of Living Courses. Little did they know that I wasn't spending all that time behind closed doors meditating, but glued to a computer screen, typing away at my story. Thank you for your kindness, love, and support, and for all the good food.

I'd like to thank the editors of this book: Jeffrey Ainis, who was more like a partner in a start-up business than the creative wordsmith that he is, and who patiently edited revision after revision; and Carol Kline, for her professional guidance, as she edited my original and then rewritten draft.

I also thank Ellen Herr for her early review of my manuscript, Tulasi Perry for suggesting my title, Judith Penner for my subtitle, and Denise Everheart for her loyal friendship, support, and suggestions.

I thank my agent, Bill Gladstone, for his clear belief in the value of this project, and Kim Ainis, Claudia Arellano, Denelle Eknes,

Bill Elkus, Sam Glazer, Joan Goodrum, Eve Hardy, Sharyn Henslovitz, Jeff Houk, Sandeep Karode, Michéle Krolik, Tara Mathur, Pamela Miller, Asha Mulchan-Onofri, Vicki Pearson-Rounds, Lloyd Pflueger, Jennifer Basye Sander, Gautam Vig, Laura Weinberg, and the others who contributed their time and valuable suggestions to this book.

I am also grateful to the many others who, though they may not be mentioned in these pages, have added so much to my life.

Finally, I would like to express my love and gratitude to Guruji, my spiritual teacher, mentor, and best friend. His guidance, support, and unconditional love have enriched my life beyond measure or words.

Further Exploration

THE FOLLOWING ARE programs I have found valuable, most of which are mentioned in this book.

THE ART OF LIVING COURSE offers the wisdom of how to live with grace and joy in a stressful world, and provides the deep spiritual experience necessary to put that knowledge into action. Practical processes include *Sudarshan Kriya* (see below), a technique that uses natural rhythms of breath to release stress and bring the mind to the present moment. The Art of Living Course is conducted in most metropolitan areas throughout the world.

YES! PLUS challenges students and young professionals, ages 18–24, to reach their highest potential by providing tools and knowledge to eliminate stress, rid the system of negative emotions, develop strong social and leadership skills, heighten awareness, and increase mental focus. It also includes Sudarshan Kriya.

THE ART OF SILENCE is a silent retreat program that offers an opportunity to experience further refinement and growth through deep meditation. Sometimes called The Art of Living Course Part 2, it is open to those who have completed the Art of Living Course or YES! Plus.

SUDARSHAN KRIYA is a core component of the Art of Living Course and several other Art of Living programs. It is a breathing meditation that brings the rhythms of the body, mind, emotions, and inner self into harmony. Independent studies on Sudarshan Kriya and its related practices have shown significant benefits to health, energy, brain function, immune response, stress levels, depression relief, and more.

SAHAJ SAMADHI MEDITATION is a graceful and natural meditation technique that allows the mind to effortlessly experience its own unbounded depth. Through daily practice, the nervous system is cultured so that inner peace and expansion increasingly remain throughout the day. Taught on the Art of Meditation Course, it is a natural complement to Sudarshan Kriya.

THE ART OF LIVING FOUNDATION is one of the world's largest volunteer-based nongovernmental organizations. Offering both educational and humanitarian programs, it holds consultative status with the United Nations and has reached people in more than a hundred and fifty countries. In addition to the programs mentioned above, specific programs are offered for youth, students, business and government, prisons and juvenile detention facilities, people with HIV or AIDS, people with depression, people in economically and socially challenged areas, women's empowerment, trauma and disaster relief, and more. Its service projects and programs of personal development and stress relief have reached more than twenty-five million people.

THE INTERNATIONAL ASSOCIATION FOR HUMAN VALUES (IAHV) was founded in Geneva, in 1997, to foster, on a global scale, a deeper understanding of the underlying values that unite the human community. An NGO in consultative status with the United Nations, its programs include trauma- and disaster-relief, programs for youth (including youth leadership training programs), programs for government and business, and programs for personal and social development. Its 5H Program helps individuals and communities become socially and economically self-reliant, with a focus on health, homes, hygiene, human values, and harmony in diversity.

You can find out more at www.artofliving.org, www.iahv.org, and www.srisri.org.

About the Author

MICHAEL FISCHMAN is a leader in the field of personal development. He is a founding member and current president of the U.S. Art of Living Foundation, a global non-profit educational and humanitarian organization, and he is also the CEO of the APEX course, the corporate-training division of the International Association for Human Values. A former advertising executive with Ogilvy & Mather, and an inspiring speaker, Fischman travels across the U.S. and around the world leading personal-development seminars that bring greater peace, awareness, and fulfillment to daily life. He currently lives in Boca Raton, Florida.

Downloads, links, a Reading Group Guide, and other features are available at www.stumblingintoinfinity.com.

CPSIA information can be obtained at www.ICGtesting.com
Printed in the USA
BVOW02s0500040815

411723BV00006B/246/P